SLOVO
The Unfinished Autobiography

[handwritten inscription]
Nov. 28, 1995.

SLOVO
The Unfinished Autobiography

With an introduction by Helena Dolny

Ravan Press

Hodder &
Stoughton

First published in 1995 in South Africa by
Ravan Press (Pty) Ltd
PO Box 145 Randburg 2125

First published in Great Britain in 1996 by
Hodder & Stoughton
A division of Hodder Headline PLC
338 Euston Road
London NW1 3BH

Hodder & Stoughton   ISBN: 0 340 66566 1
Ravan Press   ISBN: 0 86975 485 8

'At Revolutions End', from the collection of poetry *A Dead Tree Full of
Live Birds* by Lionel Abrahams, published by Snailpress and Hippogriff
Press, 1995.

'White hero of black revolution faces up to his final struggle', by Philip
van Niekerk. This article first appeared in *The Observer* 4 December
1994. Reproduced by kind permission of Philip van Niekerk.

'Slovo: They came to claim their hero', by Mark Gevisser. This article
first apeared in the *Mail & Guardian*, 20-26 January 1995. Reproduced
by kind permission of the *Mail & Guardian*.

Cover design, page design & setting: Ingrid Obery, Ravan Press
Picture and cover repro: Centre Court Studio
Cover photograph: Joe Sefale
Pictures are from the Slovo family collection, unless otherwise credited.

Printed and bound by Galvin & Sales, Cape Town

Contents

Foreword

It has become a cliché to refer to a departed friend as having lived a full life. Yet one cannot think of any other way to describe the life of Joe Slovo. From his early days he committed himself to one major goal – the removal of the racist regime and power for the people. That became a guiding light throughout his life. On 27 April 1994, with only eight months of Joe's life left, that objective was achieved.

At the time Slovo made this commitment, others must have dismissed it as misguided youth militancy which would evaporate as the realities of adult life set in. When he finally qualified as an advocate in white-dominated South Africa, many expected that goal to recede into the background. But to Joe and Ruth First, it was a target to be realised at all costs. That commitment sent them to detention, exile and finally claimed Ruth's life. But Joe, the commando, soldiered on until the mission was fulfilled.

Joe did not only interpret the world; he helped change it. The South Africa to which the eight-year old Yossel Slovo immigrated in 1934 was completely different from the one he left on 6 January 1995.

He had been part of the Allied Forces that defeated Hitler and saved humanity from Nazi domination. He had a hand in drafting the Freedom Charter and was part of the legal team that quashed the National Party's attempts to characterise our struggle as treason.

His dedication to the ideal of liberation saw him rise in the ranks of the ANC to become a member of its National Executive Committee and Chief of Staff of the People's Army, Umkhonto we Sizwe, while he served as General Secretary and later National Chairman of the South African Communist Party. This concentration of senior positions in one individual sometimes puzzled our friends and always infuriated our enemies. What they failed to understand was that Comrade Joe was not an armchair politician but a revolutionary who practiced what he believed in. They could not comprehend the chemistry that made up the ANC-led alliance and that JS was, in many ways, a personification of that alliance.

For more than three decades the National Party regime laboured hard to blemish his image. But to the oppressed majority, Slovo remained a brave military strategist, intelligent politician and dedicated patriot. That is the Joe Slovo we knew, and that was the Joe Slovo for whose burial thousands turned up, and many more lined the streets of Soweto, on 15 January 1995.

As a founder of Umkhonto we Sizwe, Joe contributed to the building of the People's Army and, as its Chief of Operations, he was instrumental in opening infiltration routes for MK combatants. As its Chief of Staff he made a sterling contribution to establishing MK firmly inside South Africa.

Together with other leaders of our people like Comrades Oliver Tambo, Duma Nokwe, Moses Kotane, JB Marks and Moses Mabhida, he worked tirelessly to rebuild the ANC into a formidable force following the post-Sharpeville repression. His contributions at Politico-Military Council and NEC meetings were invaluable.

What a joy it was to listen to Joe during a political debate. An avowed Marxist, Joe was at home with other intellectuals who could be characterised as conservative. I was fortunate to meet him in our younger days at Wits University. With his future wife, Ruth First, Ismail Meer, Harold Wolpe, Jules Browde, JN Singh and others, we would debate many issues well into the wee hours of the morning. His sharp intellect, practical approach and incisive mind were already apparent then.

Joe Slovo will be remembered for generations to come for his appreciation of the strategy and tactics necessary at various stages of the struggle. Though he was firm in his beliefs, he was not steeped in dogma. When circumstances changed, he was the first to propose new tactical approaches.

In 1990, after the unbanning of the ANC and the release of most political prisoners, it was Joe Slovo who came to me to suggest that we should review the continuation of armed actions by MK. We debated this fully and I took the matter up with the NEC, which accepted the proposal to suspend armed actions in July 1990.

Joe was creative and he was bold. On the basis of continuing discussion in leading structures of the Alliance, Joe was the first publicly to broach the idea of 'sunset clauses' and generate what became one of the most spirited debates within the Alliance. Ultimately, Joe's formulations, about the kind of compromises needed to be made in negotiations to achieve a qualitative movement forward, were accepted. As such, he can be credited with having played a seminal role in the transition that South Africa has undergone and is still experiencing.

Despite the pain and agony of terminal and debilitating bone marrow cancer, JS seemed to draw greater strength and evince even more energy and enthusiasm when he became Minister of Housing in May 1994. He toured many parts of the country, and sat in endless negotiations that culminated in the compact between the government, the banks and civic organisations. He thus set the stage for most of South Africa's house-building programme now under way.

We were together with Joe at the 49th National Conference of the ANC in December 1994; and one of the most moving experiences of my life was when I conferred the ANC's highest honour, *Isithwalandwe-Seaparankoe*, on him for his life-long and distinguished contribution to the struggle.

However, as the month and the year drew to a close, it became clear that his robust will could no longer resist the rampant assault of the disease. When I received reports about his health, I decided to interrupt my holiday to visit him. Despite the pain, he was strong and inspiring.

I again visited Joe, Helena and the family on 5 January 1995. His condition had worsened. He could hardly speak and was evidently in severe pain. Just before my departure, he struggled to lift himself up, and embraced his wife, Helena Dolny, for a long moment. Before I left, I kissed him on the forehead; and he bravely forced out the word, 'Cheers!' I could see his day had come ... and that was the last time I saw him alive.

At 3 o'clock that morning, he departed. When I arrived an hour or so later, Helena and other family members were there: hurt and grieving, but also as hardy and indefatigable as they had been during Joe's last days.

Joe Slovo was no more. Yet in the peacefulness of his final sleep, his body was to me full of life, of the joys and pains of struggle, of the love that he had for his wife and daughters, and of the experience that he has left behind for generations to come.

The story of Joe's life will not only illuminate the history of our liberation struggle for future generations, but also help equip them for a full life of service to the people.

Mandela

State President Nelson Mandela
18 September 1995

Maputo, Mozambique, 1982. The burly man paces the parquet flooring. Home has become a place of solitude, silence and waiting. The woman Joe Slovo had loved, the person who filled these rooms with a charismatic vivacity, is cruelly dead, extinguished in an instant like a stubbed-out cigarette. The letter bomb bore her name. The intent to kill was clearly personalised: Ruth First – anti-apartheid activist, revolutionary intellectual, research director of the major policy studies centre serving the Mozambican government. There was no doubt that along with Dulcie September, Joe Gqabi and others, she was classified as one of those who qualified to die in the lists drawn up by the apartheid assassins.

But there's a disquiet about Joe and a restlessness as he paces. 'Why Ruth, she never had anything to do with the armed struggle?' – a silly, plaintive, rhetorical question really. While MK special operations clearly aimed at economic and military targets, Pretoria's generals never really seemed to care who they killed. A catch-all label of 'anti-apartheid activist' sufficed, with children included if they happened to be in the way. The restlessness manifests itself in what becomes known in Maputo as 'Joe's Route 66': his seeking company, downing a whisky, then another, and then moving on to the next stop. The first year after Ruth's death becomes Joe's drinking year, when 'just another for the road' seems like just another to numb the pain. And yet he knows he must regain his equilibrium; otherwise the bomb will have claimed two victims – one physically and the other psychologically.

Some weeks after Ruth's death, Joe travels to London. It is a turbulent visit: grieving daughters, bureaucratic encounters to put in motion the settlement of the estate, the meeting of old friends for the first time since Ruth's death. There is a walk on Hampstead Heath with Barney Simon; they weep together, seeking solace in shared grief. 'You must write', Barney tells Joe, as others also advise.

On return to Maputo, Joe Slovo alias Jose Antonio de Pinto (Mozambican passport) takes out a Club Navale sports membership card in the name of Joe Kaplan and begins a new life rhythm, the regularity of which gives his friends heart failure for the easy surveillance opportunities he offers to his enemies. For the next year Joe will be up at five-thirty, Club Navale by six, back at seven, ablutions, coffee with a friend and then the working day begins, including whenever possible a stint of writing.

Joe had just stopped smoking before Ruth's death and, in spite of the tremendous stress he was under, managed to hold his own and resist the desire to start again. 'Ruth had asked me to give up' – this was to be his own quiet tribute, and it would be five years before he began again. Exercise, no smoking and therapeutic 'writing' about 'fragments' of his past life are components of Joe's recovery process.

The choice of inverted commas for 'writing' serves a specific purpose. Joe didn't write these chapters in the sense of sitting at a desk with pen and paper or a computer with a keyboard. These chapters are spoken. I can hear the rhythm of the spoken word, the cadence of Joe voice and soft inflections as I read the prose. He has a small notebook in which he has jotted down the main points of a story he wishes to recount, and a micro-cassette recorder. He sits sipping coffee, frames the story in his mind, puts down the dark blue cup and begins to pace the room, speaking into the little machine. Every few minutes he rewinds and listens, and sometimes reworks the phrases.

I've been fascinated on the occasions when I've discreetly witnessed these recording sessions; he is put off if he senses he is being watched. There is a never-ending fascination of the ability-to-hold-a-story of those brought up in an oral culture – whether Inuit, black African or Jewish – and a facility and power I envy.

Joe is very clear about what he will write about. This writing is quite distinct from the political writing of Joe Slovo, or that produced under his pen name of Sol Dubula in the *African Communist*. Among the pages of his jotting-down notebook there is a note, 'General Intro', with just one scrawled sentence: 'My selective memories have a predilection for the ludicrous and the comic which lightens and makes it possible to bear more easily the heaviness and often tragedies of struggle.' There's no political treatise tackled here, and an avoidance of the politically sensitive; what is mainly offered are the entertainment anecdotes, the after-dinner conviviality which often followed the norm of fairly heavy political discussion.

I have the notebook in front of me, and in my mind's eye I read the unwritten chapters – into exile with JB Marks, with Samora Machel hitching a lift on the same plane; arrival in Tanzania with Joe the only one carrying legitimate travel papers, but said the customs official on dealing with Joe at the end of the line: 'Joe Slovo – you chose yourself a funny name!'; the attempt to land a boat of MK soldiers on the Transkei coast in the early 1970s. There's the anecdote about Joe's detailed presentation of a plan to send Chris Hani back into the country on a bicycle, which Chris tries unsuccessfully to interrupt. When he finally gets his chance, Chris points out the basic flaw of the plan – he doesn't know how to ride a bicycle, and so then Joe coaches him!

There are the Angolan days of camaraderie and powdered eggs; a remarkable, memorable, diarised, strategy-influencing study trip to Vietnam undertaken with OR (Tambo) in 1978; a tender portrait of OR. There are the heady days of planning Special Operations from Maputo; the time he was introduced as a *rascista progressista*; the story of Hotstuff and the sabotage of Sasol; the hilarious story of Ronnie-in-disguise at Mbabane airport. There's the disappointment of the Nkomati Accord and retreat to Lusaka. The beginnings of negotiation endeavour finally achieve the return from exile, 'As I was saying before I was interrupted so rudely 27 years ago!' Codesa I and Codesa II at Kempton Park and the rewording of a popular song, 'Give me a deal to build a dream on ...'; the Transitional Executive Council; elections, inauguration and, finally, office-with-power! All chapters are humorous, anecdotal and personal but not in the sense of being intimate – that's not his style and would be infringing the fiercely private persona.

The chapters included here are as far as Joe got in that first period after Ruth's death. The writing and time for reflection were a healing experience. I found this note he wrote to me on the first New Year alone:

'Maputo was a bit deadly during the remainder of the festive season. Drink, good food and other jollities but for me also a time of sadness. Went alone to the graveside on New Year's morning with a few flowers from the hedge of my new house.

'Listen, H, don't get sad for me: these are times of sweet and tearful memory ...'

His work life carried on as normal. There was the continued planning and execution of the next big special ops' attack – this time a missile attack on Voortrekkerhoogte, although none of us knew of anything until the actual event took place. The South African response to the Voortrekkerhoogte attack was to send in an air strike on Maputo suburbs which was very, very scary. Otherwise, in his hours alone at home, Joe put in substantial amounts of time into his 'writing' project. Sue Rabkin took on the laborious task of transcribing the cassettes, squeezing in the time between working flat out in the political machinery and caring for her two young children; and Pam dos Santos also helped.

But Joe never completed all the potential chapters. In the second half of 1983 several things happened which affected his working life, and the personal space which had been availed for the writing of what he always called 'Fragments' was swiftly curtailed. First, after the death of Yussuf Dadoo, Joe became chairperson of the SACP. Now suddenly there was the possibility of a different role, a new range of activities to be undertaken with the challenge and authority of the new post.

Secondly, Frelimo's secret *rapprochement* discussions with the SA government gathered speed and came to a rapid climax. In March 1984 the Frelimo government and South African regime signed the Nkomati Accord which included the expulsion from Mozambique of all ANC full-time cadres excepting a diplomatic' office staff of ten. In the earlier stages of the talks (December 1983), Samora Machel called Joe to Bilene where he was on holiday and swore to him, 'Whatever happens, you will always have a home with us in Mozambique. Our relationship to you is special; your wife was killed on our soil.' But Machel was unable to hold his own in the talks. A few months later, in July 1984, after buying time to ensure the best possible exit of cadres from this forward area, Joe once more packed his suitcase and guitar which years before had travelled with him from London to Angola; this time he headed backwards to Lusaka.

The months before and after the Nkomati Accord were traumatic, but a trauma of a different nature from that of the bomb that killed Ruth. The foundation of forward area work undertaken from Mozambique since 1976 was threatened. The Joe that stood up at the ringside after this latest round of apartheid blows was weathered, reflective and probably a better long-term political strategist as a result. But although Joe continued writing during the Nkomati period, anchoring his life in these months of uncertainty, the introspective personal period that followed Ruth's death ended. Involvement in the political struggle of the moment regained ascendancy along with his normal even keel, his humour and delight in living. From Lusaka, he sent off the chapters of personal writing to friends for comment, and later he posted a couple of sample chapters to publishers to gauge their response. But that period of retrospection and writing had passed and the unwritten chapters retreated into life's background and never quite regained the upper hand.

In the next ten years of his life – the last ten years of his life – Joe very much lived in the *now* of the political struggle, the *carpe diem*. There was an increasing urgency to life in the struggle and a greater share of responsibility as the years progressed. In 1985 he was the first white to be elected to the ANC's National Executive Council. After Moses Mabida's death Joe became the General Secretary of the Communist Party. He was actively engaged in Pan-African efforts to deepen the Marxist content of some African political parties. In 1986 I finally made the move to join him in Lusaka and took up a greater space in his personal life – another time pressure and, whatever the compensations, the opportunities for personal writing receded even further.

He wrote a great deal during these years – much more than between 1976 and 1984 when his main focus was the practical organisational side of Special Operations – but after 1984 his focus became targeted on political strategy, and his writing geared itself to this. Comrades remember the verve and enthusiasm with which he would approach the drafting of each editorial of *Umsebenzi*, the pamphlet the SACP launched for underground distribution. I suppose that ability to focus his entire energy on one task has been noted by some of his comrades as both his strength and his weakness.

His strength was to concentrate on something if there was the means and authority to achieve it. If you were involved with something that Joe was doing, you saw how he put his whole energy into it. If he delegated something to you to do, the space was then yours, there was no equivocation. He applied this line of single-minded pursuit to himself. He gave up the position of Chief of Staff of MK on becoming General Secretary. He gave up as General Secretary when he realised not only the need to have Chris Hani in the main SACP leadership position but also that the negotiations struggle would infringe on the time needed to carry out the duties of a GS properly.

The weakness – should it be called a weakness, or a recognition of limitations – was the reluctance to spread himself. While he refused to accumulate a range of responsibilities, he also found it difficult to be engaged in more than one writing project. He said it was impossible for him to kindle along a piece of writing, for example his autobiography, on a sporadic and part-time basis. On the level of the mundane, for example, he laboured to cook a more complicated meal and have all the dishes hot and ready to be served at once!

In mid-1991, when Joe first learnt of the diagnosis of his cancer, his absorption, his tendency to live in the present became stronger than ever before. He had begun to cooperate on a biography but abruptly ended this. There were many reasons for this, not least that he was uncomfortable reflecting on his past life when he had just been formally presented with a death sentence – and a death sentence that was somehow all the more certain than that of the unseen assassin of the shadows. The threat of death by assassination is in some way easier to deal with than death through terminal illness. The latter requires quite a different level of personal responsibility about how you handle, accept and/or stave off the threat.

Joe continued to write a great deal, but it was all to do with responding to requests and the politics of the moment. He had his monthly column, 'Red Alert', in *Business Day*; he wrote political input papers for the ANC and SACP such as, 'Negotiations: What room for compromise?'; he produced papers for the many seminars he was asked to participate in, including a notable article on religion and socialism for a University of Cape Town summer school. And he attentively prepared himself for the many interviews with journalists, as he regarded the media as an opportunity to work for advantage when at all possible. In fact, his work life was much more publicly interactive than it had been in exile, and he revelled in the zest of a non-exile life!

He enjoyed the negotiations process, the stretching of his mind as delegates delved into issues; he enjoyed the challenge of working together towards an agreement with political opponents. His court experience came into its own again as he used his cross-examination skills to unpick proposals made by the other parties. He was regularly frustrated, saying Kempton Park often seemed so like the setting for a Lewis Carroll, *Alice in Wonderland*, fantastical story, that you had to pinch yourself sometimes to believe what you were hearing and seeing. His greatest fear, voiced in an interview at the time, was that, 'we will snatch defeat from the jaws of victory'. He regretted he hadn't kept a diary, as he was an avid reader of biographies, and during this period read Tony Benn's *Office without Power*. I heard people criticise him vigorously for not having kept a journal; they suggested he was being historically irresponsible.

But Joe had to make a choice between time for recording and time for strategising. It came down to personal decision about what his most fruitful contribution might be and how to best use his time. I would often find Joe sitting on the *stoep* after breakfast, gazing down the folds of the lawn and the jacaranda tree, deep in thought. 'Don't assume I'm loafing,' he once said. 'This is the most important time of my day, it's my thinking time.' And that's the choice Joe was faced with – out of meetings, yes, there could have been time for recording, but his choice was to spend his time strategising, ferreting away at the problems occupying his mind at that moment, whether an SACP problem, an ANC problem or more usually the next Kempton Park obstacle.

Was it the correct choice? I'll sympathise with historians and biographers that it would be wonderful if there were more of his personal writings; but my regrets are minor. I am comfortable with the choices Joe made; they were true to himself. His efforts went consistently towards getting the best possible deal for South Africa's future – even if he was not going to be part of that future.

In August 1994 Joe reached the beginning of his final cancer crisis. The chemotherapy treatments were no longer effective and the doctors wanted him to try heavy doses of steroids. The prognosis was ten to fifteen months, if the new treatment worked – but it didn't. Now he began to consider his biography semi-seriously! He said that years having passed and *perestroika* having taken place, he felt he would like to express his views on some of the more sensitive political issues. But he also said (forever the forward-looking activist) that what he would really like to have time to write was a sequel pamphlet with the title, 'Has capitalism succeeded?'

But how to write an autobiography when most of your life is focused on developing a new housing policy and your body is not exactly co-operating? Joe had a quick-fix idea which could have worked if he'd just had those few extra months. His plan was to sit every morning from seven to eight with his press officer and record an interview. These would then be transcribed and then he would work at reshaping them. Unfortunately these recording sessions had only just begun when a traumatic fall catalysed his speedy end.

But I am glad that those dozen or so years ago, Joe had taken the space to describe the lighter side of the struggle. The chapters presented here, which Joe carried round in a folder on which he had written Fragments', provide some testimony of the daily humour and wit that flowed so freely with Joe that was part of the joy of living with him. I'm pleased that at least some personal writing came into being that can be shared and savoured by others.

So what do you do with an incomplete biography – which even the author has entitled 'Fragments'? At first I thought it should be entrusted to a biographer who would somehow incorporate it into his/her project, but others argued against this and said there was enough to publish just as it stood. But even so, there is the issue of 'rounding-off' something which ends in the early 1960s – a full 30 years is missing. My suggestion, accepted by the publishers, was not to try to do any sort of summary

– the styles would clash – but rather to add a Part 2 to Joe's account. The voices of other people speaking or writing about Joe could come forward and be shared. He had received a great deal of correspondence in the last months and then, on his death, there were many, often wonderfully written, public and private tributes. A selection from this material complements the autobiographical writing, provides glimpses into his life and character, and shows something of what Joe meant to other people.

I want to thank everyone who agreed to this sharing process; it has been a salutary experience and I will be pre-emptive and apologise in advance for any oversights!

Helena Dolny
August 1995

Part 1

Autobiography

Return to Obel

I always think of the village in which I was born as Obel and not Obelei, its real name. In the ghetto community in which we lived Yiddish was the mother (and for me the only) tongue. By the time I left at the age of ten I had learned to count only in Lithuanian and to sing the words of the national anthem, which ended with a claim for the return of Vilnius, the capital city, then still under Polish rule.

I have no idea whether it was out of choice or because of some legal or social bar that we were all kept away from local schools. The synagogue was our school, and an ear-twisting, sadistic rabbi forced whatever he could into our heads from the Hebrew version of the Old Testament, which was our only textbook. Lithuanian towns and cities were known to us not by their indigenous names but by Russian variants, which reflected the fact that Lithuania had been part of the Tsarist empire until, with the help of interventionist forces, it (with the other Baltic states Latvia and

Estonia) proclaimed its independence from the newly-won Soviet power. I knew Vilnius as Vilna, Rokisckis as Rakeshik, Chavli as Shavill and, of course, Obelei as Obel.

The first obstacle in the search for my village was that 'Obel' did not appear in any of the numerous atlases I consulted. It was Guilliane Pajetta, a leading Italian communist and an amateur geographer, who pinpointed it for me under its Lithuanian name. It is situated in the north east corner of Lithuania near the Latvian and Byelo-Russian border. I was a frequent visitor to the Soviet Union as a member of ANC and Communist Party delegations, and I looked forward to the possibility of a visit to the place of my early childhood.

The first opportunity presented itself in August 1968. I was a day away from my journey when I was informed that it had to be cancelled. The reasons emerged a few days later in the shape of the events in Czechoslovakia, which led to precautionary measures along the whole Soviet frontier. In December 1981 I waited once again in Moscow, this time successfully, to journey back 45 years into my past.

If I had been asked whom I wished to accompany me on this journey, I would have chosen the very man who was in fact selected, Alexei Makarov.

Alexei has a homely, sentimental warmth so typical of the Russian personality. He was an appealing kind of communist; his contributions to discussions were not caked over with deadening clichés. His defence of socialism was all the more convincing because there was no utopian pretence that all problems had already been solved. When Alexei came with the news that the trip had been arranged and that he would be accompanying me on the following day, he seemed as excited at the prospect as I was.

The evening before departure I took a long walk through a nearby birch forest area and tried systematically to collect my childhood memories of Obel. The winding pathway to our dilapidated wooden house. Beyond it, fields of mauve and yellow wild flowers leading to a river bank. Dark winter mornings and winter nights, through the snow with paraffin lamp in hand, trudging to and from the synagogue school. The sauna-type ritual public bath house (*mikva*) where we all went to bathe before the Friday synagogue service. The slope which marked the beginning of the village from the direction of Rakeshik. In winter snow dozens of us uncontrollably sliding on a large, packed sledge. At the top of this slope the only double-storey building, which was somehow connected with a relative who owned apple orchards whose pinkish-cream fruit was stored in the loft. The frozen lake on which we skated with sharpened bits of wood tied to our soles. The house in winter dominated by an outsize brick cooker (*pripachik*) which supplied the central heating and which warmed a brick ledge above it to provide a place into which the whole family crawled and slept during the cold nights. A few festive occasions such as weddings when crying was intermingled with the singing of the celebratory song 'Let us all together, together, drink a small glass of wine' – an endlessly repeated refrain. Snatches of recall of our departure; a horse and cart to the railway siding at Rakeshik; a farewell present of a home-made toy cart and the necklace of miniature bagels for the journey from the beard that was my grandfather. People came all the way from Dishat, about 20 kilometres away, to wish us God-speed. I could invoke no memory of faces of friends or relatives. In any case, I did not expect to find anyone familiar; the news had long reached us that when the Nazis came in 1941 they slaughtered every Jewish man, woman and child in the region. I was led to believe that the only relative who survived was my father's elder brother, who had joined the Red Army.

These, then, were the shadows which floated across my mind on that walk through the birch forest on the outskirts of Moscow. The next morning we boarded the overnight sleeper to Vilnius. We arrived in the early morning, and I was anxious to move on because I was booked for my return to Moscow 36 hours later in order to catch my flight back to Africa. Some hours later, after a brief welcoming speech at the Party centre, we were on our way in a chauffeur-driven Volga accompanied by an official of the International Department of the Lithuanian Party. It was a clear late summer's day which showed off the countryside in its verdant best, with rolling green hills, long stretches of woodland and an unending necklace of blue-water lakes. Until we left Obel I do not recall having ventured outside its limits for more than a few kilometres, and I had no conception of the natural beauty of this republic. On the way we stopped a few times to walk for a moment or two in forest edges. In 1968, when I returned to southern Africa after an absence of five years, it was the smell of the veld which so aroused my nostalgia, and here, too, the fragrance of the undergrowth beneath which we scratched for wild berries came back to me.

In Rokisckis, now an industrialised district centre and seat of the region's administration, we were welcomed by all the leading municipal and Party dignitaries. A *shas* of honour for a returning son was placed around me and the speeches expressed pride that the small village of Obel, 18 kilometres away, had been the birthplace of a leading communist from southern Africa. They were sure I would be interested in finding out about economic achievements in the region, and in rediscovering something of its cultural heritage. A programme was then suggested which included a visit to a school, a tour of museums, an inspection of a cheese factory, photographs to be taken in front of statues of some of the local heroes, a tour of the totem-like wood carvings which were scattered over bits of countryside, and for which the Lithuanians were famous, and so on. My heart sank. It was already two in the afternoon, and we were due back in Vilnius that same night. My mind was really bent on a relaxed stroll through Obel. I whispered to Alexei that he should hint about a possible shortening or cancellation of the programme. He was quite prepared to translate my request, but it had to come from me and I could not pluck up the courage to dampen the well-meant earnestness and enthusiasm of my hosts. So, in a convoy of black official cars, we proceeded according to plan.

In the school I was moved by the children who had themselves created a museum dedicated to a famous local son who had fought in Spain and who had, thereafter, become head of the Soviet Air Force. Understandably, when we toured the statues and the museums the internationalist contribution of local people was emphasised with enormous pride. On this occasion, of course, the theme was relevant to my own visit. But it was consistent with the spirit of internationalism which we, in our movement, have come to expect as part of the Bolshevik tradition. It was, however, nearing four o'clock in the afternoon and the cheese factory was still ahead of us. My hosts had already begun to sense my controlled impatience. We completed the last stage of the tour, including a cheese-tasting climax, in five minutes flat.

We were ready to move to Obel. I had already decided I did not want to enter the village in a convoy of official cars, or to be met with pomp and protocol by the village officials. I wanted to browse around unnoticed, to stare rather than to be stared at, to find landmarks which would lead me to our house, to the synagogue school, to the bath house, the river and the lake. My appeal was successful and Alexei and I were dropped some distance from the village.

There it was: the top of the hill; the beginning of the sledge ride; the double-storey structure; and the familiar shape returning to me of the main street descending steeply for some distance as far as the bridge of the narrow river and then flattening out into a winding road skirted by fields and pine forests. I was at once stirred by the distinctive smell of the apple trees which grew in abundance. I was to discover that day, for the first time, that in translation the name of the village is 'Apple'.

We strolled around the back paths chatting occasionally to old people (they all seemed to be women), trying to find someone who remembered the Slovo family and us as children. The old ladies consulted even older sisters, but we continued to draw a blank. 'The synagogue? They burnt it to the ground.' 'The ritual bath house?' 'That also.' 'The people, are there any Jews?' 'Those that didn't run away were all slaughtered, even children.'

We started again at the top of the hill, my only remaining point of orientation. I tried a number of pathways leading to houses from the main street, and we eventually came to a cluster which seemed almost familiar. The peasant houses looked pretty much alike, and I attempted to place the house in which I had lived by its position in relation to the fields and the river. I was concentrating on one in particular when we heard the screech of brakes from the road. While we were meandering about, our other companions had busied themselves with their own enquiries.

They brought with them a woman from the collective farm who remembered the Slovo family. She must have been over 70, but spoke and carried herself with a rustic freshness. As she spoke she examined me sceptically. She could not associate the portly, grey side-whiskered gentleman with the thin, scraggy youth that I had been. Yet she remembered a women with two children. The girl's name was Sonia. There was no husband and the family was poor. They lived in a series of hired rooms in houses on the other side of the street near the lake. By then I had already formed a strong belief that we were standing within a stone's throw of my family house, and that on this point the collective farm lady must be mistaken.

As I stood there something else came back. A window had broken and a heavy piece of iron had been placed against it to keep the weather out. A night of heavy storms with frightening peals of thunder and flashes of lightning. A sudden crash and I lay terrified, screaming that we had been struck. The terror remained with me even though my mother carried me to the window and showed me that it was the piece of iron that had been blown over.

Pointing to the house which seemed most familiar, I said to Alexei, half-jokingly, 'Let's walk round the back. If there's a broken window which is protected by a piece of iron, then this is it.' We moved towards the back and, to our astonishment, there it was – an ancient, rusty piece of iron blocking the whole window.

I rushed back to the group. 'Who lives there?' 'I do with my sister,' said the collective farmer. 'This has been our family house since 1930.' I asked if I could look inside. She agreed. The small house had been divided into two; the portion protected by that piece of iron was now a storeroom piled high with potatoes. The brick oven and the ledge were

7

still there. It seemed to me that I had entered the house of my early youth.

We emerged from the house to find that my hosts had unearthed another elderly inhabitant of the village who remembered the Slovo family. He was a leather-aproned blacksmith. He stood tall and erect, avoiding my handshake because he had obviously just been interrupted at the forge and was covered in soot. Even before his Lithuanian was translated into Russian and then into English by Alexei, my interest was aroused; I heard him mention 'Wulfus' – my father's name – more than once. But once again the balance of the picture seemed confused. He insisted that the Slovo family he knew had had a family of five daughters and three sons. When I questioned the reliability of his memory, he assumed an expression of resigned indignation. Two of the daughters, he said, had left the village in 1940 to pursue studies at the Moscow University. He recalled that officials of the security services had arrived in the village soon afterwards and had questioned a number of people, including himself, about the character and political reliability of these two girls, who, he understood, were the only family survivors of the Holocaust. He mentioned that Wulfus was a fisherman, my father's occupation before he left in 1928. But my scepticism about the accuracy of his memory was aroused even further when he described the situation of the Slovo house in a part of the village which seemed completely strange to me. When we were saying our farewells he added that I must surely be Wulfus's son, because the physical resemblance was striking.

I was tantalised by the accurate recall of some of the details by the collective farm worker and the blacksmith, and the disappointment of other references which put in question whether they knew us at all. In the case of the collective farm worker the ungenerous thought had flashed through my mind that her insistence that we lived in various rooms on the other side of the street was perhaps related to a suspicion that her occupation of the house I had identified might be in jeopardy. But in the case of the blacksmith, an event in Vilnius on the following day was to make me feel ashamed that I had questioned the good sense of this warm and wonderful old man.

It was now twilight and we moved from the open clearing to the village administrative building to end our visit with the ceremony which should have begun it: a welcoming address by the head of the village officials. She turned out to be an extremely pretty girl in her early twenties. She was, I suppose, the Western equivalent of mayor, but she had none of the polish which we have learned to associate with a municipal boss. This was her first public occasion. She nervously emphasised the link, through me, of Obel with the world struggle against imperialism and racism. She repeated this theme a number of times, and it became apparent to us that she didn't know how to stop. It was a combination of nervousness and inexperience. On Alexei's whispered suggestion I chose an appropriate moment to assume that she had finished and thanked her for her kind words. She was greatly relieved. We all embraced at the door of the building, and I was once again garlanded with a white linen tassel spun from local material. With a bouquet of flowers in my hand I moved towards the car in the presence of groups of watching villagers.

Our Vilnius driver stood holding the car door handle ready to receive me. He was a lanky youngster in jeans, and up to then had either been uninterested in all of us, or overawed by the middle-aged company. From when we left Vilnius until this moment when I was moving towards him, he had not said a word to me or to anyone else. His face had an emotionless expression with no hint of a scowl or a smile. Suddenly the ice was broken. To him I must have looked like an opera duke. His face remained impassive, but as I was about to slide into my seat and when he was certain no one else would see, he gave me an enormous wink. I responded spontaneously with a loud guffaw and, for the remainder of the journey, the mood between us (since language was not possible) was warm and friendly.

We sped to a workers' rest home on the lake's edge about 15 kilometres from the village. A sumptuous feast was waiting for us. Several dishes evoked memories of tastes of long ago, especially the combination of boiled potatoes, fresh cucumbers, spring onions and salted herrings floating in a soup plate of rich sour cream. After an interminable number of toasts we all adjourned to the sauna where the cycle of enormous heat, cold pool and a reviving vodka seemed never-ending. There were moments in the sauna when, closing my eyes, I was back in that bath house in which the whole Jewish community gathered to cleanse themselves before the Friday evening synagogue service.

I felt enormously privileged to have had the opportunity of indulging myself with such a large dose of nostalgia. At the time one recollection puzzled me, and continues to do so. The village is dominated by a hundred-year-old Catholic church whose tall spires can be seen for many miles around the village. Why, then, was my memory completely blank on this feature? Was it distaste and contempt for non-Jewish religious belief which wiped out this object from the mind's eye of my early youth? The ghetto Jew's anomalous response to religious persecution was tribal bigotry. As children we were terrified to walk past the Christian cemetery, and to this day I remember the rhyming chant: *Yoshke Pandre*

9

liekt in drerd, oisgepagered vi a ferd, meaning 'Jesus Christ lies in the earth dead like a horse.' (In Yiddish different words are used to describe the death of human beings and animals, and the word *gepagered* refers to the death of an animal.) We, the chosen (for persecution?), were taught that we were superior to *goyim,* and for boys the greatest taboo was the *shikshe* – a non-Jewish girl. Those who married one of these creatures were forever beyond the pale. Antipathy towards, and fear of, the ethnic 'enemy' instilled into us from childhood undoubtedly helped erase that Catholic spire from my memory.

It was close to 4 am when we started on our return journey to Vilnius. We were escorted for some distance by our hosts, until we reached an unmarked point which they claimed was the frontier of the district. A few bottles of champagne were opened and we embraced in final farewells. It was indeed difficult to believe that I had arrived in the district only some 14 hours before.

When we returned to Vilnius, it was obvious that we could not possibly fulfil the tour which had been arranged for us for the rest of the day. We slept most of the morning and then strolled around the old part of the city, spending much time in Vilnius University, one of the oldest seats of learning in Europe.

Back in the hotel room, an hour before our departure, I hear the phone ring. I ignore it; Alexei is next door, and, if it is anyone else, I will not be able to communicate. A minute later it rings again. The caller is not to be discouraged, so eventually I pick up the receiver. The language is at once both strange and familiar. It takes me some moments to realise that the woman at the other end is speaking Yiddish, and is asking me whether I am 'Yoshke'. I have last spoken Yiddish some 40 years before, and, in the confusion, I say in Portuguese *'Um momento'* and rush next door to call Alexei. He speaks to the caller in Russian and his face beams with excitement. 'We must rush,' he says. 'That was your cousin, and she and her sister and their families are waiting for us at the station.'

And here they are, Bela and Sareta; the latter bears an uncanny resemblance to my sister Sonia. The old blacksmith is completely vindicated. These two ladies are the daughters of Wulfus, my grandfather's younger brother after whom my father was named. They are the two who had gone to study at the Moscow University and who, by this accident of fate, survived the Holocaust. Every other member of the family on my mother's and father's sides, together with all other Jews in the region, had been wiped out.

During the half-hour before our train leaves, we chat excitedly in a mixture of Yiddish (much of which surprisingly comes back to me) and

English, with the help of Bela's daughter who has learned English at the university. The two families are now settled in Vilnius, and the Party apparatus there has traced them that very afternoon after receiving a message from our village host.

Both Sareta and Bela are a few years older than me and remember more than I do of our life in the early 1930s. They remember me clearly, but I am totally unable to place them. One of the first questions Sareta asks is whether I recall those reckless rides on the sledge down that snow-covered village slope. They still make an annual pilgrimage to Obel to lay a wreath on the monument to those massacred during the occupation. They know where my house is, and they are sorry indeed that they had not been with me the day before. I am thankful that it has turned out this way – a journey of half-completed rediscoveries.

Joining the Communist Party

A s I look back on my life in a broad sweep, I can see it as a succession of journeys, each constituting a significant divide in the course of that life.

My father, Wulfus Slovo, took the first journey in 1928 when I was only two years old. He left Lithuania to find a place for us somewhere beyond the village ghetto in which we were trapped. Why he chose Argentina I shall never know. Many East European Jews went there for their exile. Perhaps a friend's letter came filled with promise; perhaps another relative had prepared the ground.

I learned later that within a year or two my father sent for the rest of us. We were on the point of starting our own journey when he joined the millions of unemployed during the recession of 1929 onwards. Disillusioned with Argentina, he decided to try somewhere else and travelled to South Africa. There he hawked fruit in the streets, and when he had saved enough money for our fare, my mother, elder sister Sonia and I joined him in 1936. He was a man I first remember seeing when I was ten.

What would I have become if my father's journey had ended in Argentina? Certainly steeped in Spanish culture and language. What influences would have shaped my social consciousness? An establishment sympathiser or a rebel? These intriguing thoughts have endless permutations. But, self-indulgent speculation apart, it is clear that my father's journey back across the Atlantic to South Africa shaped the course of my life more than any other journey. What I am now was created in the 27 years that I spent in South Africa before embarking on my next journey.

When we arrived in South Africa we moved into the suburb of Doornfontein, which was the lowest rung of the Jewish residential ladder. Those upon whom fortune smiled trekked northwards via Hillbrow to Yeoville, Bellevue and parts of Observatory. The great leap forward from lower to upper middle class was symbolised by Orange Grove and Highlands North. In these suburbs screamingly vulgar wrought-iron burglar proofing appeared to cover every square inch of access to the house, transforming the *stoep* into something resembling a gorilla cage and announcing that the occupants had at last accumulated enough items worth stealing. Beyond Orange Grove, suburbs like Parktown, Lower Houghton and Dunkeld were legends in the mind of a Doornfontein lad. We knew nothing at all about the black ghettos; they seemed to be in another world whose function was to belch servants.

Our first family house was a rambling, tin-roofed structure in Beit Street, Doornfontein, very much in the style of the houses portrayed in the photographs of Johannesburg during the early days of the Gold Rush in the 1890s. The house was soon to be demolished and replaced by the Apollo Cinema and Crystal Bakery and Delicatessen for which my father later worked as a bread delivery man and my sister as a shop assistant.

Within a few weeks of our arrival in South Africa I was sent to the Jewish government school very close to Doornfontein railway station. Most of the pupils came from East European immigrant homes but this did not save me from being targeted as the latest butt of the school wags. And who could blame them? My completely shaven scalp (as part of a delousing process) and my recent arrival from a region which they assumed was run by the Bolsheviks earned me the nickname of 'Bald Bolshie'. The headmaster, Mr Harris, whom I remember with great affection, did his best to help me through the awkward transition period. But his well-intentioned habit of stroking my bald head when he passed me gave the school clowns new ideas; when they saw me coming one or other of them would ostentatiously stroke an object such as a smooth, large pebble, a hard-boiled egg from a lunch box, and so on.

By the time my family had made the first journey north towards Bellevue I had become sufficiently assimilated not to feel like a freak at my new school, Observatory Junior. The school went up to Standard 3 and I completed my primary education (Standards 4 and 5) at Yeoville School for Boys.

In Bellevue we lived in a semi-detached house at 26a Rockey Street immediately opposite our newly acquired fruit shop. At this point the single-track tram system became double in order to allow trams from opposite directions to change places with one another on to the single track. A fair proportion of the passing trade came from the passengers in the tram which was forced to wait. Among these passengers was Ella Kaplan, my very first passion, who regularly jumped off to get her daily fix from the sweet counter.

As the child of a shopkeeper, I was seldom without an ill-gotten supply of valuables such as sherbet, bubble gum and, even more impressively, cigarettes. Our smoking club in the school lavatories flourished for a while until it was uncovered by the headmistress who rushed there during one of the school breaks to investigate a suspected fire, only to discover about half a dozen of us locked into a small lavatory puffing away for all our worth. My father's vigilance after receiving a complaint from the school abruptly cut off our most reliable supply source of cigarettes. Henceforth we had to make do with our own manufacture made out of *stompies* (discarded cigarette ends) reinforced with dried leaves according to season. And we found another venue in which to indulge our pleasures. In Bezuidenhout Street, on an abandoned construction site, we built a den out of rubble and spent much of our leisure hours coughing out our lungs and experimenting with the forbidden.

Our guru was Benny Michel, a musical polymath, who was adept in half a dozen or so instruments. He was already 14 (about three years older than most of us) and, so it seemed to me, had virtually completed his education of the world and its ways. His polio-crippled leg somehow added to his charisma, and in our den when he was holding court he would unstrap the iron support and lean on it in a sceptre-like pose.

But Benny and the den soon lost me to my first love, Ella Kaplan, an accident-prone young lady of about 12 whom, in my fantasies, I was incessantly rescuing from burning aeroplanes, sinking ships, landslides and other such perils. I now spent most of my free time hovering outside her Rockey Street flat in the hope that, Juliet-like, she would appear on her balcony. If she is alive today she would be most surprised to hear of my deep affection for her since, despite my unflinching heroism in my daydream situations, I never mustered up courage to actually speak to her. To this day I remember the last four digits of her telephone number which I never once completed dialling.

My earliest awareness of the reality of death came with Spotty, a stray mongrel fox terrier, who one day followed my sister home and decided to stay. I was consumed by guilt when he was killed by a motor car when rushing to greet me as I came home from school. Improvising a coffin made from one of my school bags, Sonia and I buried him in the shop yard and placed a headstone over his grave on which we scribbled 'Spotty 8th April 1938'. And yet I do not remember the day or even the month of my mother's death in the same year.

I was not told of her death. I suddenly woke up in the middle of the night to find the mirror covered with a white sheet. The walk around the coffin, the hysterical wailing of women and, above all, the yellow, yellow face haunted me for years. But the shaft of horror and the shock which struck me on our return from the funeral still evokes a shudder within me. As we entered the dining room, staring at me from the mantelpiece was a large doll (a present for my sister Reina) completely wrapped in bright yellow cellophane paper. It was particularly horrifying since my mother had died in childbirth and I expected to see the still-born child in the coffin.

Apart from a feeling of warmth, I have only the vaguest recollection of my relationship with my mother during the two years that elapsed between our arrival in South Africa and her death. The strands that do remain are of a woman who worked from 5 am until 8 pm in the fruit shop; of her seemingly continuous state of pregnancy; of the exact position in the room where she sat when she hugged me before going to hospital; and the sight of that yellow face in the coffin.

The period of ritual mourning began with a week of 'sitting *shiva*' during which one is obliged to use very low supports (in our case fruit boxes) when seated. Prayers were held daily at which I, as the senior male offspring, was obliged to recite *kaddish*, the prayer for the dead. Prayer sessions could not begin until a *minion* had gathered. A minion was constituted by a minimum of ten adult Jewish males. Some of those who came for the prayer sessions were complete strangers to me, and I discovered later that they were part of a professional reserve of 'minionites' who augmented their income by moving from one bereaved home to another.

Women did not count as part of the *minion*. They could only get through to the Lord through their menfolk. In the synagogue, they were segregated in the 'gods' from where they could observe the goings-on in the stalls. Sonia resented the fact that I was the one to say *kaddish* and, in the privacy of our shared bedroom, she defiantly chanted the prayer before going to sleep. I feared that terrible things would be visited upon her for this blasphemy.

Within a short time of my mother's death a third tragedy occurred. The gentle, smiling African delivery man Jonas (I assumed that like all Africans I came across he had no surname) was killed in a head-on collision. My father and sister were upset when I informed them I had begun to say *kaddish* on behalf of Jonas and wail at the daily prayer sessions which I was now obliged to attend at the local synagogue for a whole year following my mother's death.

Unlike Job, the blows visited upon me during 1938 found me wanting and I didn't last the course. As the year dragged on I began to look for rationalisations to escape the burden of the daily service which dominated my life. It was at this point that my break with God began. By the time I stood on the *Bimah* of the Berea synagogue to chant my allotted *barmitzvah* portion from the Bible, I had already begun to question whether He existed at all.

Without my mother's input the shop slid towards bankruptcy. Reina was sent to Johannesburg Jewish orphanage where she remained until her late teens. Sonia, already a 14-year-old, left school and began her career as a shop assistant. My father went back to the uncertain occupation of selling fruit from various pavement open sites. These were allocated by the City Council on a rotational basis, determined by a monthly lottery. In those months when the luck of the draw went against him, he had no income.

The Rockey Street house was given up and we started on our return journey to Doornfontein via Hillbrow. In Hillbrow we lived in a boarding house in Esselen Street run by a Mrs Leiserowitz. There I met my first real-live member of the South African Communist Party, a Dr Max Joffe, who was courting his future wife Socky, one of the Leiserowitz daughters. Max was the younger brother of Louis Joffe who had reached high office in the Party and was expelled during one of the many 1930s purges. Louis was a mild, mournful-looking soul who didn't appear to have the stomach for the rough and tumble of Party in-fighting. But detractors claimed that when in office he grew fangs. He persisted in his efforts to have the expulsion order rescinded, and I was convinced that his unsuccessful annual applications to the Party's national conference contributed to his death in the early 1950s. The Party was already underground when he approached Bram Fischer to intercede on his behalf. His renewed appeal was discussed at an underground central committee meeting and a decision was taken to readmit him, but he died before it was conveyed to him.

In the Leiserowitz house I remember listening to Max shocking the boarders (most of whom were voteless aliens) when he talked of votes for blacks and of his opposition to the 'imperialist' war. He planted the first seed of political interest in me. I met Max again much later when I attended my first political meeting at his surgery in the Lewis and Marks Building which was used as a venue for the afternoon sessions of the Junior Left Book Club. Because of its proximity to the Johannesburg City Hall steps the surgery was also used as a casualty station in the middle 1940s during the regular Sunday night battles between Communists and Grey Shirts.

Our relatively short stay in the Leiserowitz boarding house was, in other ways, an uncomfortable experience. Apart from the uncertainties of the fruit stall business, my father was still being hounded by the Bellevue shop creditors. Since civil imprisonment for non-payment of debts was still enforced, he spent a number of short spells at The Fort prison, with which I was later to become more acquainted both as a lawyer and as a detainee.

It was humiliating to go to the dining hall of the boarding house when we knew that our food and lodging bill had not been paid for months. I am not even certain whether we were actually told to leave or whether there was a different reason for our move to Mrs Sher's boarding house in Van Beek Street, Doornfontein.

At Mrs Sher's boarding house my father and I shared a tiny attic room. Apart from school bus fare the only spending money I received came from an aunt who gave me half a crown every Friday afternoon. To receive this sum (it meant bioscope at The Alhambra on Saturday morning at the cost of sixpence, 'Tickey' – three pence – hot dogs, half-penny bubble gums etc), I was obliged to make the journey from Van Beek Street to the top of Harrow Road where my aunt lived in a rambling, decaying house dominated by two steep gables and surrounded by large grounds which were completely covered in wild vegetation. I don't remember ever seeing her walk. She always received me in a large, throne-like chair in her bedroom. When the greetings stage was over she tended to sit still, merely looking at me, sighing and nodding her head from time to time in completely silent conversation. In the meanwhile the sole object of my journey would be resting on a bedside table towards which my eyes would move surreptitiously as if in fear it would disappear. Eventually, to my relief, she would point to the gleaming coin and this was the signal for me to take it and say farewell. Much later, when I saw Bette Davis's portrayal of that mysterious and frightening recluse in *Baby Doll,* I had a strange sense of *déjà vu.*

One day I was quite bewildered by my father who shyly told me that I could now have the attic room to myself since he was going to marry Sophie Silberman, a buxom young lady who lived across the road. I resented this and distanced myself from both of them and my half-sister Rachel who was born soon after.

My father died of liver cancer in 1957, when I was still an accused in the Treason Trial. Between him and me there was hardly ever a father-son relationship. Until I was ten he was a complete stranger to me and, in the remaining years of my childhood, we tried to get to know one another. But it was somehow too late and the atmosphere was one of detached formality. I don't ever recall being praised or punished by him. He could never express himself in English and, since I quickly lost my capacity to use Yiddish, the communication between us became more and more restricted. He was a gentle man, a worker all his life; his last job was with Crystal Bakery doing bread delivery rounds from about 4 am each day except Sunday. Perhaps the one thing that did rub off on to me was his enjoyment of card games. The only other form of recreation which he seemed to have was playing the horses. I saw and spoke to my father on the afternoon of his death, and among the things that I could hear him express through the haze of his pain was his belief that the complete outsider he had backed had just won the race. The Treason Trial was postponed for a day to enable me to attend his funeral.

When we moved to the Sher boarding house I was in the middle of the first year (Standard 6) of secondary school (Observatory Junior High) which was to be my last year of full-time formal studies. My father gave up the losing battle of his attempt to support me, so I found work as a dispatch clerk at Sive Brothers and Karnovsky, almost invariably referred to by the predominantly Jewish staff as 'Syphilis Brothers and Ganovim' (crooks).

Thus my adult working life began at the age of 14, and it was inaugurated by a pants-wetting ceremony on the first day. My confidence was gained when I watched my work-mates win quite a number of half-crown pieces by balancing them on their foreheads and successfully flipping them into a clinical funnel which they had inserted under the belt buckle of the inside of their trousers. The inevitable happened. As I stood there, balancing the half-crown on my brow, a torrent of eau de cologne was poured into the funnel, not only destroying the shape of my freshly laundered pair of trousers, but also causing me much embarrassment on my return to the boarding house still surrounded by the sweet smell.

Mrs Sher's boarding house had many of the characteristics of a Sholom Aleicham East-European *shtetel*. Yiddish was the official language, and even Bazaar, the African who helped serve at table, developed Jewish mannerisms and used Yiddish expressions. Apart from the occasional excursions to the left-inclined Jewish Workers Club (burnt to the ground by Grey Shirts during the war), social life for the inhabitants was restricted to the double-storey house which was ringed by a large *stoep*.

There were very few Yiddish books in circulation and there was little or no reading. A typical night would begin with a heated pre-dinner political discussion. The original topic was invariably diverted by the staggered arrival of lodgers who joined in. The dinner tables were cleared by 8 pm (when the weather was good they were put out on the stoep), and the nightly schools of rummy, poker and *klabberjas* (the most popular of all) would go into session until the early hours of the morning. Wednesdays and Saturdays were horse-racing days and there was usually a winner who provided a bottle of brandy to share with the bigger group of losers. Sunday morning outings often ended up on the broad pavement outside Cohen's cafe around the corner in Beit Street, where small groups debated horse racing, dog racing and the world situation.

The landlady, Mrs Sher, could have been a model for a Toulouse Lautrec lady in decline. Her cheeks and lips were always thickly smeared with clashing shades of red; when she stood her arms were akimbo, and when she sat her hands rested languidly on her spread-eagled thighs. Perhaps it was her appearance and the fact that Mr Sher was hardly ever there (he was a resident chef in one of the kosher Warmbaths hotels) which led to persistent rumours among the teenagers that she was having affairs with the elderly bachelor lodgers.

There was hardly any turnover of the boarding house population during the period I lived there. A few guests paid for board only, and lodged in their own rooms in the vicinity of the boarding house. Among these was a man by the name of Koppel, a dealer in scrap metal. Koppel had a gargantuan appetite and, without asking, Mrs Sher used to refill his soup plate five or six times. I always tried to avoid sitting at the same table as Koppel because, when his plate was clean, his eyes followed one's every forkful from plate to mouth. He was generally known as a Peruvian – 'Peruvnik' in Yiddish – a word which for some unaccountable reason came to be used by immigrant Jews to describe a person of boorish and uncouth habits. One day Koppel disappeared, and we heard he had been sentenced to five years jail for receiving stolen property. There was much speculation whether his stomach would adjust to prison rations.

The right-wing lobby at the boarding house was led by Mr Soshkolsky, who had the shape of a pink snowman. But, in addition, the top ball which was his head had a large, round growth emerging from below the right ear. He had a daughter, Ada, who was my age, and when the old man discovered that we had been to a matinee film together he warned her to keep away from the 'Bolzhshivik trash'. Ada was a budding pianist and was preparing for an exam or an Eistedfodd which required her to perfect Lizst's Hungarian Rhapsody No. 2, the strains of which assaulted our ears for what seemed like years.

The most musical lodger was Natie Belyaikin (he changed his name to Bell) who, particularly before the important days in the Jewish religious calendar, would be heard practising synagogue cantatas. Natie was a youngish adult with a fine tenor voice. Although a militant atheist, he was also the full-time choirmaster of the Berela Ghagi synagogue, so called after the name of its famous cantor. Natie, a most likeable man, arrived in South Africa when he was too young to fit into the village culture maintained by the older generation of immigrants, and too old to become part of native-born circles.

One of the quietest lodgers was a Mr Baker, who had retired from a lucrative coal agency business whose employees never actually handled a bag of coal. A customer who wanted coal would phone up the agency placing an order, and the agency would instruct the wholesale supplier to deliver direct to the customer. When Mr Baker first came to South Africa he was penniless and lived in a shack which had an outside lavatory. We all knew that when Mr Baker started to hum to himself and to put his hat on, he was off to relieve himself. It was clear that the years during which he had to make the journey to the outside toilets on cold winter nights had created such an association in his mind with the wearing of a hat that without it bowel movements would have been extremely difficult.

On the whole, I enjoyed the eccentricities of the inhabitants of this colourful oasis of immigrant life. I was really chuffed and regarded it as a recognition of manhood when, soon after I left school and started work, I was invited to take my place at one of their card tables. But my permanent integration into our boarding house routine was averted by my early involvement in radical political activism.

One of the important influences in my political formation was John O'Meara who was my form master in the year I was forced to leave school. At that time O'Meara was a committed Irish rebel, and he took every opportunity to rail against imperialism generally, and more particu-

21

larly its British variety. The English Left Book Club Associations had already spread to South Africa, and O'Meara arranged for a few of us to attend meetings of its junior section at Dr Joffe's surgery. My leaning towards left socialist politics was also formed partly by the bizarre and paradoxical embrace of socialism shared by most of the immigrants who filled the boarding houses in which we lived. I say 'bizarre' because they tended to combine a passionate devotion to the Soviet Union with Zionism and vicious racism towards the majority of the South African population.

In Lithuania I had been a member of *Habonim* (builders), the Zionist scout organisation into which every Jewish child was conscripted. Most summer weekends we camped in the surrounding forests and, around camp fires, we listened to tales of Palestine and sang nationalist songs in Hebrew and Yiddish. It was while living in Mrs Sher's boarding house that I was influenced to join *Hashomer Hatsair*, a Zionist organisation which claimed to be Marxist. The leader of the Doornfontein branch was Itchke Skikne, a passionate follower of Trotsky, who regularly harangued us about the permanent revolution and the role of the Jewish proletariat in far-off Palestine. Never a word about the black South African proletariat from whose exploitation we were all benefiting in one form or another. (Itchke was thoroughly ashamed of his brother Larry who deserted our 'great cause' and, under the name of Laurence Harvey, became a millionaire film actor.)

The combined inheritance of Zionism and boarding house armchair socialism (in terms of which a 'kaffir remains a kaffir'), and the absence of any relationship with blacks other than in master-servant form, made my transition to real radical politics a difficult one. I well remember the discomfort I felt when I found myself seated between black youths at that first meeting of the Junior Left Book Club to which my teacher O'Meara had taken me.

My first attempt to join the Communist Party was unsuccessful. I applied to become a member at a meeting on the City Hall steps chaired by Issy Wolfson. Issy smiled warmly, eyed my short trousers, and told me that I should perhaps wait a year or two. Eventually, in 1942, I was made a probationary member.

Issy, General Secretary of the Tailoring Workers Union, was a most impressive evangelist for the communist cause. He had a highly articulate, simple style and sounded as if his voice box was endowed with its own private megaphone. He invented an original answer to the most unoriginal question inevitably asked by one or other sex-frustrated white racist in the audience: 'Would you like your sister to marry a kaffir?' To which Issy (who had no sister) flashed back: 'If you knew her you'd realise that no self-respecting kaffir would ever marry my sister.' Later, when we both served on the Johannesburg District Party Committee, I envied him his capacity at meetings to fold his arms and fall asleep while sitting rigidly upright in a straight-backed chair.

I threw myself into Party work with a great vigour in the certainty (which I still have) that the revolution was around the corner. It is this triumph of optimism of will over pessimism of intelligence that has always sustained me.

One of our most popular teachers at the bi-weekly Party study classes was the veteran Solomon Buirski, an immigrant clothing factory owner whose East European-accented English was wonderfully clear even though it expressed itself in rather novel syntax. When he spoke on a public platform he used every trick in the book, and it was his habit to parry hostile questions with ridicule.

The leading Trotskyite, Fanny Klennerman, who was also a well-known practising nudist, was told when she demanded that Buirski tell the truth: 'I suppose you are hasking for de naked trut, Fenny?' At another meeting Benny Weinbren, a white labour politician, was offended by Buirski's assertion that marriage in capitalist society is nothing more than legal prostitution. To emphasise that, at any rate, his own marriage could not be so classified, Weinbren alluded to the fact that his wife was seated right next to him at this political meeting. 'So vot!' quipped Buirski, 'Mr Weinbren has brought wid him his cor, his vatch and his vooman.'

In our study classes Buirski gave the impression that he knew most of the classics off by heart and, without a note in front of him, would often reel off lengthy quotations. We later learnt that, when Buirski began a sentence with the words 'as Lenin said ...' we should not assume that it was indeed Lenin (rather than Buirski) who said it. All the same, he seemed to have such a profound grasp of the workings of the capitalist system that it came as a shock to us when his factory collapsed in bankruptcy.

In the black urban complexes the written word had already become the most important channel of contact with people, and weekends were set aside for literature drives. We used to catch trams or buses to townships such as Alexandra and Sophiatown and trudge the dusty streets selling pamphlets and the weekly newspaper, *The Guardian*. We sometimes spent hours with customers, discussing the news items and trying to cultivate them as potential recruits.

But the main focus of my Party activities was at my workplace where I recruited quite a number of members (mainly black but also a few whites including Mannie Brown), and we formed a factory group. We put up a literature stall in the black lavatory structure where we regularly sold Party publications, more especially the vernacular bi-monthly newspaper *Inkululeko* (freedom). We also operated an illicit wall newspaper in the same structure. Since we new that no conventional white man would ever have the stomach to enter a black lavatory, it became quite a useful base for aspects of our work.

The factory group helped create the Black Chemical Workers' Union and, some time later, one of the recruits, Nkosi, became its general secretary. I became an active member of the National Union of Distributive Workers. Within a year our workplace was almost totally unionised, and after negotiations under the Industrial Conciliation Act broke down, we embarked upon a legal strike in October 1942 which lasted for a few days and was completely successful. I had been earning £4 a month, and under the new agreement my wages rose to the handsome sum of £14 per month!

The decision to strike was taken at a meeting in the Kerk Street Trades Hall. Before the meeting I had been introduced to Bill Andrews who was visiting a trade union office in the same building. I stood in awe of Andrews, a great historic figure, one of the communist leaders of the 1922 General Strike and now the white-haired and moustachioed chairman of our Party. I excitedly stumbled over the main questions confronting us in the impending strike vote. To my surprise, he agreed to come down to the hall and address the workers. He did so with assurance and charm. He sounded and looked the very epitome of a British engineering worker, with the extra confidence of decades of trade union experience. Andrews left the hall before the vote was taken. The strike vote was almost unanimous. I could hardly wait to rush upstairs to tell Comrade Bill how well both he and I had done in the cause of working-class militancy. It soon became clear to me that I hadn't quite made the impact I had imagined on our chairman. When I found him he looked at me with a half-puzzled expression and said: 'Haven't we met somewhere before?' Only later was I to learn that Bill was already suffering from some of the symptoms of the illness which took his life a few years later. At the time my self-importance received a much-deserved jolt.

In retrospect, our strike at Sive Brothers and Karnovsky provides a good illustration of the complex link between national and class struggle in South African conditions. I belonged to a union registered under the Industrial Conciliation Act whose provisions excluded all Africans from the definition of 'employee'. Africans could neither belong to a registered trade union nor use the strike weapon in a dispute with an employer. (By some bizarre legislative quirk, Africans still had the right to take part in strikes in support of political demands, a loophole which, as we shall see, was fully utilised by the liberation movement during the mass campaigns of the 1950s.)

Our firm was something of a microcosm of the relationship between white and black workers. I was approaching 15 when I started work there, yet I immediately commanded mature African men (some of whom had worked there for many decades) who called me 'Baas'. No black could be a member of our union branch so long as it remained registered under the Act. Our picket line was manned by whites only and the negotiated settlement which ended the strike referred only to the white staff; in law no agreement which included Africans was enforceable. This was the objective reality of the law, but unfortunately it was also a reality which would have been defended by the overwhelming majority of my white fellow-workers. Indeed, the white working class had already fought and won its battles to 'keep the kaffir in his place' at the point of production.

In the early 1940s, during the democratic flush of the war against Hitler, the Party once again attracted quite a number of skilled white workers to its ranks. Some of them held positions in white unions such as the Amalgamated Engineering Union (Vic Syvret), the Building Workers Union (Piet Huyser), the Boilermakers Society (Issy Rosenberg), Garment Workers' Union (Johanna Cornelius), Typographical Workers Union (Joe Podbrey) and a few others. We also seemed once again to have a strong presence in the predominantly white trade union federation, the Trades and Labour Council.

In the end it all came to nought. One by one the newly recruited white workers dropped out of the Party. White workers helped the Nationalist regime come to power, and organised white labour accepted with hardly any protests the government measures to remove all militants and communists from their positions in the white trade union movement. In 1954 the Trades and Labour Council dissolved and reformed itself as the Trade Union Council of South Africa (Tucsa) which excluded all African unions from membership.

In 1943, when we all linked arms on that picket line and sang trade union songs about the evils of capitalism, the prospect of eventual white and black unity seemed promising. But, certainly at Sive Brothers and Karnovsky, nothing changed except the size of the pay packet of the white worker.

For me personally even the financial success of the strike was short-lived. I had been elected as the chief shop steward and I became the obvious target of the bosses. They were even more worried about my association with the African workers and the activities of our Party factory group. I was warned about this by one of the main directors, Sammy Sive. He was truly sad that 'a nice Jewish boy' like me, who was given the privilege of working for 'such a nice Jewish firm', should behave in such an ungrateful fashion. He was aware, he said, that I spent all my spare time in the 'native lavatories writing newspapers about communism'. He maintained that 'at heart we are all communists', and if I wanted proof I should ask Michael Harmel, who, only two weeks before, had been given a donation of 50 guineas from his own pocket for 'Medical Aid for Russia'.

'So stop making trouble with the natives and leave us alone,' he said, with his very thick East European accent. Being (as we shall see later) a rather 'cheeky boy', I didn't make things any easier by pointing out to him that I belonged to the Party and not to an insurance company and that he must not think that his 50 guineas to Medical Aid for Russia was a premium which would ensure that Sive Brothers and Karnovsky would be untouched by the coming revolution. My torrent left him speechless. He just pointed a shaking finger towards the door and, as I moved towards it, I heard a deep sigh accompanied by that most expressive all-purpose Jewish lament '*Oi vay*'. Added to the strike, this interview was the last straw and, on the false grounds that I had replaced someone who had joined the army and was now returning, I received my marching orders in March 1944.

The union invoked the Industrial Conciliation Act to try to force my reinstatement, by further strike action if need be. This personal experience taught me how the IC Act prevented effective action through devices such as long delays, cooling-off periods and so on. To survive while waiting for the outcome of the application for a conciliation board, I took work as a checking clerk in the patent medical department of another wholesaler, Elephant Trading Company. The manager soon began to suspect that I was beginning to Bolshevise some of his black workers, so, after a few months, I was again on the streets.

To war and to university

A t about the time of my second sacking the Party had taken a decision to encourage all able-bodied white members to join the South African Army. I was 18 and needed the signature of my father who, a year or two earlier, had joined the army for financial rather than political reasons. He refused his consent, but promised that if I succeeded in bluffing about my age he would take no steps to pull me out. He reasoned that if something were to happen to me, it would not be through his signature.

The recruiting office was clearly aware of such conspiracies and, after I received a cursory medical examination, my declared age of 22 was not questioned. Together with two other comrades who also had to add some years to their ages, we took the oath of allegiance to King and Country and signed the special volunteer form for service outside South Africa's borders, which entitled us to wear red tabs on our shirt lapels.

In line with Communist Parties everywhere our Central Committee had changed its stance on the war after the Nazi attack on the Soviet Union on 22 June 1941. But this somersault was more difficult for us than for most parties. How did you tell a black man to make his peace with Smuts – the butcher of Bulhoek and the Bondelswarts? To the average member of the rightless and voteless majority, the regime's exhortation to 'save civilisation and democracy' must have sounded like a cruel parody. And fight with what? At no stage was a black man allowed to bear arms; if he wanted to serve democracy he could so do so wielding only a *knobkierie*, as a uniformed manservant of the white soldier. The entry of Japan into the war on the side of Hitler provided a ready-made slogan to mobilise the racist whites: 'Fight against the yellow peril'. It was easy to understand those among the blacks who inwardly speculated that the arrival of men of colour might bring their own salvation nearer. Despite all these realities we spread our unpopular message in terrain which, on this question, remained unfriendly to the end.

The Party did its best to create a constituency among the whites to demand that blacks be given something to fight for and something to fight with. Astonishingly enough, when Tobruk fell, we managed to pack the Johannesburg City Hall with a white audience which enthusiastically cheered the Party's demands. But our ruling class feared democracy in South Africa more than fascism in Europe, and it did nothing to give the black majority a stake in the anti-Hitler war. The energy for real change could only have been generated by the blacks themselves outside the sphere of the constitutional framework in which they played no part. But in practice the Party commitment to the larger cause of the global struggle against fascism influenced it not to rock the war-effort boat too much. For example, Party activists in the black mineworkers union influenced a decision against strike action during the war years.

If medals for bravery and dedication displayed during this period were to be issued, they would in my opinion go to persons like [Yusuf] Dadoo who trudged the country with the unpopular mission of explaining the new line to the inhabitants of South Africa's ghettos. Dadoo had already been interned by the regime for his anti-war speeches. In 1940 he was sentenced to four months imprisonment for issuing a leaflet which said 'Don't support this war where the rich get richer and the poor get killed'. He was not initially convinced that we should now propagate support for South Africa's white war cabinet. Yet, albeit unhappily, he felt bound to act (as he had always acted) like a disciplined musket-bearer.

During my trade union days I entertained the forlorn hope that my white fellow-workers would learn in the course of fighting the boss that they should fight the system also. Now I found myself in an all-white army fighting fascism. It was an army riddled with racist attitudes; in Italy, most members of my unit would quite happily have forgotten Hitler and turned their weapons against an American black walking arm in arm with an Italian blonde. And experience taught me that this type of gut feeling was not just an Afrikaner syndrome; if anything, the purse-lipped racism of the English gentlemen from Natal was more irreversible. The Jew was slightly less rabid, but even he saw little connection between the Jewish ghettos in Europe and the black ones in South Africa.

Yet for a brief moment in time thousands of white ex-servicemen became members of the Springbok Legion, led by a radical group which included Party members such as Jack Hodgson and Jock Isaacowitz. The Springbok Legion was a brave attempt to keep alive the spirit of the anti-fascist struggle among white ex-servicemen, and to wean them away from the extremes of racism. As the years rolled on the comfort of white civvy street once again began to dull the idealism of war years and, by the end of the 1940s, the Springbok Legion was on its last legs. But that day at the recruiting office, when we were all packed into lorries and driven from the recruiting office at Union Grounds to our training camp in Potchefstroom, it felt like the first leg of a journey towards a brave new world in South Africa.

We were in the same batch as 'two-eye' Smith, whose nickname celebrated the fact that he had only one working eye. He managed to get an A1 medical clearance by the covering up the same blind eye (but with different hands) when asked to read the optical chart. I was allocated to the Signal Corps. After a few months of training in radio and telephone morse communication, we travelled by train to Durban from where we eventually embarked for Egypt. After a spell in the Hellwon Camp outside Cairo, we crossed the Mediterranean, landed at Bari in Italy and proceeded to the frontline just south of Florence. By then the war was in its final stages. Apart from spectacular artillery bombardments from our side and some stray bombing by German aircraft on road convoys, I neither experienced nor witnessed any major war action. I never saw a dead or wounded body, although I knew that we were suffering casualties from the messages I received and forwarded in the brigade signal communications centre.

The signing of the Armistice found us just outside Turin. On that night, 8 May 1945, we all linked arms with the local peasants and workers. We moved from street to pub and back again, exchanging flowers, laughing, weeping, singing and talking about the beautiful future.

I was to spend a further nine months in Italy, billeted in holiday hotels on the Italian Riviera and waiting for my turn to be repatriated at the beginning of 1946.

On our journey back to South Africa we once again stopped in Egypt. While waiting for our troop ship a few of us decided to visit Palestine. At the time Zionist guerrilla organisations were active against the British occupation, and an instruction had been issued restricting our trips to the area. We discussed this problem with our rather sympathetic commanding officer who made out route forms for ten days leave to Alexandria and suggested that if we added 'Palestine' nobody would be the wiser. We negotiated the use of a typewriter in the Cairo Officers Club and, despite the fact that I had recently spent six weeks on a shorthand and typing course at a soldiers' school south of Florence, the forgery was abominable. Since it was clear that the route forms would not be accepted by the military checkpoints at the railway station, we decided to hitch-hike.

The promised lift in a military cargo plane from a New Zealander we met in a pub came to nought. We decided to travel to the other side of the Suez Canal at Ishmailia in the hope of finding a convoy which was going through the Sinai desert. Eventually a jeep stopped, and the driver told us he was responding to a radio signal about a broken-down truck 'somewhere in the middle of the desert'. If we wanted to risk it, we could climb aboard. In utter ignorance of the vast distance between Ishmailia and southern Palestine, we didn't take seriously his reference to risk. After three hours of travelling he reached the broken-down vehicle and informed us, pointing to the vast expanse of desert ahead, that we still had hundreds and hundreds of kilometres to go. In the army you come across so many queer fellows that, after a while, you learn not to probe into the deeper recesses of their minds, and when we rejected his offer to travel back to Ishmailia he just shrugged, gave us a tin of bully beef and wished us 'the best of British luck'.

The drop in desert temperature when the sun disappears is dramatic. The sun was already low in the sky, and we were cold and hungry. There was no sign of life from approaching traffic in any direction. We had almost given up hope and had decided to curl up for the night in the sliced 44-gallon drums which had originally contained bitumen for the road surface, when we noticed a pin-point of light travelling towards us in the direction of Palestine. We jumped into the road, waved frantically, but to our utter disgust the big army truck ignored us completely. As we stood there cursing the occupants, the vehicle suddenly made a U-turn and returned to us. It was a British engineering unit truck. The driver explained that he had experienced a 'double take': he had realised only after passing us that there were soldiers hitching a lift in the middle of the desert with no apparent life on either side for vast distances. It seemed to us that he must have suspected an ambush and returned to us only when it was clear there was no firing. In any case, he drove us to his engineering outpost and provided us with food, tent and blankets. Late the next morning, through a combination of army trucks and civilian buses, we reached Tel Aviv. One of my companions had relatives living in the city who arranged for us to spend a week on a kibbutz which, coincidentally, was run by my old organisation *Hashomer Hatzair*.

Looked at in isolation, the kibbutz seemed to be the very epitome of socialist lifestyle. It was populated in the main by the idealistic sons and daughters of rich Jews who had amassed their fortunes in the Western metropolis. They were motivated by an Owenite passion and the belief that by the mere exercise of will and humanism you can build socialism in one factory or one kibbutz and that the power of its example will sweep the imagination of all men in society, worker or capitalist. Social theory aside, the dominating doctrine on this kibbutz, as well as on the others, was the biblical injunction that the land of Palestine must be claimed and fought for by every Jew. And if this meant (as it did eventually mean) the uprooting and scattering of millions whose people had occupied this land for over 5 000 years, more's the pity.

Within a few years the wars of consolidation and expansion began. Ironically enough, the horrors of the Holocaust became the rationalisation for the perpetration by Zionists of acts of genocide against the indigenous people of Palestine. Those of us who, in the years that were to follow, raised our voices publicly against the violent apartheid of the Israeli state were vilified by the Zionist press. It is ironic, too, that the Jew-haters in South Africa – those who worked and prayed for a Hitler victory – have been linked in close embrace with the rulers of Israel in a new axis based on racism.

Although I did not feel like a conquering hero (my contribution to the war seemed less than significant), my army journey brought another major point of departure in my life. I applied for and, to my great surprise, was granted a five-year scholarship to study law. This was an extremely generous gesture by the Discharged Soldiers Demobilisation Committee and the university authorities; in general loans and support for ex-servicemen to study were granted only to those who had interrupted an academic career to join the army. In my case, I had not even matriculated. I was obliged to take a matriculation exemption exam, which, as I recall it, was a pure formality; it was especially designed for illiterate ex-servicemen.

The few years that followed my admission to Witwatersrand University were perhaps the happiest of my life. The joy of relaxed discovery of knowledge, the excitement of sharp but safe student politics and the finding of new friends. My life friendship with Harold Wolpe began at the university, a friendship with the rarest of qualities. We had actually first met in 1938 on a football field adjacent to the Yeoville Boys School where we were both pupils. Harold was a year ahead of me and was a star sportsman. One day when I tried to join a football kick-around, Harold warned me off the field on the grounds that the game was for senior boys only, and not for pipsqueaks like me. In fairness to him I should record that to this day he denies my version of the circumstances of our first encounter! At the university he became a key figure in the student movement, serving as President of the Student Representative Council and becoming a leading activist in the National Union of South African Students (Nusas). He was arrested soon after the Rivonia raid and, but for his dramatic escape (together with Arthur Goldreich), there is little doubt that he would have been sentenced to life imprisonment. In exile in England he returned to academic work in the course of which he made a stimulating contribution to the development of the theory of our revolution; a contribution which helped inspire some of my own forays into theoretical writing.

At the university we had the usual divisions 'within the left'. Trotskyism attracted a sprinkling of whites, some of whom were adherents of the Unity Movement which had a following among middle-class coloureds in the Cape Province. Like their counterparts elsewhere, they claimed to be the sole custodians of the 'pure' revolutionary line. Nothing we ever did was good enough for these purists. If we called a strike it was 'premature' or 'adventurist'. If the workers were not brought into action we were 'dragging in the tail of the national movement'. If we supported passive resistance we were 'middle-class Gandhiites'. If we toyed with the idea of armed struggle we were 'left-wing adventurers'. And, of course, the worst sin of all was that we were still gullible enough to believe that the Soviet Union was a socialist country. At this time the most exciting debates which raged within the group was whether the Soviet Union was a 'bureaucratic workers' state' or a 'workers' bureaucratic state' – a difference whose import continues to escape me.

It seemed to me then (subsequent events have confirmed my impression) that in quite a number of cases the protests by these 'leftists' against 'continuing betrayals' by those involved in day-to-day activity against the regime were really a rationalisation to stay out of trouble. It enabled them to exude an aura of revolutionary charisma but, in practice, to surround themselves with an ideological cocoon which protected them against actual involvement in confrontations with the powers-that-be.

At Wits I counted among my friends three such characters whose subsequent history fits in well with my prejudices on the subject. One of them emigrated to the United Kingdom, invested his inherited fortune in large-scale landlordism, and eventually joined the Conservative Party. Another who followed him became a social democrat and was an official candidate on behalf of the Labour Party in a London local election. The third returned to what was then known as Rhodesia and, when Ian Smith declared UDI, became his attorney-general.

Post-war protest

O utside the university, the immediate post-war period saw a spate of hectic radical political activity whose legitimacy was still being shored up by the short-lived momentum of the victorious struggle against fascism.

The Party organised food raids in Fordsburg as part of a campaign against the black market, forcing shopkeepers to open their reserve stores and sell the goods at controlled prices. I have two fond memories of this episode: Bram Fischer with a crowbar in his hand opening a box of Sunlight soap which he had removed from a recalcitrant storekeeper and was selling at controlled prices to a queue which had formed, then meticulously accounting for every penny to the irate shopowner. And well-fed and plump Patsy Gilbert standing on a street corner shouting in her high-pitched voice: 'the people are starving'.

This vision of Patsy reminded me of an incident which dates back to the early 1930s. The Party had organised a hunger march of unemployed who eventually occupied the tables in the plush restaurant of the Chamber of Mines. Among those who came was Mrs Woolf, an old East European Bolshevik type and her daughter Rosa (you can guess after whom she was named!). The waiters had refused to serve this 'mob', but the tables had already been laid with baskets of freshly-baked rolls which were eagerly consumed by hungry marchers. By all, that is, except six-year-old Rosa who had left home only an hour earlier after a most ample breakfast. 'Eat some bread,' whispered Mrs Woolf to Rosa. 'I'm full, we have just had breakfast,' squealed Rosa loudly. Mrs Woolf looked round at the embarrassed smiles of her fellow-marchers and in a loud crisp voice enunciated the classic Yiddishism, 'Rosa, just shut up and eat.'

Participants in the hunger marches of the early 1930s (such as colourful communist barber, Issy Diamond) recounted to me their unique experiences of black and white unemployed marching together and linking arms in Johannesburg's streets. But by the middle 1940s white worker participation in confrontation with authority was already a thing of the past. It was becoming clearer than ever that the catalyst for real change in South Africa could only come from a challenge by the racially dominated. And this challenge was growing, more especially from the black workers.

The pace in the growth of the black proletariat was much accelerated during the First and Second World Wars. Soon after each of those, strikes of miners took place (white miners in 1922 and black miners in 1946) which acted as major catalysts in the pivotal shifts which ensued in South Africa's political spectrum. The cardinal figures in both strikes were communists, Bill Andrews and JB Marks, each of whom subsequently served as Chairmen of the Communist Party. General Smuts, who was Prime Minister in 1922 and 1946, responded to the miners' actions as if they were major rebellions and used the state's armed forces to drown both strikes in blood. He suffered defeat in the general elections which, in both cases, followed two years after the events. But here the resemblance between 1922 and 1946 ends and the epoch-making contrasts begin.

1922 was a strike to entrench the race privileges of the white worker. After the victory of the Pact government (an alliance between Afrikaner nationalism and the all-white Labour Party) in 1924, race privileges were institutionalised and the white workers became appendages of the ruling class. The political monopoly of mining capital was broken and a new alliance emerged which continued to stand in solid defence of white supremacy but within which secondary conflicts surfaced in relation to such questions as competing claims of access to cheap black labour by the different segments of capital.

In 1946 it was the turn of the black miners. Their great strike was led by JB Marks, President of the African Mineworkers Union. The union, like so many other of the African trade unions, was built up by Party members. (But, in contrast to the position in 1922, the Party's membership was overwhelmingly black and its ideology had moved a long way towards an understanding that the main immediate content of the South African revolutionary endeavour is the national liberation of the African people.) The 1946 strike shook the system to its very foundations; it sharply brought home to the regime the awesome potential of the new social force which was emerging – the black proletariat with its collective instruments of struggle. The white electoral turn, in 1948, to more extreme forms of racist repression was undoubtedly influenced by fear.

Within the black opposition movement, the strike had the effect of encouraging more radical and militant policies. Even the cap-in-hand Nationalists who dominated the Native Representative Council were forced by this event to resign their seats. But, more importantly, the period immediately following the strike saw the emergence of the young turks of the African National Congress Youth League. The youthful revolutionism of people such as Mandela, Tambo, Sisulu, Lembede and others, supported by the communist veterans who were members of the ANC leadership, began to transform the ANC from its relatively conservative beginnings into a radical revolutionary nationalist organisation. Commenting on the miners' strike in 1954, *Fighting Talk* (under Ruth [First's] editorship) said that it was one of 'those great historic incidents that, in a flash of illumination, educates a nation, reveals what has been hidden, destroys lies and illusions'.

During those days in August 1946 when a hundred thousand miners fought it out with the bosses and the police, the Johannesburg District of the Party threw all its resources into support activity. Progress Buildings in Commissioner Street (which housed the District Party offices) was the scene of an endless stream of Party members and sympathisers who, at the end of a day's labour, had come to pick up leaflets and then spend most of the night attempting to distribute them in the beleaguered mine compounds. There was no time for sleep; during the day Harold and I helped cyclostyle material at the Party and the union offices and at night we manoeuvred our way in a borrowed car around the mining areas between Springs and Braamfontein, looking for opportunities to put up posters and throw leaflets over the guarded work-prisons of the black

miners. Fifty-two accused, including all the members of the Johannesburg District Committee of the Party, were subsequently found guilty of
assisting an illegal strike. Our Central Executive Committee was acquitted on a charge of sedition at the end of a trial which dragged on for over
two years.

In 1946 we were also deeply involved with the squatter movement
which mushroomed soon after the war with the enormous influx of
homeless blacks into the city of Johannesburg. Hundreds of thousands of
Africans moved into the open veld in defiance of the law and built their
shacks in a chain of shanty towns similar to Crossroads. Memories of
colourful Mpanza on his white charger leading one of the big squatter
groups, and the Rev Michael Scott installing himself as a resident in a
squatter camp called Tobruk and surviving on sixpenny packets of fish
and chips, remain. One of the biggest concentrations of squatters was
situated near the present Moroka Township which had just been proclaimed by the Johannesburg City Council as an official housing area.
The facilities were known as 'site and service'; each successful applicant was
allocated a small plot on which a single pre-fabricated lavatory had been
erected. Communal water taps were available at scattered points. Permission to enter this fenced area was much sought after by the squatters; it
held out the promise (which was the dream of every black) to have the
'privilege' of a legal presence in the urban areas. There were bitter complaints from the farmers that the cities were depriving them of their even
cheaper labour. Under the generalship of Colin Legum, who was chairman of the Labour controlled Non-European Affairs Department of the
City Council (and who in later life posed as the liberal friend of Africa),
the post-war assault on the homeless and the hounding of city blacks
under pass law, influx control and curfew regulations was greatly intensi-
fied.

The popular leader of the large squatter camp near the newly proclaimed Moroka Township was Schreiner Badhuza, a prominent Party
activist. Most of the people in his camp were 'illegals' in Johannesburg,
and the strict screening procedures prevented them from obtaining a plot.
When it became clear that the authorities were preparing to launch a
major offensive against the squatter movement, the camp committee took
the desperate decision to move *en masse* and occupy the plots in Moroka
Township without permission. Badhuza brought this news to Ruth's
newspaper office in the later afternoon of the very night when the march
was due to take place. Rusty Bernstein, Ruth and I, the only District
Committee members who could be contacted, decided to go to the squatters' camp for discussions with our Party unit there. On the way we

reconnoitred portions of the perimeter fence of Moroka Township and discovered that a massive contingent of police stood in formation facing the direction of the veld from which the marchers would approach. It was near midnight and the march was due to take place at approximately 2 am. We parked our car some distance away and walked towards the squatters' camp where we again noticed a large police presence.

Our experiences of the next hour convinced me, as never before, that racism and backward nationalism can be transcended in the brotherhood of struggle. Our journey through the labyrinth between the hessian sacks which walled the squatters' shelters was guided by a young man who every now and again whispered that we were '*Ikomunisi*'. It seemed like a magic password; more than once we were shuffled into shacks by vigilant occupants to avoid discovery by the police patrols. On reaching a small square where the committee had assembled we reported what we had seen of police strength outside Moroka Township. We were among a minority which questioned the wisdom of proceeding with the march (which was already under way) under these conditions. But we couldn't really blame the majority; despair and reason are not always harmonious companions. The mood was well expressed by one young man in words which sum up why so many keep going for so long: 'Let's try, one day we'll get through.'

The inevitable happened. Wave after wave of squatters were charged down by the baton-wielding squads of police. The three of us decided we should follow the marchers' route in order to give whatever assistance we could to any badly injured. We saw a few stragglers and bits of abandoned clothing, but we did not come across anyone who needed our help. We eventually emerged from the veld on to the tarred road. Facing us was a massive formation of police, batons in hand, and presumably awaiting the next order to charge. The police command group moved crisply towards us and the officer in charge ordered us to halt. He asked us what we were doing so late at night in the veld. Suddenly it seemed to dawn on him. Even before we could stutter out an answer, he leered at Ruth from top to toe, gave Rusty and me a winking look and giggled out: 'Jesus, and with all those natives too, next time you's better find a safer spot. *Weg is julle* (on your way).'

In the early and middle 1940s electoral politics were still of some importance in the life of the Party. In 1944, for the first (and only) time in South African history, a white constituency had elected as city councillor an official representative of the Communist Party. At the time it gave us all a heady feeling, although it seems uncertain whether the Hillbrow electorate was persuaded that Hilda Watts (Bernstein) would lead

39

them towards a socialist millenium, or whether her victory was due to the impact of the Red Army in its post-Stalinist advance against the German fascists. In retrospect, it was most probably the latter factor which played the more important role. I remember canvassing for Hilda's re-election and being told by one voter soon after he opened his door that he did not need convincing and he would vote for Hilda Watts because 'the government is already giving too many rights to the "kaffirs".'

The question of whether we should continue to contest this kind of election in the white suburbs of Johannesburg was vociferously debated at every District Party conference. The veteran Solomon Buirski once described our first and last success in Hillbrow as an unusual 'conglomeration of coincidences that result in a fluke'. And to those who maintained that we should fight white working-class rather than white middle-class constituencies, he made the point that there would be no difference if 'Ronnie Fleet stood in Rosettenville and did not stand in Hillbrow.

The Party also continued unsuccessfully to contest elections for the Native Representative Council, which had only advisory functions and was indirectly elected by a college consisting, in the main, of tribal chiefs. The NRC was set up under a 1936 Act of Parliament which removed the remaining small group of blacks from the Cape Province Common Voters' Roll. This was perhaps the most cynical of the long line of attempts by the racist autocracy to fob off black political aspirations by the creation of dummy institutions. The NRC ended its completely useless life when it dissolved itself in protest against the regime's 1946 massacre of black miners. One of its members, the trader Paul Mosaka, summed up well the real character of the NRC when he said just prior to its collapse: 'We have been asked to co-operate with a toy telephone. We have been speaking into an apparatus which cannot transmit sound and at the end of which there is nobody to receive the message.'

I was never attracted to the lobby (both inside and outside the Party) which invariably argued for the tactic of boycott in relation to all unrepresentative institutions. Our common objective was to destroy such institutions or, at worst, to make them unworkable. There were (and continue to be) instances when militant forms of rejectionist participation serve this objective much more effectively than complete, passive abstention. However, if there was ever an institution which deserved to be completely shunned and boycotted, it was the NRC 'toy telephone'.

The 1936 legislation also gave an elite group of black voters (who had been removed from the common roll) the right to elect three white members to represent the black population in a parliament of 150 MPs.

One of these constituencies was represented by Sam Kahn who stood as a communist in 1948 and won by an impressive majority. He was holding the seat when the Unlawful Organisations Act was passed in 1950. Among other provisions, the Act gave the regime the right to expel elected Members of Parliament who were communists. Soon afterwards he became the first MP in South Africa's history to be expelled from Parliament for purely political reasons. But before the machinery of the law could bring this about, Sam managed to insert in the record of Hansard the full text of the *Communist Manifesto*, ostensibly to demonstrate to the select committee the true nature of the aims of the Party. And this most fundamental text of communist theory is available for all time, by courtesy of the Government Printer.

Sam's performance as an MP provides an excellent example of the way in which critical participation can sometimes do more to expose the iniquity of an institution than a thousand boycotts. He was a brilliant parliamentarian with much cunning and shrewdness. As an orator he ran rings round most of his opponents. He was a thorn in the side of the most powerful of white institutions – the House of Assembly. His eventual removal was therefore inevitable. He was also a source of annoyance for the South African Jewish Board of Deputies, dominated by big business and claiming to guard the broader interests of the South African Jewish community, the third largest in the world.

At the height of Sam's public activities he was requested to meet the Cape Town committee of the South African Jewish Board of Deputies. He had agreed to meet them and heard that, 'of course, we don't want to interfere with your politics, and we would be the last to question the democratic right to choose to be a communist, etc etc, but being both a prominent communist and a Jew, and bearing in mind the anti-Semitic record of the government, should you not have regard for the interests of the large Jewish community which is potentially threatened by the fact that a Jew happens to be the most prominent communist?' But at this game they were no match for Sam. He conceded that the link between communist and Jew was a traditional fascist ploy to encourage both anti-communism and anti-Semitism, but, he reasoned, the linkage between Jews and business was also exploited for anti-Semitic purposes, and he was sitting in the presence of the business personalities whose names appeared in neon lights along a good stretch of Adderley Street. 'I'll tell you what, gentlemen,' he said, 'as a gesture of concern for the Jews let's enter into a bargain: you give up your business and I'll then give up politics.'

The Indian Congress defiance campaign against the 1946 Ghetto Act was a tactic much debated at Johannesburg District Party conferences. The campaign was launched at a conference of the South African Indian Congress (held in Cape Town in February 1946) in response to legislation which prohibited all land transfers between Indians and non-Indians. Passive Resistance Councils were set up in Natal and Transvaal and in June 1946 the first batch of volunteers, headed by Doctors Dadoo and Naicker, was sent to prison for defying the new law. The significance of passive resistance as a struggle technique will be touched upon when I reach the 1952 Defiance Campaign.

But in 1946 abstract 'theoreticians' such as Buirski derisively dismissed the campaign as creating the illusion that the revolution could be achieved by sitting on your backside and squatting on a plot; this was a reference to the form which the defiance took, whereby Indians occupy plots of land from which they were barred by the Ghetto Act.

It was during this period that I first met Dr Yusuf Dadoo. But I came to know him more intimately only after 1963 in London when we were both part of a group of Party activists who were trying to do something about the organisational chaos which followed in the wake of the Rivonia disaster. Yusuf was truly one of nature's real socialists; he not only believed in the aphorism that all property is theft, but also lived by it. The eldest son of a wealthy merchant in Krugersdorp, he shunned the family fortune which was his for the taking and lived his frugal life on the modest subsistence allowance of a professional revolutionary. I had always respected Yusuf as among the giants of our national and working-class movement. But it was during our close association in exile that I learned also to love him as a friend and comrade. I have no doubt that when it becomes opportune to set out the events of the awkward ten years that followed the Rivonia arrests, the name Dadoo will appear at the top of the list of those who saved the Party from complete oblivion.

Yusuf died of cancer on 19 September 1983, a few weeks after his 70th birthday. I was on my way to attend a plenary session of the Central Committee and it was decided that I should travel via London in order to visit our chairman.

Soon after my arrival on Sunday 18 September, I went to the Whittington Hospital. I had already been warned that there was no hope of recovery and I therefore expected to find him much changed in appearance. He was very thin but otherwise very much like the old Yusuf. He was sporting a neatly-trimmed Lenin-type beard which suited him very well. He was obviously excited and pleased to see me, and, for a while, it seemed no different from the occasions when we came together after some break. What is happening down your way? Any news about the IPC and the forthcoming conference of the 12 parties? I hear there's pressure in Lesotho, is it serious? Are you safe in your new place? And so on and so forth. He was the Yusuf I knew, his face registering all the nuances of joy and frown depending upon whether the news was good or bad.

He raised a number of special questions that needed to be discussed between us. He had dictated a message to the forthcoming Central Committee meeting which he wanted me to comment on. He told me that there had been an offer from Ismail Meer to tackle his biography, and we both thought that, subject to ultimate editorial control by the Party, he was a good candidate for this task. We also touched on financial questions. The Sunday visitors started arriving in larger numbers and we decided that I would get special permission to come back the next morning (out of visiting hours) so that we could discuss these and other questions without interruption.

When I arrived the next morning he seemed to be asleep and I was reluctant to wake him. After a while the sister said that he needed his medication and that she would prepare him for my visit. When this was done I was called. He was sitting up and somehow looking flushed. His eyes looked sharp and darting, his hair was sticking up slightly. But he was clearly still in agonising pain and he agreed to my suggestion that perhaps I should return later in the day. A few hours later I received a call from Gill that I should rush over immediately.

When I arrived at about 2.30 pm, Yusuf was in a deep coma, and it seemed clear that the end would come within a very short time. His sisters and sisters-in-law asked permission to pray at his bedside and to mumble litanies in his ear. Winnie, brave but extremely upset, objected to their ritual and did not want Yusuf to die with a prayer on his ear. But we all felt that in any case he was already at the stage where he could not possibly register what they were saying. Winnie agreed, but when they had finished she nevertheless whispered a more militant message into his ear, telling him to ignore the prayers.

It now seemed a question of just waiting. But suddenly and inexplicably the life in Yusuf started fighting back. He opened his eyes and started moving his head, looking at each of us in turn with a smile on his face. When he looked at me I raised my fist in a salute. His smile deepened and he raised his own fist. He then started waving his hand, indicating clearly that he wanted to write. He whispered that he wanted to sign his statement to the forthcoming Central Committee meeting and he did so in a hand which was steady and flowing. As the moments went by he became more and more lucid. He called his daughter Roshan. He told her that death is part of life and life is part of death, and that if you have fought all your life and continued fighting until the end you can accept death and that others who continue with the struggle will continue your life. He spoke to Winnie about their life together and in between he raised his fist with the word '*Amandla*' on his lips.

He clearly knew that he was in his last hour. I had the feeling that in that short revival everything we knew about Yusuf which made him into such a great figure and a warm human being showed itself: his courage, modesty, humour and, above all, his passionate dedication to the revolutionary cause. More than once he turned to us and said: 'Keep on struggling, never give up, fight until the end.'

After a while he asked everyone to leave the room except his brother Abu and me. When the others left he talked to us about his funeral. He said that ideally he would like to be buried in South Africa, even if it meant defying the authorities and carrying his body across. We must fight even with our dead bodies, he said. But he explained further that he realised that such a course might be practically impossible and that he would be imposing a burden on the movement which it would find next to impossible to carry out. What he was telling us was merely an expression of his dream and not something he would like to impose on the organisation. He also said that normally the form of burial did not worry him. But he added that we must be sensitive to the strong abhorrence by the Muslim community of a cremation and that it would therefore be politically important for him to be buried in the normal way. He hugged us and expressed his love.

When the others came back the air was once again filled with laughter and relaxed communication between Yusuf and the others, despite the whispered voice. The smile never left his face during this short rally. At one point he seemed so much with us that I said, jokingly: 'Yusuf, what about a Scotch?' And with that shy, naughty, smiling face of his he turned to the doctor to ask for permission. The doctor thought it was a wonderful idea and said to him: 'You are surprising us all.'

Yusuf always loved to hear singing and it was the regret of his life that he felt quite incapable of holding a tune. He blamed this on his early upbringing and the absence of music in his Krugersdorp childhood home. I had gone outside the room for a moment when we were all told to return because Yusuf wanted us to sing '*Amajoni*'. We tried our miserable best, and although we sounded very tuneless his hand moved from time to time with the rhythm.

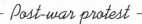

And then, as if he had done everything he wanted to do, he slowly relapsed into another coma and passed away some hours later. Death is the ultimate defeat but Yusuf managed to transform the moment into a victory of pure will. It is wonderful to be able to remember a friend and comrade in this way.

Joe Slovo's mother Chaya. She died a few years after arriving in South Africa.

Joe's father, Wulfus Slovo, wearing army uniform during the First World War.

Below: The village of Obelei in Lithuania, where Joe Slovo was born.

Above: Wulfus Slovo, four years before he left Lithuania to look for a better life, 1924.

Below: Joe Slovo (middle, back row) as a young schoolboy.

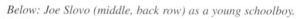

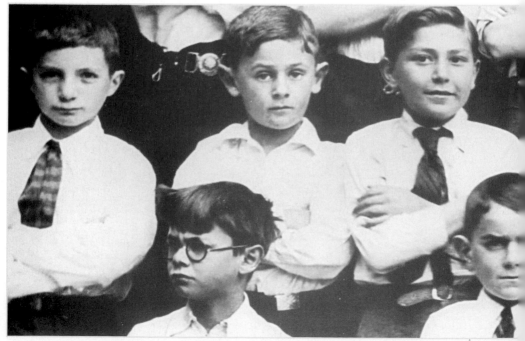

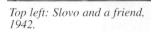

Top left: Slovo and a friend, 1942.

Top right: 'Rapallo, 1945.' An inscription on the back of the photo reads 'Don't you think this is a good snap? Joe. PS. Note my new frameless glasses.'

Above: Joe as a South African signal corpsman, 1944.

Right: Italy 1945. With war buddies Mike Feldman (left) and Barney Febler.

Above: Ruth First, Bram Fischer, Joe Slovo and 'Rusty' Bernstein on the podium at a CPSA meeting in the late 1940s.

THE STAR, JOHANNESBURG, THURSDAY, MARCH 29, 1951

Awards to University Students

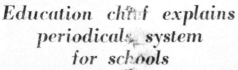

Education chief explains periodicals system for schools

From Our Correspondent

Pretoria, Thursday.

THE general position regarding subscriptions from pupils at schools for various periodicals was explained to-day by

Degrees will be conferred on 510 students at the annual Graduation Day of the University of the Witwatersrand on Saturday. The Society of Advocates prize has been awarded to Mr. J. Slovo. (left), and will be presented to him at the ceremony, when medals which have been awarded to students will also be presented. Mr. D. L. Keys (centre), will receive the Alexander Aiken medal in commerce and Mr. C. L. de Jager will receive the Dental Company gold medal.

Left: 29 March 1951. Graduation day at Wits University. Joe Slovo receives the Society of Advocates' prize. A young Derek Keys — later Minister of Finance in the cabinet in which Slovo served as Housing Minister — receives the commerce award.

Above: Cape Town 1954. Slovo and daughter Shawn on the beach.

Below: Joe and Ruth on holiday with children and friends.

Above: A campaign to save the **Guardian** newspaper. On the podium Yusuf Dadoo (standing) with Ruth First on his left and Moses Kotane seated to his right, Slovo is seated alone, in the front row right, c. 1958.

Below: Slovo as a young advocate in chambers, early 1950s.

Nelson Mandela and Ruth First, c. 1958.

Slovo at work during the Treason Trial, December 1956.

Left: Slovo and Ruth First leaving court during the Treason Trial.

Right: Slovo (with cigarette) and others accused in the Treason Trial take a break during proceedings, 1957.

Ruth First, 1961.

Below: Taking time out to relax. (Left to right) Joe Slovo, Mary Turok, Ben Turok, Sonya Bunting, Jack Hodgson, Ruth First, Brian Bunting, Rica Hodgson, late 1950s.

Ruth First, boarding a plane to leave South Africa with Gillian (left) and Robyn (right), 1964.

Gillian and Robyn with their grandfather, Julius First, in London, March 1964.

Yusuf Dadoo (left) and Slovo (right) protest against the Rivonia Trial, London 1963.

Twelve years at the Bar

I was yet another journey which brought the most important point of departure in my whole life – my relationship and subsequent marriage in August 1949 to Ruth. While studying for my LLB I was employed in the offices of Jack Levitan, an attorney. Early in 1948 he sent me to assist Advocate Fred Zwarenstein in the defence of the Lefela brothers in Maseru, Basutoland. They were charged with sedition arising out of the activities of the Basuto Peasants' Organisation – *Lekgotla la Bafu* (League of the Poor) – of which they were the leaders. With a peasant directness the Lefela brothers dismissed Zwarenstein on suspicion that he was collaborating with the enemy; during one of the early adjournments he was seen to be having tea with the prosecutor!

Ruth had been sent to cover the case for *The Guardian*, and it was there that our relationship began. I had known her from the very early 1940s. She was a key figure in the newly created Young Communist

League and editor of its newspaper, *Youth for a New South Africa*. I was, at the time, part of a small clique, all of us workers, who considered 'university intellectuals' (including Ruth) to be inferior revolutionary material. They were articulate, talented with the pen, knew the literature – in short, they seemed to be too clever by half. They made us feel inadequate, and so (as has happened so often before and since to quite a number of activists) we tried to live with our complexes by attaching them to high sounding revolutionary content. We made a virtue out of our inadequacies. Later, when I started my university career, I was sometimes made to feel like a traitor to my class! From then on winning an argument was (with a few of my comrades) no longer a question of reasoning but the exploitation of 'intellectual' tricks.

Ruth and I were elected to the Johannesburg District of the Party in, I think, 1946. At that time and until the end of 1947 she was having a close relationship with Ishmail Meer, a law student and one of the brilliant young men in the newly radicalised Transvaal Indian Congress. When Ishmail finished his studies his right, as an Indian, to be in the Transvaal expired and he was sent back to Durban. Ruth decided not to join him, and by the time we took the trip to Lesotho a combination of the Immorality Act and Group Areas Act had contributed to the destruction of their personal relationship.

We decided to start living together at the beginning of 1949, and eight months later we each took off half an hour from our respective offices to get married. Our three daughters, Shawn, Gillian and Robyn, were born between 1950 and 1954.

When Ruth was assassinated by a racist death squad on 17 August 1982, we were 12 days way from our 33rd wedding anniversary. This is not the time or the place to detail the course of our life together and our relationship with our children. But, taken broadly, I would say (however smug and complacent it sounds) that we enjoyed a stimulating companionship and mutuality through most of our period together. It was certainly not without friction, competitiveness and phases during which our political disagreement reached threatening proportions. Nor was it free of other, more or less serious, involvements. But the basic fabric of our relationship stood up to all this and more, including many forced separations connected with our duties in the revolutionary movement.

We were each aware of the important role we played in one another's intellectual development. Even if it meant the most spirited confrontations (which often frightened those of our friends who were not yet aware of the chemistry of our relationship), she never allowed me to get away with the clichéd catechisms which tempt all who become part of an apparatus; and I never allowed her to float comfortably in the sea of criticism against so-called orthodoxy which characterises the changing fashions of the critics on the left, particularly those with an academic background. She was a woman of style and elegance, both in wit and vanity. She was a comrade whose intolerance of hypocrisy and humbug won her the respect even of those who were discomfited by the razor sharpness of her thrusts. She was a companion with a rich, albeit private, passion and one who had the extraordinary capacity to postpone the traumas of work conflict and fully relax with us or with friends in private and social situations. She summed up very well the flavour of an important aspect of our relationship in a letter written just after her release from detention in 1963 when I was already in London and she was about to come with the children: 'Oh for a good solid row in close proximity.'

Back to 1948, standing outside the *Rand Daily Mail* watching the election returns. The avowed supporters of Hitler had won with a minority of votes but with a majority of rural seats. We were all stunned. But most of us, like me, thought it would be a matter of five years. Memories of a delegation from the Federation of Progressive Students to visit some of the old men in the defeated United Party to get them to take part in a rally at the University. We wasted our time. They sat there with bloated bodies and bloated minds and blamed that 'liberal' Hofmeyr for their defeat. Then came Malan's triumphant demonstration in Johannesburg and the last flicker of organised white energy against fascism, as we marched in the counter-demonstration and clashed with jubilant Afrikanerdom.

For me the only good that this ill wind blew was that we no longer had to spend our Sunday evenings on the steps of the Johannesburg City Hall, which the Party used as a weekly public platform. There was a time when one used to look forward to these Sunday evening outings. There were usually one or two entertaining curtain-raisers addressed by left mavericks of various kinds. The colourful blacksmith Dunbar held forth regularly until he was disabled by the kick of a horse he was trying to shoe. Another orator, whose name now escapes me, was a devout follower of Henry George (for whom original sin began and ended in the private ownership of land) and never deviated from his single theme of immediate land nationalisation. The class enemy was always represented by a rather mild-looking, baldish and pot-bellied Special Branchman by the name of Sergeant Sapperstein, who must have been the only Jewish policeman in the force. After the meeting a few of us used to catch a tram to Hillbrow and spend an hour or two sipping top-quality milk shakes at the Golden Ray Café.

Benny Sischy was among those who occasionally spoke at the City Hall steps. He has a place in my memory not so much because of the quality of his oratory, but because of his Jewish grandmother. Benny was a keen amateur actor who helped run a Party-inspired theatre group called the African National Theatre (ANT). They were always scratching around looking for stage props, and to the chagrin of his grandmother, Benny often disappeared with bits and pieces from his own home. On one memorable occasion the person who was to preside at the City Hall steps meetings was unable to come and a comrade was delegated to ask Benny to come as a replacement. His grandmother answered the phone:

'Is Benny there?'

'Is he ever here?'

'Please, Mrs Sischy, if he comes soon tell him we want him to take the chair at tonight's City Hall steps meeting.'

'Look, lady,' burst out his long-suffering grandmother, 'not anodder shtick forniture is going out this flat.'

During the 1930s the Black Shirts had made a regular habit of attacking our platform. But during the war and for a few years thereafter the scene at the City Hall steps was very similar to [London's] Hyde Park Corner on a Sunday morning. The audiences were all white because of the curfew regulations. It was not until 1946 that I was invited to speak from this platform, and my maiden effort was not altogether successful. It was my first year at university and I was fresh from a series of social anthropology lectures by Professor Jefferies, who was a great protagonist of the diffusionist school, which believed that all the world's civilisations could be traced to an original source in the Nile's fertile valley. I had also started going through the prescribed reading on race theories. I combined these two themes with the sole intention of taking a swipe at white arrogance.

Many of the ex-servicemen in the audience who had spent time in Egypt flustered me with continuous banter about King Farouk, 'gippo guts' and so on. But the matter took a more serious turn when I started 'demonstrating' that the Caucasian (white man) is, in most respects, closer to the ape than the negroid (black man). The white man is more hairy, has thinner lips, larger ears and further monkey-like characteristics which I have now forgotten. The interjections were no longer good-natured and I became the target for an assortment of missiles, including well-aimed gobs of spit. I pleased neither the audience nor my comrades, who, for some time thereafter, did not invite me to continue my didactic exposition of dubious social anthropological theories which had momentarily excited me.

Organised fascism was once again beginning to show itself some years before the Nationalist victory in 1948. The City Hall steps increasingly became a physical battleground between defenders of the platform and the thugs who were given free rein by the token police contingent in the vicinity. Under the command of ex-servicemen such as George Clayton, Monty Berman and Jack Hodgson, we organised ourselves into defence squads, with fixed positions on the 'battlefield'. I was grateful to be under the command of Natie Marcus. He and his two brothers not only displayed a high level of courage, but they also had the brawn to back it up. When the signal was given for a manoeuvre, I managed (perhaps more by design than by coincidence) always to find myself behind Natie, who seemed able to grab and deal with at least three opponents at one time. After a while the meetings no longer served a political purpose; no one listened to the speeches and we were all on alert for the moment when we would be forced to defend the platform. A casualty station was set up in Max Joffe's surgery adjacent to the steps.

It was sad to see this historic forum of free speech close down. But at least one could now wake up on Sunday morning without experiencing the nervous cramps brought on by the expectation that the day would end with yet another street fight. As if in remembrance, our milkshake excursions to the Golden Ray continued for some time on Sunday nights.

It was part of the Nationalist election platform that they would ban and destroy the Communist Party, and, true to their word, they promulgated the Unlawful Organisations Act by the middle of 1950. Most of us were stunned by the Central Committee announcement that in the face of the ban the Party had no option but to dissolve itself. I recall the meeting of the membership in End Street (opposite Dadoo's surgery) where Kotane had come to announce the decision. Many of us assumed that it was merely a ploy and that behind-the-scenes preparations for underground revival were in hand. I remember on the final day helping Danie du Plessis, a bricklayer and full-time District Party Secretary, pack up the office equipment in Progress Building, Commissioner Street, and burn some of the papers. He wept continuously and inconsolably. Later he presumably saw some old light of reason and atoned for his sins by becoming an elder of the Dutch Reformed Church in Bloemfontein.

When the axe fell on our Party, I was in the final year of my legal studies. The study of law appealed to me both as an exercise in deductive logic and as an instrument for the assertion of social and political rights. A combination of my interest and an instinct for examination technique won me a degree with distinction and the prize for the best student of the year. I as also awarded the GA Denny Scholarship for part-time research into the status of African women in the conflict between common law and native law and custom. The demoralisation when the Party was dissolved led me to consider postgraduate study in England. The GA Denny Scholarship was an interim award so as to enable me to prepare for the topic under Professor Julius Lewin at Wits University. But I was not to undertake this journey, which would have turned me into an academic.

It was during my final year at law school that I met Nelson Mandela. We spent many hours arguing about the Party's tactic of supporting the call for a general strike in protest against the Suppression of Communism Act and the subsequent day of mourning – 26 June 1950 – which again led to clashes with the police. In time, Nelson and I found ourselves thrown together in many important and historic projects. I liked and admired him, more especially the way he battled to resolve the conflict between the emotional legacy left by the wounding experiences of racism and the cold grey tactics of politics.

At the beginning of 1951 I was admitted to the Bar. I was not qualified for admission to the side bar. I was an alien, and by some legislative quirk an attorney (solicitor) had to be a British subject, whereas an advocate was merely required to express loyalty to the Queen. Our courts had already decided that an alien could indeed express loyalty to and affection for the monarch. The problem had previously arisen for me in a different form when as Chairman of the Student Law Society I had to be the master of ceremonies at the annual law dinner attended by judges. After a heated debate in the Johannesburg District Committee of the Party, it was decided by a narrow majority that I was to be permitted to utter the words at the beginning of the banquet (without which the proceedings, traditionally, could not start): 'Gentlemen, I drink to our lady the Queen.'

My 12 years of legal practice proved to be useful and enjoyable. Life at the Bar, compared to the constraints of worker-boss relationship, was relaxed. The advocates constituted a community, all housed in one building and sharing administrative staff. Teas and midday meals were taken together in a common room. The conversation rarely touched subjects other than Bar and courtroom gossip. To reinforce the illusion that the law is above politics, leading and well-known communists, such as Bram Fischer and I, shared tables and exchanged formal pleasantries with leading Nationalist politicians such as John Vorster, who spent a short spell at the Bar before going on to become Minister of Justice and then Prime Minister.

But this fraternal legal spirit did not even pretend to cover black colleagues. The Group Areas Act prohibited the entry into the common room of Indian and African advocates who were not legally permitted to occupy premises in the only building which housed all the advocates. Even the black elite (such as the three black advocates who had reached the Bar, out of a total of 120 or so advocates) were not equal in the eyes of the law. Imagine then how empty the hallowed legal maxim was when it came to black workers and peasants! I appeared on behalf of Duma Nokwe, the first African to be admitted to the Transvaal Division of the Supreme Court. One of the big issues was whether he would be permitted to use the change rooms at Pretoria Supreme Court to take off his normal collar and put on his robes, the advocate's fly collar and bib. In the end a special room was set aside to enable Duma to perform this 15-second operation without 'sullying' the all-white change rooms!

Yet the law took a little longer to catch up with the fascist excesses which were to be the hallmark of the new regime. Judges, until they retired or died, were still of the old school. They had a belief in some of the historically evolved and fought-for principles of what they understood to be the Anglo-Saxon legal tradition. But the judiciary did not in the end escape the process of pollution which was to spread into every strand of the social fabric. Judicial appointments became overtly political and the quality of justice steadily deteriorated. The Bar, initially indignant, soon adjusted to the debasement of the legal coinage.

The Afrikaner equivalent of the Jewish mother's proud boast 'mine son, the doctor' was certainly 'my boy, the advocate'. Even if one was a communist advocate, one was still an advocate, and it gave one a special advantage when dealing with authority, including the police. What is more, if one was an advocate, as I was, whose practice became more and more dominated by cases with a political aspect, access to prisoners and the broad freedom which still remained to hit hard at authority in open court, was a great opportunity.

The Bar itself was basically a posh trade union. To prevent undercutting, minimum fees were obligatory. Collective sanctions were imposed against any attorneys who failed to meet a advocate's bill within three months and seven days. The annually elected Bar Council was the custodian of Bar ethics. It must be said to the credit of the Bar Council that it was quite vocal about the regime's early attempts to erode the rule of law and to pack the bench with political supporters, many of whom did not have the talent or the experience to sit in judgment. But a combination of cynicism and acceptance slowly crept in. And if a new appointee did not make a fool of himself at the most simple, routine level, the common room was peppered with remarks like 'they are not so bad after all'. Mick Schneider, a colleague with an above-average turgidity but also with a wry sense of humour, put it all into perspective when in his lisping style he said: 'Things have come to a sorry path in South Africa when the simple fact that a dog can bark has become the subject of surprised comment.'

There was something guild-like about many of the traditions of the Bar which had been transplanted from the British system. There was the gown with its symbolic back pocket into which clients, if they wished, used to put a sovereign or two in recognition of the services of the gentlemen advocates – a procedure which, as we have seen, was no longer discretionary. As with the teenager's preference for dilapidated jeans, the older the gown was in appearance, the more prestigious it was. We were spared the wig but not the bib or fly-away collar. All this paraphernalia had to be carried through the streets in a sack (blue for juniors and red for seniors) when one was moving to and from chambers and the Supreme Court.

Colleagues referred to one another by their surnames without any prefixes. A particularly arduous task which faced every new advocate was the obligation to move from office to office introducing himself personally to every single member of the Bar, necessitating about 120 embarrassed and boring interviews. But until this was done, those you had not met were completely oblivious of your presence and would not so much as greet you. Since it was impossible to remember whom one had already met, it became necessary to carry around a long list in one hand and a pencil in the other. I was carrying out this arduous procedure when I knocked at the door of one of the most celebrated civil lawyers, Norman Rosenberg, who also had a reputation for being mean and ungenerous. I opened the door and shuffled inside, holding my sheet in one hand and my pencil in the other. His creased face was covered with an enormous frown and, apparently thinking that I was one of the numerous collectors for Zionist charities who plagued our building, he growled: 'I don't give,' and continued studying his papers.

Even hardline fascists like Vorster were tainted with some kind of sentimental slush about the advocate's oath. When Vorster was already Minister of Justice, a deputation from the Bar Council, led by the then chairman, George Coleman, flew to Cape Town in order to discuss a ban which had prohibited me from leaving the municipal area of Johannesburg and which was interfering with a large slice of my rural practice. On its return the deputation informed me that Vorster had made an eminently reasonable proposal. He had said to Coleman: 'Tell Slovo that if he gives me his word of honour from one advocate to another that he will stop all his subversive activities, I will immediately lift all his restrictions.' It was indeed a shrewd offer. Coleman emphasised that all I was required to do was repeat my advocate's oath of fidelity to the laws of the land. I refused this offer and explained that Vorster and I had a completely different understanding of the meaning of 'subversive', and that he would undoubtedly exploit such an undertaking to the detriment of the cause in which I believed.

I recall an amusing sequel to this episode when another colleague, Charlie Rosenthal, met Vorster over a drink after a rugby test match in Bloemfontein. He asked Vorster why he continued persecuting Slovo, 'who is just a nice guy and not really a communist'. Vorster said to Charlie that he had made me a most reasonable offer and that the answer which reached him from Coleman was 'just tell Vorster he can go and get fucked', language which I did not use, but which nevertheless reflected my thoughts rather accurately.

After I reached England in 1963, during a period of great uncertainty about the future of our struggle, I took a Master's degree in law at the London School of Economics. It was not my intention to practise in the United Kingdom. But I did toy with the idea of law as an academic discipline, which could have provided me with an interest and a means of support. As it turned out (and I do not regret the outcome), the law was never again to be my vocation. But I retain fond memories of my 12 years of court confrontation in South Africa. They served a purpose which was closer to my heart than the normal pursuit of law as an appendage of the business world ... and now and then it was good fun.

Fragments from the courts

My courtroom career started somewhat inauspiciously. We emerged from law school with our minds crammed full of legal theories and case law but totally ill-equipped to carry out the advocate's main function of preparing and pleading a real cause before a live tribunal. One felt like a fully certified motor mechanic who sees an actual engine only when he lifts the bonnet on his first repair job. It was left to each of us to pick up the essentials of court craft as best we could. The little I had picked up came from observing in the Magistrate's Court the rather flamboyant style of my solicitor-employer, Jack Levitan.

My very first supreme court trial was before Mr Justice Malan whose reputation of terrorising junior counsel had not yet reached me. The charge was one of house-breaking and theft. The owner of a warehouse had been asked to step out of the witness box in order to examine and identify the pile of exhibits that filled the well of the court. While he was doing so and for reasons which now escape me – perhaps it was to assure my client that I was really on the job – I got up and started ambling towards the witness. Before I had completed this manoeuvre I felt burning eyes piercing my back, and I turned to face the judge. For a moment or two he continued staring at me in absolute silence, and then the high-pitched, sermon-like words poured upon me: 'Mr Slovo, in case you are still suffering from an illusion of your childhood, I'll have you know that his courtroom is not a circus where every clown can jump into and out of the arena at will. Please return to your seat immediately.'

It took some years to get to know the peculiarities and eccentricities of the judges – personal quirks which, in borderline cases, sometimes determined the outcome of a trial or influenced the severity of the sentence. Malan must have spent part of his childhood sticking pins into flies, and junior counsel now obviously provided him with a substitute sport. But fortunately for litigants, his whiplash tongue and unsmiling darts of humour were generally directed against his erstwhile colleagues and not their clients.

But eccentricities aside, the judges (including Malan) saw themselves as the personification of the lady of the law who holds aloft the evenly balanced scales of justice. It has always struck me that, in blindfolding the lady, the original creator of this symbol may have been trying to make a statement more profound than we lawyers understood; if the scales of justice were skilfully tipped she would be none the wiser! And even the most humane members of South Africa's all-white judiciary were blind to the fact that the scales of justice that they were holding were permanently unbalanced in favour of their white compatriots. Nelson Mandela said it all when he told the magistrate trying him in 1962 that every aspect of the administration of justice in South Africa made him feel a black man in a white man's court.

Until the Verwoerds and the Vorsters could no longer tolerate this, the individual trial could still be a battleground on whose terrain small and temporary social victories could be won. But at the end of the day the judicial system played as vital a role in maintaining South Africa's racist equilibrium as any other branch of state administration. Ironically, the honesty and integrity of many of the old-style judges, which made possible the occasional redress of grievance even against white authority, also helped maintain the illusion that equal social justice for all might eventually be attained through the existing framework. In this sense the touching and naive faith in the judiciary of many among the racially underprivileged played no small part in reducing the disturbances against the *status quo.*

At the personal level, my 12 years of the hurly-burly of legal practice were satisfying and politically useful. The adversary system of court confrontation, with its contest of tactics and competing styles of forensic performance, allowed for creativity and some scope for self-expression. Each trial posed its unique challenges, and the unending variety of civil and criminal cases contained elements of pathos, sometimes tragedy and, every now and then, high comedy. I recall some of these experiences, starting with one on the lighter side.

Ask me to drive a tram

This is a tale of every barrister's dream witness. Attorney Stein brought two brothers to my chambers, Abe and Julius Zwetzel Levine, who narrated the following tale of family woe.

Their parents, Moses and Sarah Levine, had immigrated to South Africa from Poland in the late 1920s and fought an endless battle to make ends meet. But suddenly their ship came home. In the early 1930s they had spent a few hundred pounds on some hectares of land outside Johannesburg and tried their hand at dairy farming. The land happened to be immediately adjacent to the Moroka Township and, since their property had business rights, its value rose to scores of thousands.

When Mrs Levine died in the late 1940s she left her share of the estate to her two sons. But her husband (who had long engaged in a bitter feud against his sons) claimed that Mrs Levine had no assets to leave since the land and the dairy business were always his exclusive property. Indeed, the property was registered in his name as sole owner, and the dairy business bank account was also in his name. The couple had been married out of community of property, which meant that there was no joint estate and that the property of each spouse was in law completely separate. If, however, we could prove that the acquisition of the land and the running of the dairy business were at all times partnership ventures between Moses and Sarah, then half of the assets would now go to the sons in terms of Sarah's will. Since there was obviously no explicit contract between the couple, our only hope was to ask the courts to infer from the conduct of Moses and Sarah that they were engaged in a partnership venture.

And this is where Peretz Gischen came in. He was Mrs Levine's brother and, in the family feud, was very much on the side of the nephews. His evidence was crucial since we had no other witness who knew the Levines intimately and continuously throughout the relevant period.

By the time I had my first interview with Peretz I already half knew what to expect. I had read the verbatim transcript of his statement which, with colourful flourishes of Doornfontein English, was little more than a venomous outpouring against his brother-in-law Moses Levine.

First of all I should like to say something which it may be irrelevant but you will see what a Peruvian Moses is. When Sarah and Moses married in Poland I sent them for a present £5 which I didn't had. So I get back a present from Moses of a book in Hebrew written on the front cover

'To my ever loving brother-in-law Peretz Gischen.'

Very nice. He's not in South Africa one week when, you wouldn't believe this, he comes and vants his book back. I vanted to give him not the book but a punch in the nose, but my sister vanted peace and made me give the Peruvian his book back. Then Julius Zwetzel is born. Moses is in Kroonstad collecting money for the *mashis kanen* (Jewish old age home). I send him a telegram saying Julius Zwetzel is born and I give him the date of the *bris* (circumcision ceremony). Vot comes is not Moses but a telegram saying 'How's Sarah and the baby?' So I send him back a telegram saying 'Mind your own business', which it may not be right from my side but it shows you what a Peruvian he is.

The statement was packed with stories in a similar vein and painted a picture of Moses Levine as a mean, tyrannical and deceitful man. I had the greatest difficulty in convincing Peretz that stories about his brother-in-law's general character were not admissible under our rules of evidence and that he would have to restrict himself to the basic issue in the trial, which was whether their conduct over the years proved the existence of a partnership between Moses and Sarah. I told him, however, that counsel for the other side might well cross-examine him to establish that his dislike of Moses was so intense that he was prepared even to testify falsely against him. I advised him not to try to hide his dislike of Moses and if counsel for the other side became imprudent enough to press for reasons for his hostility, then he had every right to narrate his favourite uncomplimentary stories about Moses Levine. He was unconsoled by this possibility and could scarcely conceal his feeling that either the law was an ass or that his nephews had chosen one for their counsel.

When the date of the trial drew near I was filled with apprehension. Peretz, my only witness of substance, seemed destined to make a poor showing in the witness box. His English was inadequate, but he reacted angrily when I suggested that it would perhaps be better for him to give his evidence through a Yiddish interpreter. His frenzied bias against Moses Levine would surely reflect on his veracity when he came to narrate the cold facts that had to be proved. On top of it all, his appearance was most unprepossessing: a small man with a transparent complexion, a scalp with dispersed tufts of fluffy ginger hair which reminded one of a Karoo landscape and a myriad of freckles covering his face and hands. But, as it transpired, Peretz was to turn the tables on all of us.

My first surprise was that he stuck strictly to the relevant facts when I led him in evidence: the joint discussion between Moses and Sarah when they were about to purchase the land and Sarah's contribution to the purchase price from dressmaking earnings, the division of labour between them in running the dairy business, with Sarah doing most of the milking and cheese-making, and Moses taking the products to the market. Sarah would always pay the wages of the few labourers with cash which was kept in a business account in Moses's name.

It was as yet difficult to gauge how the judge would take to Peretz. 'Boet' Neser, an ex-Transvaal cricketer, usually ran his courtroom with the coolness and finality of a test umpire. But instead of raising his finger to proclaim sudden death, he raised his head in a gesture suggesting that, counsel having failed, he was now seeking guidance from a higher being. Peretz would come into full sail only under cross-examination, and there was no way of telling how the polite, anglicised judge would receive the ebullient and colourful Yiddishisms of our star witness.

Then began the truly unequal battle between my colleague Marcus Mandel and Peretz Gischen, whose humour and monumental shrewdness were to take virtual command in the many hours of cross-examination that followed. The beginning was predictable.

'Mr Gischen, you don't like Moses Levine, do you?'

'Vell, my lord, I shouldn't say I'm exactly in love wid de man.'

It looks pretty promising, a hint of a smile on the judge's lips. Mandel is prepared to risk all.

'Would you tell his lordship why, as you put it, you're not in love with my client?'

'I can tell him plenty but I von't. Mr Slovo told me that I von't be allowed to say so because it makes no difference to the law if Moses is rubbish.'

Gischen said this with feeling but without rancour.

Judge Neser: 'Gischen, in the first place it is for this court to decide what questions you are obliged to answer, and, in the second place, for reasons which I need not spell out, the law indeed would not have permitted Mr Slovo to lead you in such evidence, whereas Mr Mandel, at his peril, is fully entitled to canvass the issue. Are you pressing the matter, Mr Mandel?'

Mandel refused the rescue offer and demanded an answer. It was the moment Gischen was waiting for. He clasped his hands behind his back, got as much as he could out of his five foot three inches, faced the judge with quiet relish, and proceeded to describe the Hebrew book episode, the failure of Moses to attend the circumcision ritual and numerous other punishing details about Moses. Finally, with a sideways glance at Mandel, he rounded off this part of his testimony with the words: 'Mr Mandel, you husked for character, you got character'.

Uncharacteristically, the judge exploded into a burst of laughter – the first signal that Peretz might indeed turn out to be a winning card.

On the facts of the partnership it was extremely difficult to dent Peretz, and without exceeding the bounds of propriety he somehow invariably managed to infect Mandel's questions with a touch of ridicule. He had already described (in a manner which I feared at the time would be construed as a slice of positive thinking on behalf of his nephews) how Moses Levin had in fact admitted to him more than once that he and Sarah were '50/50 partners'. Peretz was asked to explain why then the licence and the bank account were in Moses's name only.

'I didn't have to ask him that. We both knew that Sarah died without a word of English. Mr Mandel, has anyone ever give you a cheque in Johannesburg in Yiddish?'

But, above all, it was the way Peretz Gischen handled the questions relating to the cheeses which in the end frustrated Moses Levine's scheme to disinherit his sons.

'You've already told the court, Mr Gischen, that over a long period of time you observed Mrs Levine making the cheeses.'

'Exactly, my lord.'

'Can you tell the court how big were the cheeses that you used to see her make?'

Peretz with a dismissive and incredulous tone: 'My lord, how big are the cheeses?' The judge told Peretz that this was indeed the question he was being asked. Peretz, as if talking to himself, once again repeated the question and after a pause said: 'My lord, did I measure them, did I weigh them? If you vant I should guess, 15lbs, maybe 20lbs. Do me something.'

A similar exchange took place on the number of cheeses that he used to observe Mrs Levine making at any given time. By now Judge Neser understood that a Peretz repetition of the question was not an evasion but rather constituted part of the answer. Eventually Peretz told the court that he was recalling events of more than 20 years ago, that only a crazy man would have gone around counting cheeses and ended up with 'How many cheeses? If you vant I should guess then maybe 30, maybe 40.'

The reason for Mandel's insistence that Peretz should give some idea of the weight and number of the cheeses which he saw Mrs Levine make became clearer at a later stage in the cross-examination.

'Mr Peretz, my client will not deny that from time to time you observed Mrs Levine making cheeses, but I want to put it to you that the cheeses which you saw Mrs Levine preparing were solely for domestic use.'

Peretz once more rose to the occasion. With a broad grin on his face, he answered: 'So she made cheeses for domestic use? I don't know how big Mr Mandel's family is, but 30 to 40 cheeses weighing 15 to 20lbs, my lord, just work that out.'

It was earlier in the cross-examination, and still on the subject of cheeses, that Peretz gave an answer whose brilliance it would be difficult to surpass. He was still being tested on his claim that Mrs Levine's cheese-making activity was virtually a daily routine and was asked to tell the court how cheeses were made.

'You claim to have witnessed this process so often that, if you are telling the truth, Mr Gischen, you should be able to describe the process of cheese making.'

Without hesitation, Peretz turned to the judge and said: 'My lord, how are cheeses made? For the last 30 years I have been catching a tram from Doornfontein and back almost every day. If you put a Bible in front of me I will put my one hand on the Bible and my other hand on my heart and swear, may God strike me dead, that the man was driving a tram. Husk me to drive a tram.'

When the court adjourned counsel had not completed Peretz's cross-examination. But by the next morning negotiations began and an out of court settlement was reached in terms of which the two sons were to receive the value of their inheritance. In civil disputes the courts are very ready to encourage a settlement between the parties. But somehow one had the feeling that Judge Neser would have welcomed another session of light entertainment with Peretz Gischen.

An attempted judicial forgery

Witness the scene of a policeman beating someone up, and the chances are more than ever that the victim (almost invariably black) will end up in court facing a number of the charges usual in such circumstances: failing to give name and address, resisting arrest, hindering the police in the execution of their duties, and (of course) assault on the police. The late attorney Lewis Baker, also an activist in our underground, briefed me in one such trial in which the magistrate was hoist by his own crooked petard.

The main police witness was a white sergeant who made a habit of organising an incessant series of raids on the houses of the Boksburg location, ostensibly checking illicit liquor, location permits, illegal occupation, rent receipts, tax receipts and investigating a host of other 'crimes' that only apply to blacks. My client was a special target. He had previously given evidence in a case involving a charge of police malpractice and from then on the sergeant began to teach him a lesson. In the three months that preceded the incident I am about to describe, the sergeant had raided my client's house – at all hours of the day and night – more than 70 times.

On the night in question he came once again and, with the usual arrogance and contempt for black privacy, rummaged through drawers, cupboards and beds, flinging the contents all over the floor. My client had by then given up even asking what the searches were all about. They were becoming an almost routine part of daily existence, and experience teaches one not to ask too many questions of a white sergeant.

The raid was over and the white sergeant withdrew. My client picked up an iron bar which served to reinforce the door against break-ins. He was about to rest the bar on its brackets when the door was flung open and there stood the sergeant. The next thing my client remembers was waking up in hospital after an operation for the removal of a bullet from his chest. As soon as he was well enough he was charged with a cluster of offences which, predictably enough, included the charge of resisting arrest, hindering a police officer in the execution of his duties and an attempt to cause grievous bodily harm to the police sergeant.

From the start the prospect of an acquittal seemed negligible. When the only evidence before the court is one man's word against another's, it is difficult to persuade a white magistrate that the one man (a black accused) is telling the truth and the other (a white police sergeant) is lying. If you add to this the fact that the magistrate and the police sergeant are close friends, then the dice could not have been more loaded against my client.

The sergeant's story in the witness box was predictable enough. On information received (one was never allowed to ask from whom), he raided the premises in search of illicit liquor. He was about to leave the premises when the accused grabbed an iron bar and rushed menacingly towards him. In fear of his life and acting purely in self-defence, the sergeant drew his service revolver and, at point-blank range, shot the accused through the chest.

The cross-examination lasted for some hours. I attempted to place on record the long and nasty history of persecution to which my client had been subjected. We knew that this tactic could become a double-edged sword, enabling the prosecution to argue that my client's sense of outraged grievance against the white sergeant provided the motive for his alleged attempt to attack with the iron bar. But the key question was: what happened immediately before the shooting? There were no witnesses on either side to corroborate or contradict the conflicting versions of events in those few seconds, and it was proving difficult to make an obvious dent in the sergeant's simple story. A few minor contradictions did emerge which, together with disputed technical data (the distance from which the sergeant fired and the angle of firing), could, in normal circumstances, provide the defence with an argument that the prosecution had not proved the accused guilty beyond a reasonable doubt. But these circumstances were not normal and I was not optimistic about the outcome.

It was the sergeant's attempt to make doubly sure that a conviction by his friend the magistrate would not be interfered with by the appeal court that was his real undoing.

After his evidence, when we assume the state will close its case, a surprise witness is called. He is a black constable who had been guarding my client's bed in the hospital where he was recovering from the bullet wound. He tells the court that on a certain day the accused was visited in hospital by two Indian friends who advised the accused to deny that he was about to hit the sergeant when the shooting occurred, and instead to pretend that he picked up the bar solely for the purpose of securing the door.

Only about ten minutes were left before the court adjourned for the day, and I was anxious to pin down the witness immediately on a number of vital questions. It would have been extremely unusual if the plot to commit perjury had been concocted within the sight and hearing of a uniformed policeman. When the court adjourned, I glanced through the evidence which the magistrate had been laboriously recording in rather spread-out longhand. I was particularly pleased with the last entry which read: 'Could they see that you could hear?' Answer: 'They could see that I could hear.'

Although I had not yet completed the cross-examination of this witness, it seemed that the trial might well end on the following day, and I began to make notes for my argument. The next morning I returned to the court some hours before it was due to begin its sitting, in order to arm myself with more accurate references to the sergeant's evidence. When I had completed my notes on this aspect some sixth sense made me glance once again at the last page of the recorded evidence. I was absolutely horror-struck. The magistrate had, since the adjournment the afternoon before, deliberately forged the record by the insertion of the single word 'not'. The police constable's last answer now read: 'they could *not* see that I could hear'. What to do?

My first reaction was one of outrage and indignation, and I felt there would be no option than to confront the magistrate with this blatant forgery and to demand that he recuse himself from the trial. Uncontrolled indignation and anger are among the barrister's worst enemies and I was fortunate that time permitted me to count the proverbial ten before I did myself terrible harm and achieved nothing for my client. It began to dawn on me that a direct challenge of the sort I had in mind might achieve little more than my immediate committal to prison for contempt of court. The constable waiting in the witness box for cross-examination to continue would undoubtedly realise what the issue was and would support the magistrate. The prosecutor and other court officials would probably do likewise. And I would have no one but my client to back up the most serious allegation that could be levelled against a judicial officer. No, this special situation called for special tactics.

The case is called and the constable resumes his place in the witness box.

'Yes, Mr Slovo. You still have some questions?'

'As your worship pleases. Constable, as I understood your evidence you told the court yesterday that the accused's two visitors could not see that you could hear their conversation with the accused. Is that correct?'

'No, it is not correct. They could see that I could hear.'

'Then why did you lie to his worship yesterday?'

The witness protests that he is giving exactly the same evidence now as he did yesterday, and the indignant prosecutor backs him up, quoting from his own notes. The magistrate who begins to sense what is happening, flushes slightly but is still uncertain how to handle the situation. I press home my advantage relentlessly.

'Constable, if I am putting an unfair question to you, his worship will no doubt correct me.' And, turning to the magistrate: 'Perhaps your worship could refer to the record?'

Only he and I know why the flush in his face is becoming more crimson. To cope with his dilemma he is trying to buy time by paging through the record ostensibly in search of the constable's answer of the previous day. He knows full well (and he knows that I know as well) that the vandalised answer is on the last page in front of him. He finds no way of handling the terrible secret between us, and I make sure that he notices the half-smile of triumph on my lips. Eventually, he turns to the witness, reads the previous day's recorded answer to him and barks out an instruction that the witness should stop prevaricating and should answer my question.

The rest of the trial was a formality. A 'lying' constable, the smell of collusion between him and his sergeant, and perhaps the magistrate's unease about his forgery, undoubtedly combined to save my client from what would have been an inevitable jail sentence.

One of the hallowed rules of bar ethics is that it is impermissible to put a question to a witness which, to the knowledge of the questioner, contains a false statement. In my endeavour to trap the corrupt magistrate, I was clearly in breach of this rule. At least one of my uptight colleagues, Advocate Weinstock, threatened to report me to the Bar Council. I have little doubt that the Gods would have forgiven my transgression even if the Bar Council would not have.

One good turn deserves another

Faced with a catalogue of race cruelties practised against blacks, the average white South African will attempt to plead in mitigation that South Africa is not the only culprit. True enough. But is there another corner of our earth which actually legislates against a common society and which, in its constitution, institutionalises the internal separation of the races?

In the gallery of apartheid measures, the Immorality Act is perhaps among the most revolting of its exhibits. To caress or to make love to a person not of your own colour is an act of 'indecency' and 'immorality' which attracts criminal penalties. It is ironic that the most fanatical defenders of this prohibition (and, in my experience, its most frequent transgressors) are the Afrikaners – a people whose forebears fathered the bulk of the present mixed population and a goodly proportion of whom find themselves classified as white only because of a combination of luck and stealth.

In a tract published in the late 1930s George Findlay, a leading left-wing QC, demonstrated that there are indeed very few indigenous-born Afrikaners whose blood does not (metaphorically speaking) contain at least a dash of colour. Their outspoken race viciousness is perhaps a defensive reflex against the agonising consequences of being pushed across the colour line by another of apartheid's grotesque organs – the Race Classification Board.

The experience I am about to describe relates to an act of 'immorality' with an unusual twist to it. Let me start with the seemingly unconnected end to the story.

The basement of the Johannesburg Magistrate's Court was transformed into a temporary courtroom to accommodate more than 100 laundry workers who were facing a charge of an illegal strike. Under our industrial legislation only 'employees' had the legal right to strike. A withdrawal of labour by Africans could never be legal since 'pass-bearing Natives' were, by law, specifically excluded from the definition of 'employee'.

In this matter the case against the laundry workers seemed open and shut. Pay-day had come around and the promise of a pay rise had not been honoured. The workers walked out *en masse*. Lorry loads of police arrived and arrested the picketing workers. A conviction seemed virtually inevitable. The hours I spent cross-examining the manager could not erase the only relevant fact: that the workers had indeed walked out of the factory in the middle of a shift because of the pay dispute.

When all the workers were found not guilty and discharged at the end of the Crown case, neither the indignant prosecutor nor the jubilant accused could quite grasp how I had managed to pull off this minor miracle. None of them knew of the secret which only the magistrate and I shared.

It was some months before this trial when the magistrate asked me to see him urgently. As soon as I walked into his office I knew he was in deep trouble. He stuttered out an apology for bothering me, but he was feeling desperate. He begged me to help him with advice about an event which had occurred the evening before.

It was his habit to spend a few hours with his friends in his favourite bar lounge after work on Friday afternoons. The previous night a birthday had been celebrated and he had consumed more liquor than usual. When he left the bar he came across an Indian court interpreter who invited him to have one for the road at a friend's place nearby. There he found a crowd of people of all races chatting, drinking and dancing. He had never been to a multiracial party and was fascinated and excited by this new experience. He stayed there for some hours in drunken conversation, mainly with a rather good-looking black woman. They soon became a little more intimate, but nothing beyond an occasional embrace and a few kisses. Later in the evening he discovered that a well-known photographer from the *Golden City Post* had taken photographs of him and his lady friend, and he fully expected these to be published.

What tragic irony! There he was, a senior magistrate, an Afrikaner establishment figure and a devout member of his Dutch Reformed

Church congregation. I caught myself about to say 'But what you did is a crime only in our sick society' and swallowed the words because he looked too broken. We both knew the scores of couples to whom he had sermonised about the sanctity of colour before sending them to prison as criminals under the Immorality Act. He had also served on race classification boards, subjected men, women and children to pencil tests, heard evidence about the shape of their noses, the thickness of their lips and listened to the opinions of a breed of race 'experts' that only a sick South Africa could produce. I wondered whether in his agony all this came back to him. But he was too pathetic-looking for me to take this moment to drive home the deserved lesson.

He asked me whether there was anything I could do to ensure that the photographs were not published and to have the negatives destroyed. He knew by reputation of my involvement in liberation politics and he hoped that I would have more easy access to the generally radical black journalists. I decided to help him for a number of reasons. The party had been held in the flat of a quite well-known Indian Congress activist whose name might have featured in the 'exposé' even though I was certain that he would never have become party to the photographer's action. And despite the element of poetic justice, the deliberate exploitation of the ugliness of the Immorality Act somehow went against the grain.

That same day I made an appointment to see Henry Kuyper, an ex-colleague of mine who had left the Bar to take up an appointment as general manager of South African Associated Newspapers, which owned the *Golden City Post*. He made an enquiry, and the story was indeed being prepared for publication. He gave immediate instructions that it should not go ahead, and later that day he sent me an envelope containing all the negatives and prints. What innocent and harmless images of relaxed happiness and joy on the face of the magistrate and of his friend for an hour or two on that Friday night. In South Africa you burn these images – which is what I did.

Luckily for the laundry workers, the magistrate kept his side of the unspoken bargain when he freed them from a charge under another one of apartheid's indecent and immoral laws which discriminate against black workers.

South Africa's busy hangman

According to Amnesty International, only Iran and Iraq have a slight edge over South Africa in the judicial killing league. In South Africa in 1982, for example, 100 people (99 of them black) were executed and more than that number were sentenced to death.

'The sentence of this court is that you will be taken to a place of detention where you will be hanged by the neck until you are dead.'

This is the climax of the ritual which authorises and legitimates a killing. I have witnessed such a scene many times and never found it possible to avoid a wave of nausea. By the time the fate of the accused has been sealed you have come to know him quite well. You want to believe his story, however improbable. So you are always left with the nagging feeling that an irreparable injustice may have been done. And in South Africa the form of punishment is even more repugnant because it contains a racial dimension. In all its history South Africa has hanged six whites for the murder of blacks whereas hundreds of blacks have gone to the gallows for murder of whites. The cheapness of black life also often protects the perpetrator. When a capital crime has been committed against a black, the investigation is usually shoddy and the prospects greater for the accused of an acquittal.

During the early 1950s the Judge President of the Transvaal Division of the Supreme Court was 'Jerry' Maritz. If a count were taken he would probably go into the book of records for the number of murder and rape trials he disposed of in a single day. His courtroom was like Chaplin's *Modern Times* production line, and he presided over it with an irreverence for legal dogma and in a style reminiscent of the frontier judge of the early Hollywood cowboy films. 'Jerry' rarely pronounced the death sentence, because as Judge President he saw to it that the bulk of the trials which came before him involved a black accused and a black victim. We all knew that if we did not waste too much of the court's time our efforts would usually be rewarded with a reduction of the charge from one of murder to culpable homicide, and, very often, the accused would walk out of court with a suspended sentence.

My initiation into this judge's style came in a murder trial when he interrupted my flow of cross-examination with the whisper: 'Mr Slovo, if you change your plea to culpable homicide your client won't go to jail.' His show of lenience did not stem from a belief in penal reform, but rather from a relaxed, casual attitude towards violence if it did not involve the white community. In the few cases that came before him when white life had been taken, the clowning style he affected and the plea-bargaining were abandoned.

I recall one such trial whose final stages I witnessed in the Springs Circuit Court while waiting for my own case to start. From Judge Maritz's summing-up I gathered that the accused had assaulted a white policeman who subsequently died from his injuries. The policeman had apparently stopped the accused in the street and demanded that he produce a receipt to prove that a new pair of shoes he was carrying was not stolen. The accused had already thrown away his receipt. When the policeman tried to grab the shoes a fracas began.

The accused was found guilty of murder without extenuating circumstances – a finding which in terms of South African law automatically obliged the judge to pronounce sentence of death. Only one more step intervenes: the accused is asked whether he has anything more to say before the sentence is pronounced – a fairly useless part of the ritual since nothing can now reverse the process.

The accused stood motionless and gave no sign that he was about to make the usual forlorn plea for mercy or reassert his innocence. The bench, out of regard for the solemnity of the moment, did not hurry him. After a lapse of what seemed like minutes, Judge Maritz once again asked whether he wished to say anything. The accused did not answer. Instead he bent down and disappeared from view behind the solid wooden dock. When he raised himself he held aloft the pair of shoes. Slowly he turned his back on the bench and faced the black spectator gallery, his head moving along each row in turn. The person he was seeking was seated somewhere in the middle, and when their eyes met the accused beckoned him to approach the dock. The man, clad in overalls (a relative, a fellow worker?), did so. Without a word exchanged between the two, the accused handed him the highly polished pair of shoes. Then, facing the bench again, the accused merely nodded as if to indicate that this is what I wanted to say.

There can be little doubt that if the races of the perpetrator and victim had been transposed (always assuming that a black man would have had the temerity to demand a receipt from a white man), the white accused would have walked out of court in his pair of shoes with a suspended sentence, after a lecture on the court's duty to safeguard black as well as white life. And Judge Maritz would have given this without his tongue in cheek as he passionately believed that he was an instrument of equality before the law.

Mr Justice Price was another judge who would have dismissed indignantly any suggestion that his judgments were influenced by the mould of white culture in which he was permanently set. He presided over a murder trial in Queenstown which for a time was a *cause célèbre* in the Eastern Cape.

Two African teachers were on trial for their lives on a charge of murdering the chief warder of the Lady Frere Prison. The deceased had earned himself a reputation as a firm administrator or a brute (depending on whether you were white or black), and was killed by a number of shots from his own firearm. The prosecution alleged that the chief warder had gone hunting in the mountains between Queenstown and Lady Frere on the previous Christmas Day and that the accused crept up on him while he was resting and killed him. Public sympathy for the two sides in the trial was quite unconnected with the facts: if you were white you were certain of the guilt of the accused and wished them a short route to the gallows; if you were black you presumed a white frame-up and thought in any case the deceased had deserved his death.

I was instructed by Attorney Tsotsie, a prominent figure in the Unity Movement, to appear for the accused. When I presented myself at the reception desk of the Queenstown Hotel, I found out why my telegram requesting a booking had gone unanswered. The manager showed a look of utter incredulity when I announced my name, and he mumbled something like: 'Which Slovo are you?' As part of pre-trial publicity, the regional newspaper had published a photograph of defending counsel 'Advocate Slovo'. It was part of a composite picture published in the *Rand Daily Mail* of Duma Nokwe and me, fully robed, walking out of the Pretoria Supreme Court after an application for Duma's admission as the first African barrister in the Transvaal Provincial Division. But some hapless picture editor had cropped me from the photograph, and above the caption was the beaming black face of Duma Nokwe. This 'Advocate Slovo' would have had to accommodate himself in some shack in the nearby location.

The trial lasted for nearly a week and, at the end, the hangman claimed another two victims. All the evidence was circumstantial (the most damaging being the sale by the accused of a few personal items of the deceased's property within a few days of the deed), and I have always felt that if the victim had not been white, the accused might well have been given the benefit of the doubt. This feeling was reinforced by an event outside the courtroom in the middle of the trial.

The local Side Bar association had organised a cocktail party in honour of Mr Justice Price to which the prosecution and defence lawyers were invited, excluding black attorney Tsotsie. But he insisted I attend in the interests of my clients. Judge Price was hailed as a returning son: he had origins in the area although he served as a judge in the Transvaal Provincial Division. In replying to the toast, the mild-sounding Englishman spoke of the great nostalgia he had for the Eastern Cape which was 'connected with his very own blood'. He went on to explain that the original Prices were frontiersmen who were 'also murdered during one of the Kaffir Wars'. From then on I knew what was coming to my clients. Judge Price's ancestors (among the plundering frontiersmen aptly described by the Batavian Commissioner-General de Mist as 'these half-wild Europeans') were avenged once again.

Justice is of course no longer of the frontier variety; its cogs are now well integrated into a complex machine whose most vital component is the block of death cells in Pretoria Prison. On average one condemned occupant is taken to the gallows every third day, accompanied by a chorus of song from those who will follow him. What happens to those who spend their days and nights controlling, guarding and eventually executing this vast community of men and women – each victim allocated a booking in the hanging hall by an official with a chart and a rubber stamp? Certainly one of the ways of coping is to block out all sensibility of the process and, like a Belsen guard, treat it as a job like any other. This was brought home to me by an incident involving a senior prison officer who worked in the hanging block and who also presided over an internal prison tribunal which dealt with breaches of discipline by prisoners.

My client, Mathews, was the leader of the Msomis – one of Johannesburg's most powerful gangs during the early 1950s. In the post-war period there sprang up quite a few bandit associations such as 'the Russians', 'the Japanese' and 'the Msomis'. For a time Msomis ruled the streets of Alexandra Township, one of the few black ghettos on the outskirts of Johannesburg one could enter without a permit. Although Mathews could not be described as a 'social bandit', he did not interfere with those who were active in the political struggle against state tyranny. Thus our Communist Party general secretary, Moses Kotane (who lived in Alexandra Township), could walk the streets in the dead of night knowing that he would not be molested. Mathews was eventually tried on a number of charges connected with robberies carried out by members of his gang in the course of which the victims had been killed. I had not appeared at his trial which ended with a death sentence, but I was briefed to argue the matter in an appeal which was unsuccessful. It was after I had visited Mathews in the death cell to explain the Appellate Division judgment that I received a call from his attorney instructing me to appear on Mathews' behalf at a disciplinary hearing.

A special room of the death block. Prisoner Mathews marched in, looking like a shadow of his former self. He knows of course that his life will be snapped in days, perhaps hours. He looks frightened, as if they have come to fetch him for the final call. Before the tribunal enters he mumbles something about an argument with a warder. I tell him not to worry and think to myself what more can they do to a man who is condemned to death. The presiding officer enters. Evidence is given by a young warder that the prisoner called him a 'fucking shit' in the course of some trivial argument whose content I cannot now recall. Mathews does not deny the allegation and claims to have been provoked by the warder's nastiness. I argue that in any case a man about to be hanged should be pardoned for such a petty outburst. I leave the jail feeling numb. Mathews (who was hanged about a week later) was sentenced to be deprived of three meals.

The Native Commissioner's dream

Until I was banned under the Suppression of Communism Act from travelling outside Johannesburg without special permission, I had a large rural practice which often took me to the reserves and so-called Black Spots of our countryside. These are the African rural ghettos (now graced by the name of Bantustan) allocated in the final dispensation after the crushing of the long, drawn-out indigenous wars of resistance. They cover in total a land area of 13%; the balance of 87% was proclaimed as the permanent and exclusive homeland of the English, Dutch, French, German colonisers and settlers and their descendants. And the ideological folklore which emanated from the early Stellenbosch professors to proclaim the fairness of this division has yet to be surpassed in its audacity. Belief is so often a faithful servant of self-interest, and most of the white bureaucrats charged with administering the dispensation not only regarded it as fair but also believed it was in the best interests of their black wards. I came across a typical example of this in a cattle-culling trial in the middle 1950s.

I was briefed to go to Maun (a major administrative centre in what was then called Bechuanaland) to appear on behalf of a group of 50 peasants who were being charged with failure to comply with the cattle-culling regulations. Mr Gold was the administrative head of the region and, like all his fellow native commissioners, he was all branches of government rolled into one. In his legislative capacity he helped determine how many head of cattle each peasant had to slaughter or sell by a given date. In his administrative capacity he had caused the appropriate order to be served on each peasant. In his executive capacity he had determined that prosecutions should be instituted against a selected number who disobeyed the order. And in his judicial capacity he was now about to preside in a trial which would punish the transgressors.

My clients had all indeed refused to comply with the culling orders, a response which was pretty general throughout the countryside during the 1950s. Mr Gold was a courteous and quiet-spoken public official. He was obviously deeply convinced of his role as a sincere benefactor of the African inhabitants who had been placed in his charge. When I met him he spent an inordinate length of time trying to convince me that the reduction of the number of cattle in the region was virtually a matter of life or death for the community as a whole. He unrolled a map and referred to a scientific agricultural survey which had emphasised the dangerous advance of soil erosion in the region and which had provided him with a guide as to the maximum number of cattle which could be sustained on the available land.

Within the limits of Mr Gold's vision and mandate it was difficult to dispute the technical accuracy of his belief that he was indeed acting in the best interests of the peasants when he insisted on a drastic stock reduction. But, like all serving technocrats, he either did not see or did not want to see that the problem had nothing to do with too many cattle and had everything to do with too little land. Science and technology can hardly persuade a man who has been dispossessed of most of his land and then told that the forced reduction of his stock is in his deepest interests. When I gingerly made these points during this informal pre-trial exchange over tea, Mr Gold mumbled something about politics not being his business – this from a man whose working life was devoted exclusively to the application of the politics of segregation.

Mr Gold still hoped that there would be a way of resolving the problem raised by the peasants' defiance without invoking penal sanctions. As a gesture of goodwill he was quite prepared to postpone the trial for some months – an offer which my clients were ready to accept since they could lose nothing and could only gain time. To me it was clear beyond question that under no circumstances would these stolid peasants change their minds about an issue which was far deeper than Mr Gold's legitimating ideology would admit.

Just before the formal adjournment Mr Gold, displaying his infinite faith in human rationality as he understood it, made a passionate appeal to the accused to use the time he had granted them to reconsider their attitude. And the absolutely unbridgeable gap between fantasy and reality emerged from the unintended humour of Mr Gold's homily:

'In 300 years time I will not be here. There will be some other Native Commissioner. And your great great great great grandchildren will tell that Native Commissioner how grateful they are that there was once a far-seeing father who gave their ancestors the correct advice and who helped make the Maun district part of the healthy place it is today.'

He paused and looked around as if in expectation of grunts of approval and nods. He was met by an immobile silence.

The crime of teaching

Before institutionalised racism became a world issue, South Africa's white politicians did not find it necessary to package apartheid in the glossy wrappings currently in use. For example, Hendrik Verwoerd, the apostle of modern apartheid, spoke of the need to bring about an education system in South Africa which would prevent the creation of a class of Africans which 'feels that its spiritual, economic and political home is among the civilised community of South Africa'. He was speaking in the Senate in his capacity as Minister of Native Affairs in support of the infamous Bantu Education Act of which he was the architect.

On the initiative of the ANC, parents began to organise community schools in which their children could escape the new syllabuses designed to prepare an African child for his subordinate position in the social system. This effort was then met with more legislation outlawing schools which did not have official state recognition. I became involved in a spate of cases in which teachers and parents were arraigned before South Africa's courts of justice for teaching the three Rs. It seems to me that the bare publication of the verbatim records in some of these trials would do the job of a thousand speeches in exposing the nature of apartheid practice. The records of the trials were usually short and the evidence uncontested. A typical composite record of one to two pages would read something like this:

'I am a police sergeant in charge of the X Police Station. On such-and-such a day of such-and-such month I received certain information and proceeded with my men to a spot which overlooked a large tree. We took cover behind some rocks and bushes. Soon after the sun rose I noticed groups of children aged between six and 13 converging on a spot near the big tree.

'At approximately 7.30 am I observed the accused approaching the children, and they all proceeded to the big tree where the children seated themselves in its shade in a semi-circle. The accused proceeded to suspend the blackboard (Exhibit A) from a nail which protruded from the tree. He then proceeded to write on Exhibit A with white chalk and the children appeared to be writing intermittently in their exercise books. We kept the scene under observation for about 15 minutes when I signalled to my men to surround the accused and the children. I approached the accused, told him that he was under arrest for conducting an illegal school and gave him the usual police warning that he need not say anything to incriminate himself. The accused remained silent.

'My men and I then proceeded to confiscate a number of items which I now hand in: Exhibit A, a blackboard with the five times table written out. Exhibit B, a batch of 20 exercise books bearing the names of the different pupils on the outside and containing, in various stages of completion, the five times table as the last entry. We also confiscated a number of children's basic readers in English as well as some vernacular illustrated story books which I hand in as Exhibit C. The accused was still holding a piece of white chalk when I apprehended him and this, together with a number of other pieces of chalk of varying colours, I confiscated and now hand in as Exhibit D. I asked some of the children in the front row, in the presence and hearing of the accused, what the accused had been doing prior to our arrival, and one of the pupils stated that the accused had been teaching them the five times table. The accused made no attempt to deny this. The accused could not produce a permit to run a school. I took him into custody and escorted him to our police station.'

In 1976, when the Soweto revolt erupted, the authorities expressed their surprise at the persistent anger of the schoolchildren and maintained once again that behind the revolt were the communists and the hand of Moscow.

Touchè

The art of cross-examination is the cornerstone of court craft. What to start with, what to ask and (more important) what not to ask, how to tackle the different categories of witnesses, when to stop, how to incite the tribunal to put the boot in and not to see the witness as a poor victim, how to manoeuvre a witness into changing sides without his being aware of it, how and when to ask the key questions – these are among the complex pathways of the labyrinth through which every cross-examiner must find his way. Wigmore's brilliant classic volumes on evidence (in which I am sure Peretz Gischen would have found a place) are jam-packed with examples of how even eminent counsel lost their way in this maze and in the result managed to snatch defeat from the very jaws of victory.

I remember one case he relates in which a widow claimed damages arising out of the death of her husband whose car collided with a train at a level crossing during the hours of darkness. The key witness for the defendant was a railway guard who, after two days of cross-examination, could not be shifted from his simple story that just before the collision he had carried out his duty of standing at the level crossing and warning oncoming traffic of the approach of the train by swinging a lamp from side to side. After the witness was released from the marathon spell of cross-examination he wiped his brow and whispered to one of his friends: 'Whew, thank goodness he didn't ask me whether the lamp was alight or not.'

Despite occasional unfair lawyerish twists and the often unequal contest between a layman and a skilled, professional inquisitor, I know of no other method which can improve on cross-examination as a way of testing a witness's veracity. Within certain broad limits counsel should not be hampered in his probings on behalf of his client; he is there as a partisan and not as an ombudsman charged with seeing all sides of the question. It is the tribunal which must exercise its critical faculties and separate substance from appearance. At the same time experience teaches that the fiat to ignore the faculties of belief and disbelief is also a fiat to engage in a kind of institutionalised dishonesty and gives counsel an indirect power to subvert the truth. This is especially so in the abstract concept of a reasonable man who has fixed powers of judgment and observation, and to hint at dishonesty if the witness's conduct does not measure up to this mythical concept. This was pointedly brought home to me in an experience which took place only partly in a courtroom.

During the middle 1950s I used to drive myself to work in a two-tone Chevrolet which I parked in a public parking space near our chambers in His Majesty's Buildings. One day when I went into the parking lot I discovered that my car had been stolen. I went back to my chambers and immediately telephoned the car theft squad. I identified myself to the sergeant at the other end of the line and he began to take a description of the stolen vehicle. I told him it was a two-tone Chevrolet and gave him the registration number. He asked me what the colours were and I answered 'red and cream'.

'Is it red on top or cream on top, Mr Slovo?'

A pause. 'I'm sorry, Sergeant, but I can't for the life of me remember at this moment.'

'How long have you had the car?'

'About four years.'

'What is the colour of the upholstery?'

'Ah – I think it was a sort of light colour but I can't really be certain.'

'Mr Slovo, are you wearing a watch?'

'Yes.'

'How long have you had it?'

'About seven years.'

'Without looking at it, can you tell me what make it is?'

'… to tell you the truth, no.'

78

To overcome my embarrassment I went on to the offensive and asked the sergeant what the hell the make of my watch had to do with my stolen car. 'I'm sorry, Mr Slovo, but I just wanted you to understand how I felt when you cross-examined me in that case in Brakpan of the pick-pocket whom I observed for something like five seconds. You called me a liar because I couldn't remember whether he was wearing a green jersey and fawn trousers, or a fawn jersey and green trousers.'

I was relieved that this exchange took place on the phone, and that the polite-spoken sergeant could not see my deep blush.

The 'fucking police'

For a while after a sensational trial in which I was involved, the expletive 'fucking police' was widely used more as a statement of fact than as expression of anger; its use in this literal sense arose from the rather novel strategy adopted by Johannesburg's Immorality Squad in its crusade against prostitution.

At the time the two most important entrepreneurs in the brothel business were a certain Mrs Davis and a certain Mrs Peake. Competition between them was stiff and the outcome often hinged upon which side managed to establish the most mutually beneficial relationship with key members of the police force itself. At the time Mrs Peake had obviously stolen a march on Mrs Davis, most of whose employees were rounded up in a rather unusual police operation.

In the normal course a raid on a brothel netted very little for the police. More often than not, the management was given a timely tip from one of its moles inside the force. Even in the absence of a warning, the private conditions under which business was usually conducted gave sufficient time for the offending couple to compose themselves and thus deprive the police of vital evidence. Then there was also an even chance of bagging a dignitary of church, state or big business with the attendant dangers of repercussion for the officer in charge if, in the end, the case against the accused collapsed. In any case this kind of catch was highly embarrassing for the image of the white establishment since it helped provoke seditious cackles in the black ghettos.

In order to avoid some of these pitfalls a special squad was selected, presumably from among the most virile members of the Immorality Department. At an appointed time the members of this squad, armed with marked money and a packet of prophylactics, descended upon their targets as customers rather than as raiders. Their instructions were actually to engage in fornication and, while they were busy doing so, officers of a back-up force would rush in to make the arrests and provide the corroborating evidence normally demanded in the case of a crime committed at the instigation of a police trap.

I had recently appeared in a number of well-publicised prostitution cases and the brief to defend the new accused landed on my desk. As the proceedings unfolded it became more and more apparent that Mrs Peake and some of her employees had a large role in a campaign to crush the Davis chain.

The trial was punctuated with incident and melodrama, with reverberations not only in the sensational press but also in the Church, in Parliament and other establishment institutions. We asked for further particulars to the charge, and when the answers disclosed that in their quest for a conviction the police had gone to the very limits, the opening salvo for the defence was very clear. I took exception to the charge on the grounds that the case rested upon police conduct which was, to say the least, utterly repugnant to public decency and morality. The court adjourned to consider my application but the cat was already among the pigeons.

In the public furore which followed I found myself, for the first and last time in my life, quoted with approval by the synod of the Dutch Reformed Church, right-wing Nationalist MPs and other guardians of the Afrikaner establishment. But despite the public outcry it was difficult for the court to find a legal slot which would dispose of the issue before the leading of evidence. The highly embarrassed prosecution limped on with a charge against one of my clients as a test case. Apart from the police testimony, corroborating evidence was forthcoming from a number of ladies we knew to be part of Mrs Peake's stable.

Had I studied Wigmore's volumes with sufficient diligence I would have been alerted to a technique fairly commonly used by prostitutes in the witness box. Wigmore warns us that a prostitute who feels herself discomfited by the intensity of the cross-examination is very likely to hit back by innuendoes that counsel's knowledge of the goings-on in the world of the prostitute was gathered during his own meanderings rather than from his client's instructions.

In the course of my cross-examination of one of these experienced professionals I asked her to be a little more precise about the exact address of a house which she alleged had been used from time to time by my client and various other ladies (including herself) as a brothel. 'I am a bit confused about the number,' she answered, and then looking at me straight in the eye, 'but you should be able to help us, you patronised it often enough.' All I could do was to join in the general laughter, acknowledging that this round of the contest had certainly been won by the witness.

On another occasion the Sunday newspapers had a gala day describing the unusual events outside the courtroom soon after one of the adjournments. I walked out of court that day with a feeling that things were going well for my client. I had managed to make a dent in the evidence of quite a few of Mrs Peake's associates who were gathered in a huddle outside the courtroom as I emerged. It must have been my self-satisfied expression which finally determined the course of action they were debating. One of them already had her shoes off and, holding one of these aloft, she led her screaming colleagues, variously armed with shoes and swinging handbags, in a charge towards me.

I decided that in the circumstances discretion was the better part of valour, and instead of making a stand I started sprinting down the long central corridor of the magistrate's court, much to the amusement of the spectators. My bid to evade the battle was hampered by a rather heavy briefcase which I was loath to abandon. At the moment when it seemed that the group might well catch up with me, I was suddenly grabbed by a tall, wiry-looking man who skilfully whisked me into an office whose door he locked in the nick of time.

My rescuer turned out to be a police lieutenant by the name of Viktor. Later he was posted to the Security Branch and, in 1963, when Ruth was detained under the 90-day detention law, Viktor was to be one of Ruth's chief interrogators. He played the role of the friendly, sympathetic member of the team as part of the psychological assault designed to break her down. Predictably enough, the incident of the chase provided him with ready-made material in his calculated attempt to establish some kind of rapport between himself and the prisoner.

My client was eventually discharged at the end of the state case without having to give any evidence. The prosecutor was not too upset since he could now withdraw the charges against the rest of the accused and avoid the continuing public embarrassment of calling the members of the 'fucking police' to describe their sordid campaign in Johannesburg's houses of pleasure.

But there was one man whose problems were not over when the case ended: he was the detective sergeant in charge of the whole project. Some weeks later he arrived unannounced at my chambers and asked to see me on what he described as 'some very private business'. He then told me that his marriage was virtually on the rocks and that his wife refused to accept his protestations that he was not himself among the group that had actually taken part in acts of intercourse with the accused. To the best of my knowledge, on the evidence that had been produced, he was telling the truth and I saw no reason why I should refuse this plea to help alleviate his personal distress. Later they came together and visited my chambers and, at the end of a rather unusual marriage counselling session, his embarrassed and weeping wife seemed less sceptical about his denials.

Defiance and the Freedom Charter

S oon after the Party was banned in 1950, it became apparent that the decision in favour of dissolution (opposed by only two members of the Central Committee, Bill Andrews and Michael Harmel) was indeed a genuine decision and had no qualifications. But pressure mounted from the ex-rank and file. Groups were formed in various places to discuss what happened next. A few of us took the initiative at the university, and we made it plain to the ex-members of the Central Committee that unless something was done by them we would jump the gun and form our own Party underground. Unknown to us, a few meetings of the old Central Committee did take place in Cape Town, but it became clear that quite a few of its members were not ready to lead or take part in the underground struggle. Eventually an organised top-level did come into existence in a paradoxical way.

The official appointed by the regime to wind up the affairs and assets of the Party was officially known as 'the liquidator'. Among his tasks was to establish who had been members of the Party and then to compile an official list of such membership. All those whose names appeared on the list were officially regarded as 'named' and became liable to various disabilities and bans. But the common law, with its precepts of natural justice, still required that the liquidator, before he could place a name on the list, had to call upon the person to show cause why he should not be 'named'. In order to decide on a common policy all those who had received such a letter from the liquidator were called to a meeting at which a committee was elected to represent the interests of those who would be affected by the Suppression of Communism Act. The meeting, with a bravado which bordered on extreme folly, decided also that since none of us was ashamed of having been a communist, we would write a joint reply indicating that we would not resist being named and that indeed the liquidator's list was a roll call of honour! Whatever history will say in relation to the tasks of the revolution and the need to move into underground work, the gesture was less than useful.

But it was this committee which initiated steps to recreate the Party as an underground force. I was co-opted to this group, which began to organise the first underground national conference of the Party, at which a Central Committee was elected. Between 1952 and 1962 the Party had six underground conferences, and the last one, when the Party Programme was adopted after a thorough discussion in the underground units, recorded impressive achievements throughout the country after a decade of underground work. This conference was attended by delegates from every major urban centre and by historic figures whose relatively recent conversion to the cause of socialism and the Party was a positive sign that our roots were indeed spreading deeper in the indigenous soil. To mark the fact that there had been an interregnum in the life of the Party after the 1950 dissolution, the name was changed from the original Communist Party of South Africa (CPSA) to the South African Communist Party (SACP).

All the conferences were organised in Johannesburg or on the Reef. Two of them were held over long weekends at Anglo-Union Furniture Factory, which was managed by Ruth's father, Julius First. I recollect this dedicated old Bolshevik (who for a short spell in 1924 had been chairman of the Party) patrolling the ground continuously to watch over us.

Apart from the obvious structural changes, the underground period also led to an evolution in practice of a new relationship between the Party and the mass movement. The ANC and the other congresses were to be made illegal only ten years later, and, in the meantime, public political work could be carried on only through the mass movement. It was not until the 1960 Emergency that the Party felt strong enough to announce its existence in an illegal leaflet. In the event all of us, and particularly the leading African comrades, began to devote energy as never before to the broad Congress movement. It was in the 1950s that the real foundation was laid of an alliance between the Party and the ANC that Oliver Tambo has described as constituting the two pillars of our liberation struggle.

Perhaps the most astonishing feature of the whole period was that we did not suffer a single casualty at the hands of the police in the first ten years of underground life. This appears even more impressive when we remember that the overwhelming majority of those who made up the underground membership had previously been publicly connected with the legal Party and most of them were 'named' on the liquidator's list. Almost all of us, members of the Central Committee and District Committees, were subject to bans imposed upon us under the Suppression of Communism Act which deprived us not only of the right to be active participants in a list of specified legal organisations, but also restricted our movement from one city to another and prohibited us from attending any 'gathering'. The definition of a gathering was so narrow that Ruth and I would have constituted a criminal conspiracy merely by being together since we both had 'gathering' bans, but we were saved by an exemption inserted by the Minister in our banning letters which gave us special permission to consort and communicate with one another.

One of the Party activists from the legal days, Joe Mogoti showed an absolute unconcern for the new reality. He was employed as a lawyer's clerk and often frequented both the Supreme and Magistrate's Courts in Johannesburg. Whenever he noticed me in the court corridors, whether alone or in conversation with magistrates, prosecutors or investigating police officers, he invariably shouted for all to hear: 'Hi, comrade Joe. How goes it?'

In general we engaged in illegal activity but were not really underground in the traditional sense of the term. We were either known or suspected by the police as political activists, and we continued our aboveground, normal lives. The first major figure to go underground in the real sense of the term was Nelson Mandela who did so as a result of a collective decision after the 1961 Anti-Republic general strike. But in spite of the fact that we were accessible to 24 hours a day police surveillance, we managed to organise regular meetings (sometimes more than one a day) and occasionally to travel illegally beyond the confines of the restricted regions.

What explains this relative success? It, of course, did show a degree of care and planning in our work. But this was only part, perhaps even a small part, of the explanation. Torture, solitary confinement, indefinite detention without trial, executions in police cells by 'suicide' – these and other similar instruments of political coercion were not yet part of the armoury of the regime's security forces. Indeed, compared to Belsen brutes like Swanepoel [a notorious police interrogator in the 1960s and 1970s], the old-style security police, headed by Major Spengler, were gentlemen. When he was transferred from the Special Branch, he gave an interview to the *Sunday Express* in which he paid tribute to the sincerity of the political activists whom he had kept under surveillance!

In my experience of numerous political trials I rarely cross-examined a Special Branch man who lied on fundamental matters. Assaults on political prisoners were extremely rare. The right of access to lawyers immediately on arrest was still in existence and, in any case, the law obliged the police to produce a prisoner and formally charge him in a court of law within 48 hours of his detention. The right to home privacy was still entrenched and no search could take place without a magisterial warrant. I recall an occasion when Head Constable Dirker, who had come to search Michael Harmel's house, was asked whether he had a warrant. He sheepishly replied that, being in a hurry, he had taken the wrong file and Michael's warrant was still in his office. 'What, then, are you looking for?' 'Politics, man, politics,' he replied.

This kind of bumbling ineptitude was soon to end. Already by the middle and late 1950s the new crop of security officials had been sent to foreign institutions which specialised in teaching techniques of mental and physical torture and the most scientific way to break the human spirit. They went to the United States, which had begun to accumulate field experience in Vietnam, to fascist Portugal and to Algeria, where the French were still trying to resist the popular onslaught.

But in the meantime the Rivonia disaster had not yet struck. And the 1950s were punctuated by a series of mass struggles, the like of which South Africa had not previously experienced.

First the 1952 Defiance Campaign. The concept of *satyagraha* (the path of truth) was born in South Africa early in the century when Mahatma Gandhi led the struggles of the Indian people against discriminatory property and movement laws. Attempting to change the hearts of the oppressors through public sacrifices such as deliberate courting of imprisonment, fasting unto death etc, was a technique which Gandhi had tested in the South African laboratory. He had taken it with him to India in 1913 where passive resistance was to play a dominant role in the conflict with the British Raj.

Despite his humanistic philosophy, Gandhi in South Africa was unable to link the future of the small Indian immigrant group with that of the indigenous African majority. The *ashram* which he created was famous for its internationalist composition: it boasted of a Jewish businessman, an Anglican priest and some ladies from the English liberal establishment. But Africans seemed altogether to be absent. Gandhi was (and remained to the end of his life) above everything else a passionate Indian patriot and, like the founding fathers of the ANC, he still had illusions that Whitehall would side with the people against the local racists. A combination of these two tendencies in Gandhi during his South African phase tempted him to make an extremely unfortunate offer to the British colonial authorities to organise a special Indian ambulance detachment in support of the campaign to crush the Zulu Bambatha Rebellion in Natal. Presumably he thought that by doing so he would advance the sectional cause of the Indian ethnic group, which seemed to be his chief, and perhaps only, concern. There was little evidence by the time he left South Africa that he had absorbed the ancient lesson that freedom is indivisible.

Nevertheless, the Gandhian tactic of passive defiance continued to play an important role in the approach of the National Organisation of the Indian People in South Africa which, by the early 1940s, had elected leaders such as Dadoo and Naicker, who linked arms with their African brothers. The 'squatting on a plot' campaign of the middle 1940s was in the same tradition. And the 1952 ANC-led Defiance Campaign had a similar inspiration. It was called off in 1953 when the regime passed its 'Flogging Act' which introduced mandatory flogging for anyone found guilty of contravening any law 'by way of protest'. By then 8 000 people, mainly Africans but also including coloured, Indian and white resisters, had served short terms of imprisonment for deliberate contravention of the six selected colour bar laws.

Although the Defiance Campaign conformed to the precepts of Gandhian passifism in structure, it had little of the philosophical perspective of *satyagraha* in its essence. Very few of those who participated believed seriously that through filling the jails, or by other forms of self-inflicted suffering, they could thaw the ice-cold heart of white autocracy. It was a method of organisation and mobilisation well suited to that epoch, and the 'Lenins' who cavilled at this form of struggle because they had not previously read about it in the works of the founding fathers demonstrated once again that the content of Marxism is far richer than is dreamt of in the philosophy of some of its would-be apostles. Certainly, Nelson Mandela, the Volunteer-in-Chief of the Defiance Campaign, did not harbour any illusions about the ultimate possibility of converting the ruling class without a tough revolutionary struggle. The first person to defy was Moses Kotane, to be followed by Yusuf Dadoo and JB Marks – all well-known communist personalities who showed their readiness to lead from the front.

The decade had begun with hectic activities against the regime's plans to outlaw the Communist Party and ban its publications, as an obvious first step to outlawing all genuine opposition, especially from the blacks. In March 1950 the Defend Free Speech Convention, called by all the liberation organisations including the Communist Party, proclaimed 1 May 1950 as a People's Holiday; in the Transvaal about 80 percent of the black workers heeded what amounted to a strike call. The response of the police to this essentially peaceful action was to open fire on a number of demonstrations as a result of which 18 people were killed and numerous others injured. The ANC Executive declared 26 June 1950 to be a day of protest and mourning for 'all those Africans who lost their lives in the struggle for liberation'. Despite a very short period of preparation, Monday 26 June brought the first-ever national political general strike by black workers. From that day onwards 26 June was celebrated as South Africa's Freedom Day.

One of the images of 26 June 1950 that has remained in my mind is of police action in Alexandra Township. I had accompanied Ruth who was covering the events for *The Guardian*. When the police began their baton charge to break up the demonstration on the football field, Ruth rushed to the centre with her camera, faced the police and stood squarely taking photographs of them charging towards her. From 1946 onwards Ruth had become the key radical journalist in the Transvaal. At the handsome salary of £25 per month, she worked for *The Guardian* and its successors, the *Clarion, People's World, New Age, Advance:* the changes in name were necessitated by successive bannings under the Suppression of Communism Act. Her pioneering exposures of working conditions in the Bethal potato belt, the farm labour scandal (the use of the judicial system to press-gang Africans into farm labour squads through pass law persecution) and her journey to Namibia followed by the first pro-liberation book to be published, were among some of the better-known investigative successes which won her acclaim. She worked extremely hard at teaching some of the up-and-coming young left African journalists such as Joe Gqabi (who was murdered by racist gunmen in Harare in 1981).

I was able to play a modest part in one of Ruth's journalistic investigations. We had long suspected that the Fordsburg Native Commissioner's Court was being used as the main instrument for press-ganging Africans to work in near-slave conditions in the Bethal potato belt. Each morning the car park adjacent to the court was packed with lorries and vans, most of them designed like moving prisons and driven by pink-faced Boers in floppy hats and short khaki trousers who were waiting for their human cargo. For a few days Ruth and I watched the departure of these mobile cages packed with wretched men who had ventured forth into the white streets of Johannesburg without the right piece of paper. For this 'crime' they would labour 12 hours a day in the hot sun, dressed in sacks and feel the boss-boy's *sjambok*. On Ruth's suggestion, I presented myself as a student who was busy with a thesis on the conflict between common law and native law, and I was given full access to the court's records. The statistics I managed to gather reinforced our own observations during the so-called pass law 'trials' that this was not a court of justice but a slave-labour bureau. The exposure attracted worldwide attention.

Professor Matthews' call at the ANC's 1953 conference for a convention became the basis of the next phase of the mounting mass struggles of the 1950s. The Central Committee of our Party devoted many sessions in early 1954 to discussing how the call for a convention could be given organisational expression. Eventually the idea of organising a gathering of representatives of the people from every walk of life, in town and country, caught fire and a joint campaign committee representing all the Congresses began its work. A small subcommittee of banned activists which included Walter Sisulu, Rusty Bernstein and myself was appointed as a back-up group to help with the unfolding of the campaign. We really did try to ensure that every document to emerge from the final gathering would truly reflect the aspirations and thinking of the people themselves.

The thousands of meetings held throughout the country were designed to get the people to express their immediate demands and views on the sort of South Africa they would like to see in the future. Literally tens of thousands of scraps of paper came flooding in: a mixture of smooth writing-pad paper, torn pages from ink-blotched school exercise books, bits of cardboard, asymmetrical portions of brown and white paper bags, and even the unprinted margins of bits of newspaper. South African history had never before that moment (or indeed since) seen such a groundswell of democratic expression by plain and ordinary people. Some expressed broad, everyday needs such as running water, a proper toilet, a trading licence, enough pay to eat meat more than once a week, and so on.

The small group separated and collated all these bits of paper, divided them into various categories of demands and then proceeded to prepare the draft document to be placed before the delegates who were to assemble on 25-26 June 1955 in the centre of Kliptown. What emerged was the well-known Freedom Charter whose poetic ring is mainly the inspired effort of Rusty Bernstein, who presented the first draft. More than 3 000 delegates assembled to discuss the charter clause by clause. The gathering carried on, even though surrounded by a massive force of armed police who moved in and took the names and addresses of all those attending.

Most of those who had worked to bring about the Congress of the People could not be on the platform among the delegates – the bannings saw to that. But I remember lying on a tin rooftop with some of my comrades some 150 metres from the main square, observing through binoculars this festival of democracy, and hearing the cheers and the singing which punctuated the adoption of each clause of the Freedom Charter. A great day indeed!

The Freedom Charter, adopted by the ANC and by the Party as an inspirational vision of a future non-racist democratic South Africa, has been Talmudically dissected by a variety of critics on the 'left'. It has also been spurned by the Pan-Africanist Congress (PAC) mainly because of its claim that South Africa belongs to all those who live in it – black and white. Reservations about the Freedom Charter have also been expressed by various strands of so-called black consciousness, which emerged during the 1970s.

This is not the place to analyse the context in which the Freedom Charter must be understood, nor the changing historic meaning of some of its key clauses. Suffice it to say that the Freedom Charter has become one of the key inspirations of new generations of revolutionaries and that the ruling class considered it a treasonable platform for the violent overthrow of the white autocracy.

About 18 months later the regime acted. In simultaneous raids across the country at dawn on 6 December 1956, the first batch of 156 political activists was arrested on a charge of high treason. The key document in support of the charge was the Freedom Charter. After four years of sporadic court appearances the last group of accused was finally acquitted by a panel of judges headed by Mr Justice Rumpff, an unfanatical supporter of the Nationalist regime and one of the recent appointees who did have legal talent and a sense of objectivity and fairness.

As one witness after another droned on, the picture which was emerging (treason or not) was of a movement with a most impressive record of mobilising and organising at grassroots level in every corner of the country. During the early stages of the trial people in their thousands continued to demonstrate their solidarity with the accused despite police shootings. In the four ensuing years the mass upsurge reached heights unprecedented in South Africa's history.

The Treason Trial

A fter the first arrests on 6 December 1956, I had immediately become part of the legal team which handled the defence. At this early stage I worked closely with the well-known radical lawyer, Vernon Berrangè. Vernon's flamboyant court manner, his incisive and spirited style of cross-examination and his uncanny grasp of the workings of the police mind won him a reputation as the profession's most surgical demolisher of official witnesses. Vernon, a layman's lawyer rather than a lawyer's lawyer, was to demonstrate all his considerable forensic skills against the long procession of police witnesses who testified at the preparatory examination.

A day after the arrests Vernon and I began negotiating with the chief prosecutor, Van Niekerk, the questions of bail and the date for the opening of the preparatory examination. The treason arrests had hit world headlines and the gauche-looking Van Niekerk (who bore a close physical resemblance to the strip-cartoon character Lil Abner and in his court performances proved to be just as hick) was obviously delighted by the aura of publicity in which he was suddenly bathed. In his room at the Supreme Court building Van Niekerk was in a most genial mood. Over cups of coffee he informed us that it would be impossible to start proceedings until the middle of January and that we could leave for our annual holidays which had already been planned. The state's attitude to bail would be determined in a day or two. He shook my hand and wished me a very good rest. At that moment he was well aware that I would not be leaving for my vacation. At 4 am the following morning his men would arrest Ruth and me, and we joined the others on a charge of high treason.

In the ensuing four years of the trial (with its occasional peaks of drama and high comedy), there sat shoulder to shoulder in alphabetical order 156 African, coloured, Indian and white political activists (a scene never before witnessed in South Africa's history) charged, among other things, with the crime of 'creating hostility between the black and white races of South Africa'!! The amount eventually fixed for our release on bail was £250 for a white skin, £100 for an Indian or coloured skin, and £50 for an African skin, almost as if this was the price of different quality merchandise.

The evidence presented by the prosecution was often extremely garbled, unlettered and sometimes hilarious. Among the very few witnesses whose recorded notes of what was said at meetings made sense was Johan Coetzee, a short, steely-eyed detective sergeant who had learned shorthand. With his machine-like efficiency motored by a cold mind, he was an obvious candidate for a swift rise in the Gestapo-inspired security force which would be moulded at the end of the Treason Trial fiasco – a security force which would use terror, murder and the infliction of pain as its primary weapons. Coetzee (now a general) became its chief and subsequently South Africa's Commissioner of Police.

It is not the purpose of this narrative to reflect on the evidence presented or to dwell on the intricate legal issues which were handled so brilliantly by a team of advocates headed by Maisels backed up by Attorney Parkinson. It is my intention rather to touch on some personal experiences and impressions connected with our detention and recall a few of the trial's amusing and bizarre moments.

I was no stranger to the main Johannesburg jail, the Fort. But now I was escorted as prisoner and not as counsel to the interview room I knew so well. Unlike in the dock, where we sat shoulder to shoulder like a cross-section of a future people's assembly, in the jail living conditions conformed in every respect to the apartheid pattern in the rest of the country. The 17 white men accused had larger accommodation and more exercise space than was allocated to more than 120 of their black comrades. We each had a mattress and they had to make do with rope mats on a concrete floor. We had a cushion and newly laundered blankets, and they had to cover themselves with filthy lice-ridden ones.

Certain images I would have wished to have photographed for posterity: one was the picture of the three drums of prepared food standing outside the prison kitchen, to be wheelbarrowed to the treason accused. To prevent any error, each drum was marked by a large piece of paper which floated on top of the food. The first drum was marked 'Congress One'. It invariably contained well-cooked chunks of beef or pork destined for the white accused.

The 'Congress Two' drum was for the coloureds and Indians and it contained either porridge or a mess of boiled vegetables on top of which floated a few pieces of fatty meat that were most probably the discarded cut-offs from the 'Congress One' drum.

'Congress Three', the fare of the African accused, was always meatless, and the contents alternated between a porridge that looked like congealed plastic and a mixture of boiled mealies and beans.

When we asked the chief warder why a white man charged with treason was fed with meat while a black had porridge, he told us that it was common medical knowledge that a black man would have digestive problems with 'white food'. The sad thing about the chief warder was that he actually believed what he said; his mind had been fashioned, perhaps irreversibly, by state and church ideology premised on the white man's folklore that the abject conditions of the black not only accord with God's scheme of things, but are also in his best interests. The chief warder was voicing this belief in the same way as one of the Nationalist Members of Parliament had recently claimed that it was in the interests of blacks not to sleep between sheets because if they did they would undoubtedly risk losing the famous shine on their skins.

But the politics of the morbid aside, my first short spell in jail was an interesting rather than an agonising experience. Although the politicals had their own exercise yard, the segregation between them and the other white prisoners broke down because both sections used the same wash house and dining room. The white non-political prisoners were less hostile to what we represented than their community outside. In their eyes we ranked pretty high in the hierarchy of those who swim against the tide of established authority. 'What are you in for?' I asked a young man with a foreign-sounding accent. 'German shopping,' he replied. When he saw my puzzled expression, he elaborated his answer by miming a shop-lift-ing exercise and ended with 'You understand? In Germany we call it English shopping.' When I told him what I was in for he whistled with admiration and repeated the words 'high treason', with a reverential em-phasis on the 'high'. The degree of respect and chain of moral authority among them was much influenced by the frequency or seriousness of previous brushes with the law, a fact exploited by prison administrations when appointing their henchmen from among the prisoners.

At the time the 'head prefect' of the non-political section awaiting trial was a middle-aged man who had already spent a considerable part of his adulthood serving various sentences for house-breaking, car theft and other related offences. When not in prison he worked as a hairdresser and claimed to be a militant member of the National Union of Hairdressers to whose general secretary Fleet (a well-known communist during the legal days) he referred as 'Comrade Ronnie'. He was given permission to cut the hair of the treason accused, and I took advantage of this. He was skilfully snipping away at my hair, and, like any other barber, chattering about this and that, when a young man asked him for a loan of the spare pair of scissors in his shirt pocket. 'Can't you see I'm busy, man? Run off,' and he carried on. A few minutes later the same young man made the same request, and this time was told to 'Fuck off or else.' As the youngster complied, the barber looked at me, shook his head and, with a pained expression on his face, said: 'These fucking first offenders don't know their place any more.'

It didn't take long for the news to spread that the Fort had within its walls a resident advocate. Even though the advocate had patently demon-strated his own inability to keep out of trouble, the Fort population came to him unceasingly to discuss their own. Warders, it appears, are plagued by a high rate of infidelity on the part of their wives, and quite a number of them sought my advice on divorce, separation and maintenance prob-lems. I could not but feel an amused compassion for one of them who blamed it all on his profession: 'How can I prevent my wife having a good time when she knows exactly what time I am locked in, and what time I am allowed out?'

These consultations were often conducted while I stood around in our exercise yard. But I also have perhaps the unique, if dubious, distinction of being the only counsel who has ever found himself conducting a con-sultation while answering nature's calls. The Fort's lavatories were doorless and since the wash house was the only common territory be-tween politicals and non-politicals (in the dining halls we sat at separate tables), I was invariably cornered by one or other 'client' while perched on a lavatory seat. I am not sure if they benefited from my advice, but I certainly paid for it with uncomfortable bouts of constipation.

If you had ever strolled the streets of both the white and African areas of Johannesburg, you would have been struck by the contrast between the joyless pallor of the deserted white streets and the bustle, laughter and music that filled the air in a place like Soweto. It is as if there is an understanding among whites that you do not make a spectacle of yourself 'in front of the servants', and among blacks that against the odds, laughter and music are forms of defiance. In the same way, the relatively comfortable and well-fed white inmates lay mute, two to a cell, enviously listening to the vigorous and full-throated choruses which came nightly from the cells of the blacks.

There was no existing dock large enough to accommodate the treason accused and so the authorities improvised a court in the Drill Hall, part of Johannesburg's main military administrative complex. The people who lined the route taken by our guarded convoy from the Fort to the drill hall made us feel as if we were doing a lap of honour. We took turns at the tiny barred widows of the *kwela* to watch the waving placards and hear the unending roar of the slogans. At the hall itself the hundreds who managed to break through the police cordon surrounded the prison vans and banged their welcoming beats until it felt as if one was inside a kettle drum.

The confusion of that first day in the hall was monumental; it set the pattern for the farce that was to be played out during the next four years. The prosecution had forgotten to install loudspeaker equipment so the court adjourned for a few hours. Another false start and another adjournment because no arrangements had been made for interpretation.

Not a single black spectator was allowed into court and the segregated section was filled with white faces. Another protest and another adjournment. The next day a spectacle never before seen in a South African court – the dock had been transformed into a huge cage. The wags among the accused put up notices such as 'Dangerous animals – do not feed.' The lawyers who were permitted access to their clients only through wire mesh threatened to withdraw *en masse*. Again the court adjourned and the monkey cage was dismantled.

At last Van Niekerk begins once again to stumble along with his outline of the Crown case. Suddenly we are reminded that beneath the farce a real drama of social conflict is being played out. Outside the hall thousands of blacks wait hopefully for one of the 50 seats now reserved for them in the previously segregated gallery. The soft buzz of their voices forms a continuous background to the prosecutor's address. But for an instant there is an unaccountable hush from the crowd, followed by a chorus of screams and a volley of police gunfire. The grey-haired magistrate, Wessel, turns pale and, already on his feet, shouts 'Court is adjourned.' The lawyers scurry out of their seats. Shouts of indignation from the dock, which is swiftly surrounded by armed police.

But the image which has impressed itself indelibly on my mind is the back view of Gerald Gardiner (destined to become Lord Chancellor in Britain under the Wilson Labour administration). He had been sent as an observer by the British lawyers organisation, Justice. I was absolutely mesmerised by his completely unruffled composure. In all the panic and confusion he was the only one to remain seated. He took his time before slowly turning his head which continued to be supported by a cupped hand of an arm whose elbow rested on the table. He seemed at that moment the very epitome of fabled British calm and imperturbability. As a barrister Gardiner had the reputation of being a master of effective understatement, and when he returned to England he was to put this talent to good use in his matter-of-fact reporting of the Treason Trial events, and of the regime's moves to destroy the independence of the judiciary.

The shooting outside the courtroom was to trigger off a number of court confrontations. Despite my arrest it had been decided that, in order to enable me to play an active role in the court proceedings, I should appear in my own defence. In the latter capacity I was permitted to occupy a place at the defence lawyers' table which was equipped with electronic recording apparatus. The preparatory examination was already drawing to a close when the prosecutor called Colonel Grobbelaar, the police officer in charge of the contingent that had fired on the crowd, to testify that it was confronted by a threatening mob and that the action was justified. Justified or not, we argued, it could hardly be suggested that the accused had a hand in it since they were under lock and key.

When it was my turn to cross-examine, I attempted to demonstrate (since unlike Gardiner I am not a master of understatement) that the police action against the crowd constituted a murderous assault. The magistrate shuffled uncomfortably in his seat and eventually put his foot down. He ordered me to stop pursuing this line of cross-examination. I refused, accusing him of inconsistency in the light of his earlier dismissal of the defence objection that the Colonel's evidence was wholly irrelevant. Since the Colonel had been allowed to smear the people's action, I insisted on our right to set the record straight.

The magistrate had already ruled that advocates Berrangè and Coaker could not continue with their cross-examination of Colonel Grobbelaar.

The Guardian reported the following verbatim exchange between magistrate Wessel and me.

Magistrate: 'Do you want to reserve your cross-examination, Mr Slovo?'

Slovo: 'At the same time I wish to place on record my objection. I don't propose arguing it, I just wish to place on record ...'

Magistrate: 'No, no, I appreciate that. I take it you are not objecting to the court's ruling ...'

Slovo: '... My specific reason for placing an objection on record at this stage is that the court has allowed the Crown to lead evidence which would suggest ...'

Magistrate: 'I can't allow you, Mr Slovo, to reopen this matter. My ruling I have given. You must not ...'

Slovo: 'No, sir, I wish to place on record a point which was not made by Mr Berrangè.

Magistrate: 'I cannot allow you to refer to this matter any longer. You must not do that.'

Slovo: 'Well, sir, then I object to your worship's conduct of this aspect of the proceedings. I wish to place that on record.'

Magistrate: 'What is that?'

Slovo: (repeats above.) 'And I say so with sincerity and if your worship wishes to hear me on it, I will ...'

Magistrate: 'Do you understand that you question the court's conduct of this aspect of the proceedings? Is that what you say?'

Slovo: 'Yes, I say that, sir, advisedly ...'

Magistrate: 'You understand the grave consequences that the implication of your remarks now convey?'

Slovo: 'Yes, sir. I have seriously considered the remarks I am making at the moment ...'

Magistrate: 'I don't wish to hear you ...'

Slovo: 'Why?'

Magistrate: 'I regard this as contempt of court and it is a serious matter, and for contempt of court you are now sentenced to ...'

The instantaneous uproar from the accused and the black gallery drown the magistrate's last few words. And suddenly an event occurred that to my knowledge has never before nor since been seen in a South African court. A large number of the accused led, if I remember correctly by Fred Carneson, jumped out of their seats and with shouts of 'bastard' and other expletives made a charge towards the bench. Had it not been for Chief Albert Luthuli's quick response and undoubted authority, the consequences would indeed have been grave. The Chief immediately boomed out an order for his fellow accused to return, and they did so.

By now the magistrate had once again jumped out of his seat and fled to his back room. Some minutes later I was called to his office. He was in a state of shock and asked me if I could remember the amount of the fine he had imposed on me. I was unable to help him, and he then suggested he would listen to the recording but that meanwhile he would release me on my own recognisances. (In a subsequent appeal to the Supreme Court my contempt conviction was set aside.)

The magistrate obviously decided overnight to reassert his authority. When the court resumed he announced that, since I had abused the privilege of sitting at the same table as the lawyers, I would have to move back to my place in the dock. I collected my papers and returned to my vacant chair among the *S*s towards the back next to Ruth (who had not yet won her battle to sit among the *F*s).

But the game (and so much of the treason proceedings was just that) is not yet over. The other lawyers complete their cross-examination of the next witness and Wessel then looks for me among the 156 faces. I am sitting at the opposite end of the aisle that separates the two blocks of accused. When he eventually catches my eye, he nods in my direction and says: 'Yes, Mr Slovo, any questions?' I rise slowly to my feet, do a cinema walk over knees and legs, and, with deliberation, walk down the long passage to the lawyers' table, gravely look at the witness and then, leaning my head close to the microphone, I say: 'Your Worship, no questions,' and I immediately proceed to make the long return journey. To his credit, Wessel joins in the burst of laughter, and after the next tea adjournment he announces that I may resume my former place at the lawyers' table.

When the rainy season started Wessel faced another unique problem. Farid Adams not only had the distinction of having the case called after him (*Regina* v *Adams and 155 others*) but also the misfortune of occupying a position in the dock that spat water on him every time there was a downpour. The lawyers informed the court that their client would be forced to arm himself with an umbrella if the roof were not repaired. The magistrate promised to make urgent representation to the Public Works Department. When the heavens next opened Farid spent his time dodging the persistent drip-drip, and counsel complained that the situation made it impossible for their client to concentrate on the evidence. Unless something were done about it there would have to be an adjournment each time it rained. The magistrate said he would follow up his enquiries with the Public Works Department. The next storm once again made its way through the roof and on to Farid. Enough was enough; the magistrate adjourned and promised to make immediate contact with the Public Works Department.

When the rain clouds had exhausted themselves, the court reassembled and the enormity of the problem facing he Public Works Department was sadly related by Wessel. 'I have been informed by the foreman responsible for the maintenance of the building that he faces the following serious dilemma; when it's raining his men can't work on the roof, and when it's not raining, it is difficult to isolate the leaking area.' Some genius must have earned his promotion on this one because when the rains came again accused number one came out of court completely dry.

The oppressive tedium of the preparatory examination was occasionally broken by the unintended humour of some of the virtually uneducated police witnesses. One of them, Kunene, had been an uninvited guest at a farewell party for India's Assistant High Commissioner in South Africa. He testified that I had raised my glass and said on behalf of those present: 'Sir, I am very happy to say goodbye to you.' Such a remark must have inspired (Groucho) Marx's response to one of his departing guests who had said: 'I would like to say goodbye to your wife' with the quip: 'You're not the only one.' Kunene, who was no longer in the police force, let his side down badly when asked if he could identify me as one of the speakers at the farewell. Clearly waiting for this moment to make a gesture of solidarity with the accused, he answered that he would have no difficulty at all in identifying me since 'Slovo is a very popular man in Johannesburg. We Africans always talk about him. He is always ready to assist the Africans.'

A black policeman's feelings about his role as an instrument of race rule must of necessity be ambivalent. Inside the police force he occupies an inferior position by virtue of his colour and he experiences continual humiliations from the white boss. Kunene's bouquet for me was his own way of making a rebellious statement. But the evidence of Head Constable Van Paffendorf was more puzzling. It was not only his name but also his mannerisms (including occasional heal-clicking in the witness box) that suggested a Prussian family link. To the obvious discomfort of the prosecution, Van Paffendorf failed to identify me as one of the main speakers at a public meeting. He was asked by Van Niekerk more than once to look carefully at the faces of each and every one of the accused, unhurriedly and meticulously. He examined each of us in turn and stated crisply that to the best of his knowledge only those accused whose names he had already mentioned had been present at the meeting in question. And that was that.

The reasons for Van Paffendorf's 'omission' became clear a few weeks later during an adjournment of the proceedings. Berrangè telephoned me and asked me to come down to his chambers. On entering I was most surprised to see Van Paffendorf who jumped up, clicked his heels and nodded a Junker-style greeting. We sat down and he immediately explained that he wanted Berrangè and me to institute proceedings on his behalf against the Minister of Justice. Van Paffendorf was convinced that because of his well-known support for the opposition United Party the authorities had deliberately failed him in recent examinations to become an officer, and, on top of it, he had been transferred to South West Africa. We advised him that it is notoriously difficult to prove bad faith on the part of public officials and that, in any case, if the two of us appeared on his behalf he might well be suspected of having staged a deliberate lapse of memory.

The preparatory examination ended on 30 January 1958, and on 1 August of the same year, 92 of us were brought before a special court to face an indictment of high treason and alternative charges. The venue had moved from the military drill hall to a Pretoria synagogue which had been converted into a courtroom. Appropriately enough, the judges (Rumpff, Bekker and Kennedy) sat where the Torah (law scrolls) would have been kept and the accused faced them as they would have done had they been taking part in a religious service. On 13 October 1958, and after lengthy Talmudic-sounding argument, the court upheld the defence contention that the indictment as elaborated by the particulars supplied was defective. Mannie Brown made history by secretly filming the final stages of the judgment and the joyous eruption that greeted it. The lawyers were carried out shoulder high and the air was filled with song. Ruth took a snap decision that a celebration was called for and we passed the word round that all would be welcome at our house in Roosevelt Park that night.

By 8 pm our house was bursting at the seams. We should have guessed that the police would try to find a way of hitting back for their humiliating defeat in this first round of the much-publicised treason bout. The liquor laws made it a crime for any black man to be in possession of as much as a thimbleful of any alcoholic beverage. At close to midnight our house was surrounded and, through the windows and doors, dozens of police swarmed in, immediately grabbing any black who was holding a glass in his hand. They also brought with them journalists from the government press who presumably expected to be able to expose to an outraged leadership the scandalous scene of white and black drinking together, dancing together and embracing.

Under the headline 'Many colours at party', *Die Burger* described the celebration as follows:

'A party at which whites, natives and Indians were present was held in a Johannesburg suburb last night. There were about 200 people present. White and non-white drank, danced, sang and chatted together. The police appeared at 10.30 p.m. In many of the motor cars white women rode with natives.'

Die Vaderland's photographer jumped on to my dining room table to take his pictures. But as with the Treason Trial itself, the raid gave the invaders no dividend. From the gentleman who jumped on my table I eventually accepted a settlement of £200 damages in an action I instituted. Our black guests were already old hands at this game, and not a single one of them was found with as much as drop of liquor in his or her glass. Eventually, when the police left empty-handed, Ruth was extremely puzzled by the number of people who congratulated her for saving the day by her brilliant quick-thinking. When the police rushed in, our experienced guests immediately emptied the contents of their glasses into a large, beautiful vase which I had bought with my first big poker win and which Ruth and I treasured. When the pushing and shoving began Ruth's first thought was to save the vase, which was perched precariously on a narrow wooden ledge. She grabbed it (she was puzzled at the time by its unusual increased weight) and rushed it to the kitchen, completely ignorant of the fact that it now contained a few gallons of a cocktail mixture of whisky, brandy, wine, beer and other 'prohibited' substances.

One of the welcome guests at the party was the then Bishop of Johannesburg, the Right Reverend Ambrose Reeves. He was one of the most committed Samaritans in the cause of social justice. In a country in which so much savagery is sponsored by the Dutch Reformed Church's white dominees, the likes of Bishop Trevor Huddleston (accused number 78 in the Treason Trial) and Reeves himself represent the Christian motive at its best. Soon after our arrest Reeves became the leading organiser of the fund that met the costs of the long-drawn-out trial. The tragic death of his son in a drowning accident during the trial brought all the accused to a Mass in Johannesburg's Anglican Cathedral. As we watched the intricate and colourful ritual of the ceremony, with its richly-robed clergy and cherub-like altar-boys moving in various directions and swinging censers from which billowed incense, Duma Nokwe leaned over and whispered to me: 'It's odd, isn't it, that the antics of a witch doctor are sometimes regarded as clownish and primitive. Maybe General China is on to a good thing.'

I had no difficulty in understanding Duma's allusion to General China. The late General China (his real name was Letlaka) was one of these grand old stalwarts of the ANC who never missed a day of the treason proceedings. He was always to be seen sitting in court gyrating a very thin, short twig in the area of his right temple whenever the State representative was on his feet. This exercise with the magical twig was designed to help (if that were possible) confuse Van Niekerk even further. General China was clearly on to a good thing. The last batch of 30 accused who were reindicted and whose trial began in January 1959 (Ruth and I were this time excluded) were finally acquitted in March 1961.

In 1956, a short time before the treason arrests, the security police invaded a meeting in the Trades Hall. We made an urgent application for their removal which came before Mr Justice Blackwell. He issued an order that the police remove themselves, and in the course of his judgment said: 'This is not yet a police state.' Judge Blackwell obviously had a nose for what was coming in the following decade. Although the treason proceedings had a flimsy and often burlesque basis, they were an attempt to establish legal responsibility through mechanisms and procedures which had been historically evolved to minimise the chances of a wrong conviction.

The four-year trial was the last attempt by the regime to establish guilt for a political crime through the mechanism of such procedures. Henceforth a political suspect, cut off indefinitely from the outside world, would face raw violence in police cells. The Coetzees and Swanepoels would take over, and those stubborn enough to refuse to implicate themselves or to inform on their comrades would risk execution long before being brought to the judicial tribunal. And the judges would become the witting or unwitting instruments of statutes that mocked the very concept of due process and the rule of law.

Mass protest, ideology and family life

T he 1950s were a decade in which mass legal protest reached a massive peak and then exhausted itself. The South African Congress of Trade Unions (Sactu), formed in 1955, was in the throes of a national campaign around a demand for £1 a day. The historic march of 20 000 African women on the Union Buildings, Pretoria, in August 1956 was followed by years of pass-burning and other militant forms of protest by women in rural and urban areas. Protests against rising transport costs led to bus boycotts of which the most protracted took place in Alexandra Township, Johannesburg. It was also a period when the mass struggles in the rural areas reached a peak which has yet to be equalled. In Zeerust, Sekhukhuneland, Zululand and Tembuland, acts of real 'treason' were being committed; people's courts were set up which tried and executed pro-government quislings, and people's administrative bodies were being created. Especially in Pondoland, whole districts were for a short period taken over by the 'mountainmen' who set up people's courts and levied taxes on black and white in the area.

In a broad sense, the rural revolts were partly inspired by the general atmosphere of resistance which had been generated in the struggles already mentioned. But, although many of the leaders of the rural upsurge sought advice and material help (including weapons) from the ANC, it would be an exaggeration to claim that the events were either led or organised by our movement. Although there are pockets in the country areas which have been penetrated by ANC organisation (Gert Sibande and Alpheus Maliba are two examples in the Transvaal), our weakness as an organised force in the rural areas persists up to today and is even more serious in the light of the regime's bantustan offensive.

The 1950s saw the national general political strike developing for the first time as an effective weapon of mass struggle. Time and again hundreds of thousands of workers in all the major urban centres downed tools in support of broad political demands, despite the loss of pay, violent police intimidation and the risk of losing a job and, with it, the right to live in the urban area.

Apart from these major struggles, the period was also punctuated with numerous other campaigns of both a national and local character. For example, we called for a potato boycott in protest against the near-slave conditions under which the workers toiled in the Bethal potato belt. Robert Resha, whose oratorical campaign was sprinkled with figurative allegations that Transvaal potatoes contained the blood of black farm workers, became such a victim of his own passionate propaganda that for the rest of his life he was unable ever to eat a potato.

For pathos and poignancy the resistance to the removal of Sophiatown was in a class of its own. This was not only the last remaining island within Johannesburg proper in which Africans had retained ancient freehold rights to property, but it also gave birth to a special, colourful generation of spirited young political fire-eaters like Robert Resha, Patrick Malao and others. Though slums abounded, this was home, and the decades had created a distinctive Sophiatown urban culture with youth who walked with a Sophiatown swagger and wore their caps at a provocative angle. The authorities sent an army of bulldozers backed by massive armed force and, block by block, they razed Sophiatown to the ground. With an insensitivity which is so natural to white arrogance, they built a white suburb in place of Sophiatown and called it 'Triomf' (triumph). Little wonder that many of the angry Soweto generation of the 1970s are the offspring of the Sophiatown dispossessed. Our house was barely a mile from Sophiatown, and its disappearance deprived Ruth and me of the late afternoon and weekend company of many of our friends who, on their way home, paused for a snack, an illicit drink, or, like Patrick Malao, for a relaxed hour or two with us and our children. Gone too was yet another place where we could visit our friends without a special permit from the Native Affairs Department.

During the Treason Trial the one piece of evidence that worried the lawyers was a speech recorded by means of a bugging device placed in the chimney of the Transvaal Indian Congress premises. In the course of this speech Resha used the words 'murder, murder, murder' as one of the answers to the regime's cruelties. When the movement in the early 1960s began turning towards revolutionary violence (of which more later) it was in part responding to the frustrated anger of groups like the Sophiatown generation who, try as they might, could not with their bare hands stop the armed bulldozers.

We had always been taught that the Party was the vanguard of the struggle. But it was the 1950s which gave real meaning to this maxim in revolutionary practice. The Central Committee (to which Ruth was elected at an underground conference in the late 1950s) through its Johannesburg-based Secretariat often functioned on an almost daily basis. There was no major event which was not subjected to analytical scrutiny. Long before any of the campaigns waned, the question of 'what next' had already been the subject matter of many agendas. And we established our position in the liberation movement by persuasion and example – not, as our detractors allege, by caucus and manipulation.

Despite the relatively powerful organisational position of the Party, communists such as Moses Kotane saw to it that the decision-making processes of the movement as a whole were not sectarian and one-sided affairs. This was one of Kotane's most impressive qualities as a leader of the Party and the national movement. His style of work won him the respect of communist and non-communist alike. He was undoubtedly the most important factor in winning for the Party its place in the liberation alliance. Chief Albert Luthuli regarded Kotane as one of his wisest associates in the ANC leadership, placing great reliance on his views and advice.

I came to know Kotane well only during the underground period: until 1950 he lived and worked in Cape Town, seat of the Party headquarters. My first taste of his overbearing style was in 1947 when, during a university vacation, I acted as secretary of the Johannesburg District Committee (as stand-in for Danie du Plessis who was attending a conference of Empire Communist Parties in London). The District Committee had instructed me to write to our General Secretary complaining that the executive had not replied to some point or other. I did as I was told and ended my letter with an expression of hope that the executive would stop dragging its feet and respond by return. The response was indeed by return! Kotane had divided his page with a line down the centre, with my letter set out on the left side and his reply point by point on the right side. His response to my last paragraph was 'Don't be a cheeky boy' – a notorious phrase usually hurled by whites against blacks who have the temerity to speak to a white man without cringing.

Kotane's confidence in himself and his assertive, often bullying style (which knew no colour bar) made an enormous contribution to the acceptance of the Party as a truly indigenous force. White and black racists never fail to attach the label 'puppet' to any black who works with non-Africans, but no one, by the wildest stretch of imagination, could dub Kotane a puppet. Yet for me it was easier to admire than to like this awesome figure. It was difficult to disagree with him. He seemed proud of the no-nonsense, hard and domineering image of himself that he cultivated. When he was still working in South Africa under the discipline of the functioning Party collective, these qualities were, on balance, a distinct asset. But in exile there were moments when Kotane's unbridled individualism made it difficult to reconstitute the shattered Party apparatus.

Despite the post-1953 underground conditions, we continued to practise a good measure of internal Party democracy. The rank and file had the opportunity of debating major policy statements before they were finally adopted by the Central Committee. The leadership was re-elected at least once every two years at conferences attended by delegates from every district and who outnumbered members of the Central Committee. An election system was devised which was designed to achieve a balance between the often contradictory requirements of security and democracy. Every delegate was asked to fill in a blank ballot form with the names of those he wished to see constitute the Central Committee. The ballot forms were then handed to the General Secretary and Chairman, whose election had already taken place. These officials, with two others who had received the most votes (and whose names were announced), were given a mandate by the conference to constitute the balance of the Central Committee (whose names were not announced). In doing so they were not to interfere with the actual voting preferences expressed by the delegates except for reasons of security and to ensure an adequate degree of regional representation. In practice, it was very rare to exclude a candidate who had received the necessary number of votes.

Despite the collectivist and democratic traditions which were maintained even in such adverse conditions, the Party did not go through the turmoil which was experienced by so many others in the wake of the revelations by Krushchev at the 20th Congress of the Communist Party of the Soviet Union. The initial response was one of complete incredulity: was it possible that a man whom we had revered as the greatest apostle of Lenin was guilty of such horrendous crimes? And was it conceivable that he could perpetrate the crimes in the name of a party whose revolutionary achievements had no equal in the 20th century? Yet the impossible and the inconceivable had happened!

Individual reactions to the revelations varied; to this day some of my comrades believe that the version of the Krushchev speech published in *The Observer* is a forgery. But, possibly because of the quick succession of crisis events which followed Krushchev's February 1956 speech (the treason arrests and the four-year trial, Sharpeville in 1960, the turn to violence in 1961 and the Rivonia disaster in 1963), the Party did not pause to weigh up the lessons of what has been described as the 'Stalin period' and the 'Mao period' which followed it.

I believe that the perversion of socialist norms which characterised both 'periods' has put back the clock of socialist achievement on a world scale for half a century or more. Perhaps, unavoidably, we talk of 'Stalinism' and 'Maoism' to describe these perversions; and the very nomenclature hints at purely individual responsibility. But if we throw our first batch of stones at these sinners only, we are ignoring an enquiry into a social process of which they must have been instruments. By attributing to these two leaders a monopoly of sin, we are also perpetuating cultism. No cult (whether of the personality or otherwise) has ever left its mark on history without the blind devotion of congregations of worshippers. We all share in the guilt and the starting-point of any assessment must be ourselves.

We know that our ideology and the form of our Leninist Party structures do not, in themselves, protect us against the terrible abuse of power and the exercise of tyranny in office. We must no longer behave as if it is impossible or inconceivable, and in this way will help to make it so. And since the only value of our judgment on the unhappy period is to assure the future (and not to pronounce a posthumous sentence on the two accused), we should not, as is often done, dilute the lesson by balancing out the good deeds against crimes. At the same time, those who maintain that collective forms of society must inevitably breed such perversions, ignore ignorantly or deliberately not only the achievements of the class which built on the foundations of October 1917, but also the strides which have been made since 1956 to restore socialist morality.

Both Ruth and I lost our innocence in the period that followed the 20th Congress revelations. She was perhaps a little more unforgiving about our complicity than I was and, surrounded by the pressures of her colleagues in English universities, she searched for the answers more avidly than I did. In some ways she risked the worst of two worlds. Her continuing membership of our Party and involvement in its work (despite reservations about many of its foreign policy postures) put her outside the circle of those who were so shaken by the Stalinist experience that they turned complete tail on socialism and the socialist world system. On the other hand, there were those in our movement who viewed with suspicion her insistence that it is not treason to socialism if our independent judgment leads us to disagree with this or that policy of traditional and respected friends of our struggle. Ruth and I often differed in our individual assessments of these policies and, as many of our friends can testify, we gave one another no quarter in these often-ferocious verbal contests. Even if she was wrong on some of her positions (as I believe her to have been), Ruth's kind of 'deviationism' is an important obstacle to the resurgence of blind cult worship (whether of an individual, a party or a state) in the socialist movement.

For Ruth and me the 1950s were years filled with an intense and exciting activity at all levels of our life. She was busy with her investigative journalism and I, where I could, used the weapons of the law to advance our cause. But our main efforts were in the underground. Despite bans and restrictions, countless debates, discussions and decision-making meetings went on unimpeded. And through all this we somehow managed to live a normal, undisturbed personal life: dinners, dances, weekend picnics, annual holidays (usually in the Cape), concerts, theatres and so on. At the purely personal level our lives were very little different from those of the middle-class whites who inhabit the half-acre plots of posh suburbia. We had indoor servants, two motor cars, a gardener and a comfortable income, made even more comfortable by the astonishing generosity of Ruth's parents, Julius and Tilly. Short of exile, there is no way out of the trap of privilege of living in white society; nor was it really possible to eliminate the social separation between us and our black comrades imposed by the barbarism of race exclusiveness. But out commitment to total liberation was, in the end, to be tested in other ways.

The birth and raising during this period of our three children, Shawn, Gillian and Robyn, was part of the flow of the 'normal' stream of our lives. But in retrospect we came to understand the divide between the rhythm of family life and the tempo of political activism in illegal conditions was certainly more problematic than it seemed at the time.

Above: Maputo, 1982. Robyn, Shawn, Gillian and Joe at Ruth First's graveside. Seated on the right is Tilly First, Ruth's mother.

Below: The Kabwe Conference, where Slovo was the first white elected to the National Executive of the ANC, 1985.

Above: Slovo (front centre) with an ANC delegation to the Soviet Union. Others include 'Mac' Maharaj (back row, fourth from left); Ronnie Kasrils (front row, second from left), and Ray Alexander and Dan Tloome (front row, second and third from right).

Below: Inspecting an air-conditioning factory in China, Wenzhou, August 1993.

Cuba 1986. Above: Official inspection of a ceramics factory, together with comrade 'A', Angel Dalmau and 'Mac' Maharaj, and, below, a more casual moment.

Above: April 1993, at Ruth's grave which lies together with those of other fallen ANC comrades in the cemetery in Maputo.

Below: Front row: Thomas Nkobi, Joaquim Chissano, Joe Slovo, Samora Machel, Oliver Tambo and Graca Machel, at the funeral of Moses Mabhida.

Above: May 1986, Joe's 60th birthday party in Lusaka. With him are friends Pallo Jordan and Ronnie Kasrils.

Below: At home in Lusaka, c. 1987.

London 1987. Helena and Joe leaving for the registry office. Joe displays his famous red socks.

Above: Joe's return to Obelei, the village of his birth, 1981.

Below: Joe with good friends Dina Forte and Bridget O'Laughlin with her baby Ruth, 1983.

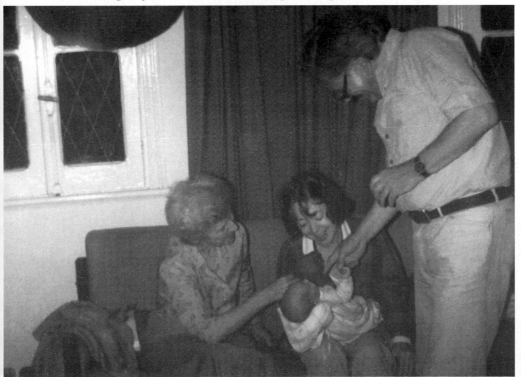

Above: Slovo and Mandela reunited. Lusaka, 1990.

Below: Christmas 1990, with Marlene Green, Nelson Mandela and stepdaughter Kyla.

Press conference on mass action, April 1992. Pallo Jordan is on the left.

Above: Slovo with old friend and comrade Harold Wolpe.

Below: Joe with the Elite Swingsters at a party in 1993.

Joe and Helena outside the Union Buildings at Mandela's inauguration as state president, May 1994.

Slovo's funeral, January 1995. The coffin leaves for Avalon cemetery, Soweto, borne on a Defence Force gun carriage.

When Shawn was six, Ruth's mother, Tilly, had to be called in at four in the morning while the children watched us being taken away by a group of police. The Treason Trial was given continuous prominence in the press for quite a few years. And by the time Gillian went to school she must have been stung by the unintentional cruelties perpetrated by fellow school children who picked up whispers from their parents about the 'Communist Slovos' facing criminal charges. Was Robyn still too young in 1960 when they came again in the middle of the night and detained me during the post-Sharpeville emergency? Certainly by 1963 all three of them were old enough to feel the trauma of my journey into exile to be followed, within a few months, by Ruth's 117 days of solitary confinement. Then there were the regular evening disappearances for meetings late into the night and the longer weekend journeys to attend conferences. Did the children sense tensions in us about some of the risks of which we ourselves were not conscious? Were they not inwardly aware that we were lying to them when we offered innocent legends to explain away some of these activities?

They lived in two worlds. Outside the home they were in an alien world; a smug white world in which nonconformism had its price. In the eyes of white society we were different in the pejorative sense of the word. At the level of pure human relationships across the colour line the problem was less complex; in the home they continually experienced the normality of this warmth and closeness. But the very nature of our activities in conspiratorial work left very little scope for intimate frankness about what we were doing and why. Fear and a sense of insecurity apart, our arrests and frequent absences must have seemed, in the eyes of our children, acts of voluntary preference; they must have felt that they came a poor second to the cause.

Were we, in the circumstances, morally entitled to have a family? And, having become a family, did we have the right to include our children in the sacrifice for a cause which had meaning only in our understanding? Such questions are not unique to our family, to our time and to our struggle. There are no simple answers to them. One thing is clear, however; the world would be a poorer place if it was peopled by children whose parents risked nothing in the cause of social justice, for fear of personal loss. If I regret anything, it is certainly not how my daughters turned out but rather that we might have found a way of easing the hidden traumas they were suffering had we been more sensitive. As it was, my optimism and euphoria about the pace of struggle made us less aware of our own future and that of our children.

Sharpeville

T he 1950s ended with general strikes and the 1960s began with the Sharpeville massacre in March 1960. The massacre for a brief moment brought into prominence the Pan-Africanist Congress (PAC).

The PAC was made up of a group which had broken away from the ANC in 1959. It was founded at a meeting held at the United States Information Library in Johannesburg where Potlako Leballo, one of the leaders of this group, was employed. His previous career as a teacher had come to a sticky end when he was imprisoned on a charge of fraud involving the misuse of school funds collected from African parents.

The PAC's first contribution to militant revolutionary action was to launch a 'status campaign' designed to obtain polite treatment for African consumers from shopkeepers, bankers, government officials etc. Predictably, this campaign turned out to be the dampest of squibs. The only strategy the PAC pursued consistently was one of unending attempts to displace the ANC as the primary liberation organisation in South Africa.

In order to achieve this, it was always ready to accommodate itself to any political posture even if it meant a complete somersault on a previously held position. Thus, it initially posed not only as anti-communist (which it has remained to this day) but also as an organisation which stood for free enterprise and a Westminster-model form of government. As soon as its leadership realised that it could profit from the Soviet-Chinese dispute, the PAC suddenly embraced the tenets of the Maoist variety of Leninism. It attacked minority participation in the liberation movement and the alliance between the ANC and the Party, which it described as a device by which the minorities dominated the organisations of black nationalism. At the same time it worked intimately with the reformist Liberal Party, one of whose key figures, Patrick Duncan (son of South Africa's Governor-General and ex-British colonial civil servant), became the PAC's chief representative in Algeria.

Above all, it assiduously cultivated two myths: firstly, that it stood for black nationalism and not populist racism, and secondly, that it was the PAC that had pioneered the new policy of revolutionary violence in South Africa. To deal in detail with these two myths would be going beyond the purpose of this narrative. Here I merely wish to illustrate the point by touching on some of the events with which I was connected immediately before and after the Sharpeville massacre.

The December 1959 annual ANC conference decided that the new decade was to begin with a national campaign against the pass laws. The first stage of the campaign was to culminate on 31 March. Not to be outshone by the ANC, the PAC (which held its first national conference a week after the ANC's) also decided that 1960 would be a campaign year against the pass laws. In line with its primary strategy of outmanoeuvring the ANC at all costs, it pre-empted the ANC's first campaign target date. At a press conference on 18 March 1960, Robert Sobukwe declared 21 March as an Action Day when Africans throughout the country must leave their passes at home and surrender themselves for arrest at the nearest police station.

What the PAC had embarked upon was an ill-organised, second-class version of the 1952 Defiance Campaign. Sobukwe wrote to the Commissioner of Police emphasising that the PAC would at all costs avoid violence. He invited police co-operation to ensure that those who would come to present themselves for arrest would do so under orderly conditions. Indeed, the only militant-sounding slogan of the whole campaign was that in the event of arrest there would be 'no bail, no defence, no fines'. But to the perpetual embarrassment of the PAC its leaders (who had not bargained for what was then a rather heavy penalty for a political offence – two to three years) shamelessly applied for bail, raised money for fines and briefed lawyers for defence. I recall receiving a letter from Sobukwe, who had been sentenced to three years, enclosing a copy of the court record and asking me to try to argue the appeal on his behalf.

Unfortunately, I was unable to pursue the matter as the time for lodging an appeal had already expired. I had met Sobukwe only once in my life, and that was when we were both prisoners at the Johannesburg Fort during the post-Sharpeville emergency. We recognised one another while standing in separate colour-bar queues waiting for medical attention outside the prison dispensary. I raised my hand feebly in a clandestine kind of greeting to him and he, thinking that my open-handed waving gesture was the PAC salute, reciprocated in kind with the ANC's clenched fist salute. This display of friendly humour made me wonder whether Sobukwe would not eventually break with the political rogues who had swarmed around him. But this speculation could not be tested as he never regained his freedom; after serving his sentence and an additional period of detention he was restricted to the Kimberley district where he died in 1978.

Only two areas responded to the PAC call on 21 March – Cape Town and Sharpeville. Those who assembled at Sharpeville were met with machine-gun fire which left 69 dead, most of them shot in the back while running away. From the PAC there was, and could be, no response. The opportunist motivation behind the sudden call meant that no thought had been given to follow-up action. It was left to our movement to pick up the pieces. The day after the massacre a clandestine meeting of Party and Congress leaders was called, and two general decisions were taken. Firstly, there was to be a call for a three-day national general strike to begin on Monday, 28 March. Secondly, advantage should be taken of the deep public revulsion at the Sharpeville murders to launch a campaign for the destruction of the pass books.

A subcommittee, including Mandela, Sisulu, Nokwe and me, was appointed to give effect to these decisions. I remember how Nelson and I waited for the other members of the subcommittee to arrive at my home in Roosevelt Park. We were both depressed and commiserated with each other about the massacre and the fact that the ANC national campaign into which so much effort had already been put had been so tragically pre-empted.

The whole movement began to work day and night to ensure that the stay-at-home would be the success that it turned out to be. The subcommittee also decided that Duma should immediately go to Pretoria to consult with Chief Luthuli on our proposals for a pass-burning campaign. He was in Pretoria giving evidence for the defence in the Treason Trial. We tipped off the press, and Chief Luthuli was photographed holding aloft his own reference book like a torch in flames. This signal was answered by thousands in most urban areas. From the PAC there was complete and utter silence.

The regime was shaken both by the revulsion of the world against the horror of the massacre and by the response of the people to the strike call and the pass-burning campaign. For a brief moment the regime panicked and the Minister of Native Affairs announced that the pass laws were to be suspended. Our celebrations were short-lived. On 30 March the whole country was placed under a state of emergency, over 2 000 political activists were detained without trial, and (almost ten years after the Communist Party had been banned) the ANC and PAC were declared illegal organisations under the Suppression of Communism Act.

For me the ten days between the Sharpeville shooting and the declaration of the emergency were packed with other commitments. Earlier that year, in the early morning of 21 January, 434 black and six white coal miners had been entombed in a sudden collapse at Clydesdale Collieries near Coalbrook. I was retained to appear at the special inquest on behalf of the black widows and other relatives. Ironically, Issie Maisels, who led the defence team in the Treason Trial with courage and brilliance, was counsel for the mining company. The British Mine Workers' Union had sent an experienced mining engineer to assist us at the inquest. It soon became clear that we were not dealing with what is known in legal jargon as 'an act of God'; the death of 440 workers was a classic example of social murder.

At this particular mine the supports consisted of pillars of coal rock which had been left intact. Between the pillars the coal had been hewn in such a way as to leave arched ceilings. The thickness of the pillars and the arched structures of the ceilings ensured sufficient support against the pressures from above. The mine had in fact been closed for some years, but with the increased world price of coal it became profitable once again to bring it up. And how much more profitable would it be if, instead of having to drill for new pathways, the pillars were 'robbed' and the arches made more shallow by chipping away yet more coal? That is precisely what was done, until the weight of the earth above crashed down on the 440 victims of capitalist greed.

A few days after the Sharpeville massacre the inquest was adjourned to enable me to honour a previous commitment to defend a doctor in Ladysmith on abortion charges. I promised to make myself available again on 31 March. I returned from Ladysmith on the evening of 29 March. I was prevented from honouring this promise. Early on the morning of 30 March I was detained under the newly proclaimed emergency regulations.

I came to learn through a newspaper that had been smuggled into our Pretoria detention centre that, at the end of the Coalbrook inquest, the magistrate forwarded the papers to the Attorney General. This is a way of indicating that the event merited the attention of the prosecuting authorities. The Clydesdale management was subsequently prosecuted and found guilty of contravening mining regulations. Some time after my release from detention I chanced to meet the inquest magistrate, who teased me about the fact that I had promised to return within two days and then disappeared for six months. He nodded sympathetically when I expressed my belief that those responsible for safety measures at Clydesdale Collieries had literally got away with 440 murders.

While the emergency remained in force the regime had the power to continue detaining political activists. The majority of those who had escaped the net on the first night were instructed to seek temporary asylum in one of the neighbouring British territories. A few senior national leaders such as Dadoo and Tambo were sent into temporary exile to represent the movement in a world that had been stunned by the regime's Sharpeville atrocities. The Party also instructed a small group, including Kotane and Harmel, to remain in the country and live and work in complete clandestinity. This group, in consultation with members of the Central Committee in detention, organised the distribution of the first underground leaflet in the name of the Party after nearly ten years of underground existence. The *African Communist,* which was first published in 1959, was not acknowledged to be the organ of the Party until after 1960.

Those of us who were netted by the police undoubtedly had an easier time than those who carried on underground or went into temporary exile.

Memories of detention – 1960

We knew that the regime was preparing to act. But when Julius Baker rushed in with a message from a friendly black police source that the arrests were due that night, both Ruth and I responded with complacency. There had been so many false alarms, and each time we had slept out and called for Tilly to look after the children. Nevertheless I did decide to make the usual check outside Grey's Building in Von Wielligh Street which was then the headquarters of the Special Branch. Previous experience had shown that if their floor was lit up late at night it was more than likely they were preparing for an early morning raid. Despite the warning blaze of lights, Ruth and I lulled ourselves into inaction by each insisting that if the police did come it would be for the other.

We had been asleep for only a brief while when I heard a gentle rap on our bedroom window. There, standing in the flowerbed, was Detective

Sergeant Herbst with a sheepish grin on his face. This was his first raid on our house and he, like colleagues who had preceded him, had failed to find the front door. It was located in the back part of the house, a zone which in South Africa normally provides access to blacks. Herbst was unable to find the 'white man's entrance'.

They had come for me. Ruth, uncharacteristically, did not display the usual combative forthrightness which, for both of us, played such an important part in bonding our life together; the natural tendency for either of us in these circumstances would have been to tell the other 'stupid ass' to listen next time. The kids woke up and looked on as the police team searched the house. Ruth and I once again shared the intimacy of seeing Herbst being drawn like a magnet towards Stendhal's *The Red and the Black*. The book's title combined the two most subversive factors in South African officialdom's struggle equation and had invariably proved too much for Herbst's predecessors: this was now the third copy we were losing in as many raids.

What we did not want them to see was nesting in the false compartment in a desk which Julius (Ruth's father) had made specially for us in his furniture factory. The children, who knew these hiding places, remained nonchalant as the police set about going through the desk and pulling out the drawers. They failed to spot the false compartment, and Shawn's ever-so-slight wink of triumph when they began putting the drawers back stayed with me as a warm memory during the subsequent period of separation from the family.

The police swoop was carried out in two stages. A week after my arrest a second batch of detainees was rounded up. Judging by the pattern, Ruth would almost certainly have been included. But she, in the disguise of a red wig to hide her own distinctive gypsy-black hair, had already crossed the border into Swaziland with the children. The decision that Ruth and a number of others should go out of harm's way was taken by a small Central Committee collective, headed by Kotane and Harmel, which had evaded the arrests and continued to operate from hide-outs in Johannesburg for the duration of the emergency.

Our period of detention began with short spells at the Marshall Square police station and the Johannesburg Fort, then a longer stint at the Pretoria Local prison. At Pretoria we displaced the white 'long-termers' from their relatively well-appointed and comfortable barracks (complete with beds, mattresses, sheets, kitchen, showers, etc.) where they spent the final months of their imprisonment in preparation for life outside.

Most of our warders seemed awestruck by the large and unusual collection of educated whites who were somehow involved on the 'side of the natives'. We were looked upon as oddities rather than as enemies. The passionate hatred and fear of 'commies and liberals' had not yet become so deeply embedded in the popular white imagination; the menace of liberation still seemed too distant and the challenge to race rule was still contained within the fairly innocuous bounds of studied non-violence.

By later standards we had an easy time in our detention, and I have few agonies to recall. My memories are of the personalities who enriched our enforced communal life; the jail battles which it was still possible to fight against authority; the bonds of family closeness that came from the circumstances of the separation; and, as always, the absurd, ludicrous and unwitting humour of authority exercising mastery through the uniform and not the mind.

A large common cell on the first floor of Marshall Square police station was the temporary detention place for the first batch of Johannesburg white detainees. Our Indian colleagues were next door, and the songs on the other side of the building told us where the Africans were being held.

On the morning of my arrest, as our cell began to fill up with the staggered arrival of new detainees, the buzz was like that at the finishing post of an athletics meeting. The clatter of steps followed by the jangle of keys would signal the approach of another arrival. As he came into view a cheer of excited greeting burst from those who already considered themselves 'old lags' because they had been deposited some hours or even minutes earlier. This excitement was little to do with the sharing of a predicament rather than facing it alone; for we were not really in any serious predicament. The mood was relaxed and almost festive; we had done nothing legally culpable, and this fact still counted then in South Africa. Those who administered the security apparatus had not yet assumed their inquisitorial fiat. So each of us experienced moments of pleasant surprise when a close friend or talented comrade joined the detainees; it would relieve the tedium of institutionalised living that stretched ahead.

Some time later in our detention I wrote to Ruth:

'To live in such conditions brings out the best in everyone and especially in people who are in any case the best ... enough variety in events and personalities to take the edge off boredom ... an odd chap who specialises in making rusks from *katkop* (the head of a cat – the name given to prison bread) and telling long stories which make him giggle ... the rehabilitated alcoholic who spends all day drinking coffee instead ... the ex-senator with the violent temper which lasts exactly two minutes ... the theatre producer whose clothes never seem to need ironing ... the pink person who exudes goodwill ... the odd fellow who adopts the boiler as his baby ...'

Later I will identify some of these co-detainees, but for the moment back to that first day at Marshall Square.

Comic relief came almost at once with the arrival of Ismail Bhana who was with us for only one night at Marshall Square. Ismail (who has since died) had a light skin and looked more Aryan than many of the 'white' police officers who had brought him in. We were quietly amused when Ismail was escorted into our cell instead of the one accommodating the Indian detainees next door. A few hours later the fun and games began. The duty constable walked in with a clipboard and counted his white prisoners several times. Each time his face took on an increasingly puzzled expression as he compared the number in the cell with the record on his clipboard. Not a smirk from any of us.

He left to make a report and was presumably told to go back and count again. This time he lined us up against the wall and, slowly pointing his finger at each of us, mouthed one number after the other. No, he had not made a mistake and he left us once again. Later the constable returned accompanied by the sergeant, who again counted the number in our cell. The constable had an 'I-told-you-so' expression on his face and it was now the sergeant's turn to examine the record and scratch his head. Suddenly, although it took an inordinate length of time, the penny dropped. He decided to call our *names*. At the end of the roll call a grinning Ismail was left standing on one side of the cell. The demands of 'white' ethics had to be satisfied and he was resettled to his ethnic group area in the Indian cell; the curtain had come down on yet another vaudeville sketch unique to South Africa.

More significant confusion was yet to come. Later the same day the cell door was opened, and names were called of a few who were told to pack because their release had been ordered by the Supreme Court. Our ever-active legal guardians had moved swiftly as soon as the round-up began. Among the lawyers was Harold Wolpe, who had not yet been detained and was still working as a solicitor with his brother-in-law, James Kantor. Counsel was briefed to make an urgent *habeas corpus* application on behalf of certain detainees in order to test the validity of the arrests. Late at night lawyers rushed to the home of the duty judge, Mr Justice Ludorf.

Habeas corpus (an ancient English common law writ requiring the body of a person to be brought to court to investigate whether it is being lawfully detained or restrained and meaning literally, 'you must have the body') had not yet been abolished for political offences. Our detention was ordered under emergency regulations and proof had to be placed before the court that an emergency had in fact been delared. No copy of the *Government Gazette* containing the proclamation had yet reached Johannesburg. While the whole world headlined the declaration of the emergency, the courts needed direct evidence. Without such evidence their eyes are supposed to be closed, and they have in the past refused to take judicial notice of much more patent facts such as the constituents of a milk shake.

The judge was told by counsel for the government that a special military jet was on its way with the necessary documents of proof on board, and he postponed the application for a few hours. Harold tells of tantalising time spent hovering around the Ludorf home very near to the airport and listening for any sounds that would augur the arrival of the vital exhibit. The deadline arrived before the jet could touch down and, since the liberty of the individual still had some meaning in South Africa's inherited system of law, Ludorf (incidentally, a Nazi activist during the war against Hitler) had little option but to grant the *habeas corpus* applications. Steps were immediately taken to prepare applications on behalf of the rest of us.

Back at Marshall Square, we decided not to wait for further legal procedures. On the face of it we were all being unlawfully detained. We demanded our immediate release, failing which we threatened massive damage claims against all and sundry. Eventually we were told to pack up all our belongings and we crammed into the ground floor charge office, ostensibly to receive and sign for items such as watches and money that had been taken from us when we were booked in. However, it soon became clear that all this was a delaying tactic on the part of the security police present in massive numbers in the charge office.

As nothing seemed to be happening, I decided to bring things to a head by asking the senior office present whether or not I was in custody. He refused to commit himself, and I thereupon announced that I was now walking out of the police station and went to the main door. They did not take me seriously even when I moved to the door and I managed to walk as far as Marshall Street past two armed, uniformed guards who drew themselves up to attention when I passed. My suit and tie must have led them to believe that I was a high-ranking police officer. But before I was more than about ten metres away from the entrance, members of the Special Branch had caught up with me, told me I was under arrest, and escorted me back to the charge office. Almost immediately thereafter we were all taken back to our communal cell – apparently that jet with the fateful *Government Gazette* had touched down.

Some of those who were freed by Ludorf's initial ruling were inept enough to go straight home where they were duly picked up again the next morning. Others such as Julius Baker made straight for Swaziland. Before he left our cell he had presented the rest of us with his small suitcase containing a wondrous collection of medications, a gamut of do-it-yourself cures and an assortment of aids to relaxation and solitude such as eye-shades, ear plugs, sleeping pills, yoga books, a variety of teach-yourself language primers, and so on. Julius's mobile pharmacy was probably on stand-by for all his journeys, in keeping with his habit of thoroughness.

The government's choice for the round-up was extremely catholic; an ancient Special Branch list which was constantly added to and never reduced must have accounted for the polyglot collection. A recent vintage of congressites, communists, trotskyites, church radicals and liberals was supplemented by quite a few who had years before retired hurt from politics. Ex-Senator Hymie Basner had broken with the Party in 1939 over the Munich pact. Frail-looking Louis Joffe had been expelled from the Party in the 1930s at a time when purging the ranks was regarded as the patent medicine for gathering strength. This was the second time the authorities ignored his enforced exclusion from political activity; in 1940 when the Party still opposed the war, the luckless Louis was interned by Smuts. Archie Lewitton (of whom more later) had kept away from political activity for years before this detention but it now roused the ire in him again and set him back on course to 90-day detention in 1963! And quite a number of other ghosts from the pre-1950 days of legality discovered that police files are seldom closed.

Among the representatives of the lesser-known political groupings to be detained was Vincent Swart, a lecturer in English literature at Witwatersrand University. His love was the poet John Donne and he indulged himself in this passion in many fascinating prison tutorials which also attracted a puzzled warder audience. Vincent had been a complete stranger to most of us. His claim to detention appears to have been his role as the main theoretical inspiration behind an esoteric political sect with headquarters in Alexandra Township which called itself 'The Democracy of Content Movement'. The name alone perhaps helps to explain why this movement failed to grab the imagination of the masses; by 1960 the only echo of its existence must have been in the records of the Special Branch. When Vincent was brought in we were all convinced there had been some administrative mix-up because he smelt and looked like part of the regular intake of 'sherry gang' drunks whose main habitat in those days was the gardens in front of the Johannesburg Library. He went through a painful period of drying out, finding solace in a virtually continual consumption of black coffee. Harold's contribution on Vincent in a limerick competition, after the hunger strike that came later, ran:

On fast was a man called Vincent
His thoughts were all towards food bent
Until at the last
He broke his long fast
For Democracy, of course, not the Content.

Vincent's fine wit and unassuming erudition played some part, I believe, in helping me to break down my intolerance towards all nonconforming leftists. I was touched to receive from him an attractively bound edition of *Candide* with an inscription of his friendship and sent after his early discharge from detention. Sadly, within a short time of his release he died from drink-related causes.

As in the Treason Trial, the left wing of the church was once again represented by the Reverend Douglas Thompson. In the early 1940s he was prominent in the FSU (Friends of the Soviet Union) and Medical Aid for Russia, organisations which during the heyday of the anti-Hitler struggle boasted sponsorship from some of Smuts's cabinet ministers. But for Douglas this was not a passing phase. Inspired by spiritual associates such as the Red Dean of Canterbury (Hewlett Johnson), he became a passionate devotee of Soviet socialism and worked out for himself a liberation theology for South African conditions.

During our days of detention Douglas's pink, cherub-like countenance was to officiate over many 'services' to commemorate our movement's 'holy days' such as 1 May and 26 June and pay tribute to the anniversaries of our revolutionary 'saints' and 'martyrs'. Douglas usually spoke healthy good sense even though he sounded Quixotic when he strained to square the supernatural with dialectical materialism. An inter-denominational church service became a regular Sunday morning activity attended by Christians, Jews, agnostics, atheists and others. It made a break in the routine of confined living and, in any case, the services always packed some political punch.

I wrote to Ruth about one of these 'services' in the Fort:

'May Day in jail was an inspiring day. After a week of miserable weather the Gods arranged brilliant sunshine and a near winter freshness in the air. Those of us who were so inclined sported appropriately coloured bits of paper with matches for pins ... we listened to an inspiring sermon (from our very own reverend) on what this day of days means ...

we were most probably among the few South Africans who could lawfully share each other's thoughts on the meaning of this day ...'

When we were transferred to Pretoria Local, Douglas's monopoly over our 'spiritual welfare' was broken. The Reverend Mark Nye, associated with the Liberal Party, was already in Pretoria as one of a local batch of detainees. No Christian love was lost between these two men of God who stood in opposite corners of the political ring. United front tactics demanded that each of them officiate over services in strict rotation, and the schismatic debate on politics and religion proceeded from week to week almost like a movie serial. Thompson preaches a political sermon one week and Nye rejoins the next week with '... now I am a man and have put away such childish things' – or some such Biblical quote, with Thompson returning to the fray the week after.

But the differences between the two clergymen were not merely on abstract doctrine; their response to detention also varied. For example, when the hunger strike was embarked upon Thompson was only too ready to carry the Cross whereas Nye consulted his conscience and was apparently informed that since it was God's purpose to put him in jail, he would be sinning if he frustrated that purpose by trying to get out! South African experience has taught me to believe that there are two categories of people who can always be counted on to make whatever sacrifices are demanded by a worthwhile social cause – a *good* communist and a *good* Christian. But membership of a church or a party does not, by itself, eliminate cant or sophistry by those who represent them.

John Lang, an attorney and liberal activist, had a lay connection with the church which was to stand us in good stead – experience with church choirs. He spent many hours teaching us the art of harmony, and towards the end of our period of detention we could render numerous choral works with reasonable artistry. I began to see how the harmonic skills of black crowds had their origins in church experiences and in a culture in which communal singing is an important form of social togetherness.

Earlier at Marshall Square it had been Eli Weinberg's arrival that encouraged us to find our voices. Eli, a Latvian-born veteran of the communist and trade union movement, had a fine trained tenor voice, perhaps slightly too operatic and dominant for casual communal folk singing. But he was to become one of the anchors of our choir. Once Eli had arrived, the mornings invariably began with arias in Yiddish, Sotho and an assortment of other languages.

Although many of us had worked intimately together over a long stretch of time, we knew surprisingly little about one another's backgrounds. I enjoyed the company of Eli in those long walks round and round the concrete courtyard (72 times = four miles) during which he related fascinating snatches from his childhood years in Latvia.

Eli was eight years old when the First World War began. In the face of the Kaiser's advancing army into Russia his mother tried to send him off to a safe haven to live with relatives in the north of the country. He got lost and was adopted by a frontline Russian cavalry unit with whom he lived in the trenches as their mascot for the duration of the war.

The unit cook assumed the role of Eli's surrogate father and, among other things, protected him from the continuous risk of sexual assault. Eli was reunited with his mother through the efforts of two German officers who undertook their search mission on the promise of a supply of *taglich* which Eli's mother baked and sold at her small delicatessen store. He had some blurred recollections of the exciting days of the October Revolution, and in particular remembered Trotsky's impressive oratory at a mass rally in his town, Riga. The Baltic States were soon (with interventionist assistance) to secede from the victorious workers' republic. Eli then became an activist in the workers' underground movement until it was agreed that he should leave Latvia.

I also heard Eli's fascinating tales of his wanderings among the Sotho people when he first arrived in South Africa in the late 1920s and of his experience as a communist trade unionist attempting to organise white workers.

From the moment Cecil Williams was brought in our theatrical company, christened 'The Fortress Mummers', was in business. Cecil, originally an English master at Johannesburg's King Edward School, had turned to the theatre and become a full-time professional producer and director. Always well turned out, Cecil managed to maintain his spruce appearance during his detention. His smooth black hair was brylcreemed into place, the creases of his trousers were mattress-pressed nightly and he sported a selection of colourful cravats; he looked very much like a stereotype of the handsome hero of the early silent films. His elegant lifestyle had been made possible by an inheritance from a lady who, in her eighties, came across Cecil in a Johannesburg street while he was rattling a collection box in aid of the Springbok Legion. They became friendly and, to his great surprise, his uncalculating kindness was repaid by a rather large bequest.

I first met Cecil in Italy in 1945, just after the war, when he was seconded from the navy to become the officer in charge of a soldiers' training and educational centre on the outskirts of Florence. As I was waiting to be repatriated, I took advantage of an opportunity to take a two-month shorthand and typing course at this centre. After the war Cecil joined the Party and was also a prominent figure in the Springbok Legion. During the years of illegality he was always ready to play his part. When Mandela became a fugitive after 1961 Cecil often helped transport him to secret rendezvous. Cecil was being driven on that fateful journey on 5 August 1962, when Mandela, disguised in a chauffeur's uniform, was captured by armed police at a roadblock.

Cecil was a close friend, and Ruth and I especially admired the way he coped with the awkward consequences (both in society generally and more especially within our movement) of his life as a homosexual.

The detainees' theatre group under Cecil's direction produced a continual flow of play-readings and performances of classical and contemporary works. I particularly remember a performance of *A Midsummer Night's Dream* and the impact it made on the warders who (whether they were on or off duty) used to gather in large numbers to watch our performances. They laughed uncontrollably at seeing some of their charges prancing about on the stage pretending to be lions, moons and hedges.

From time to time some original work was produced, and I announced one such work in a letter to Ruth:

'We had play-readings from Sheridan and Congreve but the *piece de resistance* was the world premier of *A Fate Worse Than Death*. This was a topical farce composed collectively by the detainees theatre company. The banal climax portrayed the saving of "Belinda Blue-Eyes" (acted by Ronnie Press) from the oncoming wheels of the Nylstroom Express. The hero-pilot-captain of the "helicopulator" was named after the Treason Trial senior defending counsel Issie Maisels.'

I have a special memory of this performance because it was my stage debut. I played a non-speaking role, portraying the menacing approach of the Nylstroom Express and spent days rehearsing the technique of producing the track noises of the train with my feet, interspersed with sounds of steam puffing and hooting. Regrettably, and despite the quality of my performance, I never graduated to playing a speaking role, but my train noises still stand me in good stead when I am called upon to do a party turn.

The cameos I have so far selected are about those among us who helped minister to our spiritual and cultural needs. But when Monty Berman was brought into Marshall Square we knew that our culinary needs would receive equal attention. And my letters to Ruth are peppered with references to Monty's great productions:

'..."Chez Monty" is open and it's difficult to resist the delectable dishes – spaghetti bolognaise, Suliman's Pilaf etc. etc. It's remarkable what he can do with a tin of bully beef.'

'I've so far mentioned a few names. It is difficult to pick and choose from such a fine collection. But Monty I must mention. On a day you break a hunger strike a cook is more important than the politician. He is off to the kitchen. Nothing exotic at first. Just a bit of bread and jam ... Later Monty with his under-cooks is baking scones. He rolls with a milk bottle and shapes with a jam bottle.'

But more than anything else Monty wanted to be a guerrilla commander. It was his maverick conduct in pursuit of this ambition which later soured the close personal relationships between our two families which had its origins in the school friendship between Ruth and Monty's wife, Myrtle. When MK was formed Monty was not given a position on its command structures and, together with some disenchanted Party members and radical liberals, he proceeded to create his own 'army' – the African Resistance Movement. The ARM carried out a few sabotage actions on 16 December 1961, the day when MK launched its own sabotage programme.

From exile Monty tried to maintain his army and demonstrated his romantic sense of adventure and courage by returning clandestinely for a short spell in the disguise of a priest; a disguise which must have fitted very well with his genial, relaxed and benign facial features. Soon after my own exile began in London, Monty proposed that a new joint command be established between the ARM and MK which, among other things, would have at its disposal a small ocean-going yacht acquired by the ARM. The ANC would have nothing to do with this offer. I don't know what happened to the boat but the ARM completely disappeared from the scene. Despite a political parting of the ways I retain a feeling of warmth for Monty, and understandably enough, his culinary contributions make him stand out as one of the most memorable of the diverse talents which the Special Branch had brought together during the emergency.

Archie Lewitton had a different talent, and his considerable chess skill was usefully deployed from the moment he joined us when he began to devote himself to the organisation of a continual round of chess competitions.

In the 1940s Archie had abandoned his profession as a pharmacist to become a full-time Party worker, first in the Johannesburg district office and later in Cape Town as an elected member of the Central Executive Committee. Ruth could have had no difficulty in identifying him in the following passage in one of my censored letters.

'We have a cynic among us – an excellent chess player – who wallows in his reputation of hardness, but we all recognise that he is one of the most gentle of souls.'

It took me some years to understand this aspect of Archie. My early impressions were jaundiced in 1942 in which I was the victim of his rather astringent and completely straightforward humour. At the time I thought him a wicked monster. I was a 16-year-old candidate for Party membership and my insufferable seriousness could not yet accommodate the lighter side of the Party and politics. As convenor of the Sive Brothers and Karnovsky factory unit of the Party I was responsible for the circulation of the Party's official organ *Inkululeko*. Each fortnight I would pick up our unit's 30 copies from the Party office at Progress Buildings and at the same time hand over the 30 pence proceeds from the previous sales at a penny a copy. On one occasion we discovered that our parcel contained only 29 copies, and I came to hand over 29 pence to Archie who was at the time connected with the business side of the newspaper. The conversation went something like this:

'What has happened to the other penny?'

'The parcel only contained 29 copies this week.'

'Are you suggesting that the Party leadership makes mistakes?'

'A mistake can happen.'

'How long have you been in the Party?'

'I'm still on probation. I hope to be confirmed in a few months time.'

'Now you know what we have to put up with. You are not even a member yet and you've already begun to fiddle the books and to accuse the Party leadership of being incompetent and enumerate.'

I offered to pay the extra penny out of my own pocket.

'That would not be at all right,' he said relentlessly and in a tone of voice as if I were trying to bribe him. My demoralisation by then was such that his final remark, with the merest hint of a smile, 'Listen, I believe you,' sounded to my ears as if it implied that others certainly would not.

I failed to see a signal that I was a victim of a Lewitton set-up (I later discovered that he was often tempted to direct these against starry-eyed and over-serious enthusiasts). At the time I was convinced that my future in the Party had just come to an abrupt end.

The Party factory group at SBK had another representative among those rounded up for detention at the start of the 1960 emergency – Mannie Brown. Mannie was born in Palestine where his father served as a British civil servant. He was brought to South Africa as a child soon after an incident in which he was shot in the leg during an armed action by the

Zionist underground. At SBK he was employed as an invoice clerk, and soon after the formation of our unit I recruited him into the Party. After the war Mannie made various forays into the business world which were invariably successful. Very much like my father-in-law Julius, Mannie combined an extraordinary private and social generosity with a hard-headed approach towards the 'dog-eat-dog' ethic of so-called free enterprise. Mannie's eyes twinkle with mischievous enjoyment when he relives some of his pre-emptive fiddles against competitors.

Business was a game and Mannie was above-average at most games. We used to meet often on the tennis court and over the regular Sunday night poker table. In detention he taught many of us to play bridge for the first time and he was the victor ludorum of all the sporting contests organised virtually daily in that exercise yard; he was beaten only once in a tennequoit competition by Harold Wolpe (also no mean athlete at his prime) who had the advantage of a handicap in his favour.

It sounds awful to admit this, but I had a surge of pleasure when I discovered Mannie among us, and I smilingly told him that I was pleased that he had not escaped the police net. Mannie's bantering and usually self-deprecating humour responded typically: 'You think you're a shit! This morning when they came to fetch me I insisted it was Babette (his wife) they were really after.' They both enjoyed the completely serious denial by the officer in charge that such a mistake could have happened.

Our second place of detention was to be the Johannesburg Fort situated just opposite the Johannesburg General Hospital. The wail of ambulance sirens was one of the familiar sounds which came to us regularly from the outside world. But suddenly one morning the air was pierced with what seemed like an endless scream of ambulances and police vehicles. Something special had happened. A riot? A natural disaster? For an hour or two the Fort buzzed with speculation until a paper ball was flicked towards us through the iron grilles by a non-political prisoner. On it was a scrawl 'Verwoerd assassinated at Show Grounds. Good luck.'

At the time we were not aware that the person covered in blood whom we saw being brought in a few minutes earlier was David Pratt who had fired at Verwoerd. An amended paper ball communiqué from our colleagues later informed us that Verwoerd, although shot a number of times in the cheek, would survive. Some wag among us rose to the occasion by suggesting that as a deeply religious man Verwoerd should now be called upon to turn his other cheek – a quip which surprisingly was not deleted by the prison censor from my letter to Ruth.

In Pretoria Local we linked up with David Brink, a leading and full-time activist in the Liberal Party, and learnt that he had reacted with particular apprehension when news of the attempted assassination reached him. In his case the general distaste for Blanquism as a form of struggle (which most of us shared) was reinforced by an unqualified commitment to the path of 'legality' and constitutionalism. But there was a tangible reason for his shock reaction: he had reason to fear that the authorities might attempt to link him with Pratt in the Milner Park shooting.

In the period immediately preceding the declaration of the state of emergency the Pretoria office of the Liberal Party, where Brink worked, was convinced that its mail was being tampered with by Special Branch. In order to obtain evidence of this a rather complicated scheme was evolved. Brink arranged for a letter to be posted to him couched in language that implied a plot to assassinate an important government personality. If a raid ensued to follow up the 'plot' it would go some way towards exposing police methods. In addition, the letter was specifically doctored so as to reveal whether it had been opened. When the letter arrived Brink and his associates concluded that it had in fact been tampered with, but no immediate raid took place. Before the matter could be taken very much further the emergency intervened. Brink and all the office files (including the one which contained the trap letter) were taken into police custody.

It was noticeable when we met Brink that the early stages of his detention ticked away very, very slowly. He waited for the axe to fall. But the letter never again surfaced; it must have been buried in the mountain of confiscated documents shovelled into police headquarters at the start of the emergency.

Pratt was eventually tried on a charge of attempted murder. He was found 'guilty but insane' and was committed to a mental institution where, it was reported, he committed suicide by tying both ends of the bedsheet to his bedpost, putting his neck into the loop and rolling over and over until he asphyxiated himself. We never saw Pratt again at the Fort, but at Pretoria Local we used to catch glimpses of him through the large window of our prison dormitory which abutted on the exercise yard. Reverend Douglas Thompson was the only detainee to have had direct contact with him; a warder with some compassion (at the cost of being disciplined) once allowed the two of them to play a game of chess. From Thompson's impression and the little one could gather from Pratt's appearance there seemed little hint of the volcanic passion in him which erupted that Easter Day at Milner Park.

When we first noticed him at Pretoria Local, he was still allowed to exercise at the same time as the prisoners awaiting trial. Within a few days he had organised a group of younger ones into a parade ground squad and had them marching up and down to the bark of a sergeant major's drill voice. The kids who took part in what we called 'Pratt's Army' seemed to enjoy this break from prison boredom, and the guards (equally bored) thought it was an amusing spectacle. After a while though, higher authority must have pondered over the implications of allowing an alleged political assassin to engage in 'war games'; 'Pratt's Army' was duly demobilised and shortly afterwards he was deprived of all company and had to exercise alone. It was out of desperation for human company or a desire to make a gesture of political unity that he dashed one day across the yard to enter our section for a minute or so, shouting warm greetings until they caught up with him.

Pratt's image is fixed in my memory by a moment during one of our choir practices after this incident. We were rehearsing the rather melancholy refrain 'Drink to me only with thine eyes'. Pratt, surrounded by warders, stood motionless as close to our window as they would allow, body slumped, hands in pocket and tears uncontrollably cascading down his cheeks, making not the slightest attempt to hide them or to wipe them off. A few days later he left an exercise book for us in the lavatory complex. It contained very elaborate and fanciful exhortations for joint efforts against racism. We declined to respond; Brink's dilemma aside, we could not let our inclinations to comfort Pratt in his misery provide grounds for invented charges that the assassination gesture was part of a wider conspiracy. But we often made a special point to convene the choir when he began his half-hour spell in the exercise yard.

The most experienced political figure among us was 'Rusty' Bernstein whose membership of the Party dated from the second half of the 1930s. But the respect and affection he enjoyed from virtually all the detainees did not stem from his seniority; indeed, he was that rare political animal for whom either self-aggrandisement or adulation were anathema. An architect by profession, he had spent a large slice of his working life in full-time Party work, making his most impressive contribution as a political analyst whose incisive and fresh writing style reflected a mind uncluttered by dogma and cliché. Yet Rusty in one way was an unlikely sort of revolutionary.

I always felt about him that if he granted himself the right to choose he would have opted for the quiet life, satisfying whatever instinct for excitement and adventure he had through sitting hunched in his family drawing room indiscriminately reading thrillers against the background of classical music. But reason and the social compassion in him deprived him of choice. It was the sense of service rather than of self-assertion that attracted to him so much warmth and trust in his judgment among the detainees. Within a few years of our detention Rusty was to face a possible death sentence in the Rivonia Trial. By quirk of legal fortune he was one of the two accused to be acquitted.

Rusty was naturally one of the key figures in the detainees' committee which, among other things, was the think-tank for ways and means of continuing to engage in political struggle within the prison walls. We started in a small way, continuously pressing demands connected with food and other conditions. Ronnie Press, a Sactu activist, was asked to use his skills as a science teacher to extract an assortment of creatures from the soup and prepare a chart to which the animals were stuck in order of size, with a description under each one.

When the Colonel arrived to make his routine enquiry about complaints I was appointed to tell him that the soup was not fit for human consumption. He indignantly denied our claim and immediately ordered the chief warder to bring a plate of soup. The Colonel stood there in military splendour consuming a spoonful or two and trying to look as if he were enjoying it. It was only then that we produced the chart. Colouring slightly, he stopped eating the soup and, without saying another word, marched off with the warder trailing behind him carrying the unfinished plate in one hand and the spoon in the other. From then on the soup seemed relatively free of additional insect protein.

When we came to the Fort we were initially locked into a cell, from 4 pm until 6 am, with lights out at 8 pm. The 14 hours in the tiny space seemed endless. I came to understand then how important the purely physical is in discussion and debate; without the visible hand gesture, the frown, the nod, the look of boredom or interest, the discourse loses colour and stimulus. You often find yourself cut off in mid-sentence by the sound of snoring.

It was while we were being kept under these cell conditions that an event occurred which won the great admiration of the segregated criminal fraternity in the passage opposite. Suddenly, in the middle of the night, a piercing scream came from one of our cells. It was Ronnie Press's falsetto voice shouting 'Help, help, Hymie has collapsed, he's not moving, someone open the door ...' Basner had suffered a black-out. The warder in the passage was helpless because, for security reasons, he was also locked into the passage without keys.

When no response came, all hell broke loose. All of us began shouting and banging the concrete floors with the lavatory buckets and whatever else came to hand. The bedlam achieved its purpose; a bunch of warders arrived in quick time presumably expecting to deal with a riot or a jailbreak. Early the next morning we told the Colonel we would not tolerate being detained under conditions that constituted danger to 'life and limb'. We won this battle. From then on only the large grille at the end of the passage was locked and the individual cell doors remained open throughout the night. Even more important, we were given complete control over the lights.

I wrote about these conditions to Ruth:

'... concessions have now been in operation for a couple of days, making life more bearable. We can "visit" one another. Our cell has been invited to have dinner on Wednesday with cell 35 – the best mixer of salads and dressings in the whole Fort. My cell consists of two lawyers (Wolpe and Louis Baker) and one business agent (Mannie Brown). Excellent company but poor cooks. I must get myself invited out more often.'

'... Another innovation which makes for more comfort is that we are now in control of our own lights. No more bedtime at 8 pm... it is our combined efforts which have achieved most of these concessions. At the same time people outside must have a balanced picture ... our fellow detainees are, *a la* South Africa, living under conditions fit for criminals and not political prisoners ...' (The rest is blacked out by the prison censor.)

But the protest that made the biggest impact locally and internationally was to come later when we were moved to Pretoria. Jock Isaacwitz, a leading figure from the Springbok Legion days and subsequently prominent in the Liberal Party, told Ruth after his release, 'Within a few days of my detention I noticed Rusty and Joe in a deep huddle in the corner of the exercise yard and I said to myself, "Jock, my boy, it looks like you're not going to get out of this one without a hunger strike." '
Well, Jock was only half right. The hunger strike happened indeed. But the plot was not hatched in the way he imagined; the lead was in fact given by a group of women detainees who (not for the first time in the history of our struggle) outshone the men.

From the moment of their detention the women demanded access to lawyers, contact with their husbands next door, and, above all, that they either be charged in a court of law or released. The first collective act of defiance in support of these demands took place while we men detainees were seated in the vehicles of the police convoy that was to transfer us from the Fort to Pretoria. We became puzzled by the long delay until we began to hear the defiant shouts of familiar female voices one after the other. When told of the impending transfer they had refused to leave their cells, and eventually each one of them had to be carried by a team of wardresses to the black marias. The jail authorities were terribly shaken. It was beyond their imagination that a group of seemingly respectable white women could engage in such unseemly physical defiance of authority.

When the women detainees declared a hunger strike we immediately decided to act in solidarity with them. Sundry ulcer cases, diabetics, geriatrics and other disabled individuals were exempted. But of the able-bodied, a few refused to join in: 'conscientious objectors' such as the Reverend Mark Nye and some frightened individuals such as John Lang. Lang did not think the partners in his law firm would approve, an excuse he used later to scab on a decision not to answer questions when the interrogations began. While the small minority ate, full meals for all of us were delivered three times daily by the warders, and duly taken back uneaten.

On 23 May (the tenth day of the hunger strike) I smuggled out an uncensored letter to Ruth. I draw freely on its contents to describe some of our experiences.

'I feel hilarious. This has been a glorious day. If you get this letter it has not come through the censors. I'm bloody sick of guarded language, so here goes.

'Saturday was the eighth day. An unprecedented event on such a large scale in a South African jail. We have been encouraged by news from outside. Our efforts have served once again to draw people's attention to our detention. We're all feeling generally weak but otherwise quite well. The hunger pangs have gone ... A state of euphoria ... A light, relaxed head. Wonder and amazement among us that we have managed so far.

'The original decision was that we should aim for a minimum of seven days and, if possible, 14 to 16 days. Today turned out to be a day of decision. In informal discussions we all agreed that a decision would depend on news from the women and an evaluation of working up still more outside reaction ... We were all enraged by the Minister's statement that there was in fact no hunger strike. We obtained the Colonel's permission to send a telegram to the Minister ... a copy was also smuggled out.

'The women seem to be doing their glorious best. Physically some of them were hit a bit harder than most of us. But when the history of this period comes to be written the women will rank first place. The example of their fighting spirit from the time of the physical obstruction of the removal from the Fort to the hunger strike itself was an inspiration.

'This then was the position on Friday morning. There was an air of expectancy. Surely some sort of retaliation was coming. Solitary? Dispersal to different parts of the country?

'By the evening we heard that strenuous efforts had been made to get the women to stop their hunger strike. This consisted of assurances by the Colonel that he had received a telex message from the Minister promising them a reply to their demand for release. Also threats that they would be separated and sent to different jails ... A message came to us that eight of the women were to be moved to Nylstroom at 6 am the following morning. Gloom, depression and anger. A decision to make a court application. Husbands would go first thing the next morning and ask to be taken before a judge. A restless night.

'The next morning (Saturday) the Colonel was nowhere to be found. Again no appearance at the usual 10 am parade. Something must surely happen. At 12 noon it did. A brigadier and a colonel walked in. "I've come to tell you that since last evening the women have broken their fast. They," he added, "are on a diet of orange juice and milk and they say they are enjoying it." With rage in his voice, Eli said, "That is a lie. We don't believe you." They have never heard that said to them, these high-ranking gentlemen. There must be retaliation. But no. The Brigadier speaks. "Please believe me, it's the truth. I have the assurance of the police that they are speeding up their investigation."

' "Let one of us go to them to obtain confirmation and the reason why."

' "That can't be done."

' "Have they been given any assurances?"

' "No!"

'And that was that. It stank. We decided to carry on until we found the truth.

'It was only on Monday that we discovered that the women had in fact ended their fast in the following circumstances. First, they had received a communication from the Secretary for Justice to the effect that their demand for immediate release was receiving the Minister's consideration. The second reason appears from the following statement which the women issued.

' "Tonight several women were examined by Dr de Villiers who informed two of them that their condition was serious, that if they did not stop fasting immediately they would harm themselves irreparably. One other woman had already been similarly warned. These three did not wish to stop fasting while the rest are not eating. On these medical grounds, as responsible people, we have therefore decided to call off our hunger strike tonight. We wish to make it absolutely clear that this is our only reason for so doing."

'Yesterday (Sunday) – our ninth day – nothing of importance. Uncertainty about the women. Speculation about threats. Nothing heard about our application to be taken to a judge … All conclude that if the women have stopped we should also consider calling it off unless some compelling reason presents itself tomorrow. We have achieved more than we had expected at the beginning. Investigation was being speeded up. We made our existence known to people outside.

'When this morning came with real news of women and later also news that they were on the road back to good health, we took our final decision – to have our first "meal" at lunchtime. I go with Cecil to the chief warder to ask for certain foods (oranges, milk etc.) with which to break the fast. He readily agrees and even lets me go to announce this decision to the "sacred" cells. These are the cells in which those who have been interrogated are lodged and contact with them is normally forbidden. However to help end the strike that (according to these petty liars) never was, the taboo is broken. Milk and jam is sent. A bathtub of oranges. Smiles all round while lusty throats sing *The Hammer Song*. Monty is off to the kitchen. Nothing exotic at first. Just a piece of bread and jam. Why has no-one written a poem about a piece of brown bread and jam … a banquet fit for a king.

'Finally at 7 o'clock for the first time in ten days we are all gathered around the dining room table. Soup with some bread in it. Then scones and tea … Spontaneous joy, warmth and comradeship. Song after song. From the stirring *Marseillaise* to *Underneath the Arches* to *London Burning* to *Nkosi Sikelele' iAfrika*. A sing-song to cap all sing-songs. A feast to end a fast which in a sense had itself been a feast, but of a different kind. Cries of encore from our interrogated friends across the way. The warder peering in from the cold – puzzled but seemingly enjoying our mirth … A happiness one seldom experiences … the collective joy of a struggle fought and partially won and one which we know will have a final victory in the not too distant future was what was really being expressed.

'It is past ten now. The lights are out except in the ablution block in which I am sitting. A couple of late birds stand and chat. The conversation is beginning to move away from food and sex is beginning to assert its rightful place again. One phase has ended. From prison walls the future looks bright. All my love.'

The day we ended our hunger strike – 23 May 1960 – was my 34th birthday. Birthdays were not holy days in our family and Ruth and I often forgot about our own and the others'. But this day was hard on my emotions. My fellow detainees were aware of the occasion because a few days earlier I had jokingly appealed to them to hold out until I turned 34. The fact that it coincided with an end to the hunger strike obviously added to the special warmth of the greetings. But what I valued most of all was the splendid gesture from a group of fellow detainees from whom we were completely isolated by colour.

All this time the Treason Trial was still limping on at the converted synagogue courtroom down the road from the central prison. Each night the 30 accused would be returned to their detention cells. On this day we had already been locked in when, at about 4.30 pm, the rhythm of strong African voices rose up from the lane which abutted on the outside wall of our dormitory. At first songs which did not seem congruent with the sound of African voices, *For he's a jolly good fellow* and *Happy birthday to you*. Then, for a finale, a rousing Congress song. The driver of the prison van bringing back the treason accused had been persuaded to make this special birthday stop. It was difficult to hold back my tears. But more was to come.

Leon Levy, one of our two white detainees still facing treason charges (the other was Helen Joseph), returned to us half an hour later from his day in the Treason Trial court, bearing a cake box inscribed with best wishes for my birthday and the signature of every Treason Trial accused. Inside a wedding-type cake with thick icing and two silver horseshoes perched on top. That night, our protesting stomachs notwithstanding, we all had a taste of this gift of comradeship.

Within a short time I had the opportunity to convey my personal thanks for the cake and the birthday serenade. An application that I be allowed to visit the African cells in my capacity as a lawyer and co-conspirator in the Treason Trial was granted surprisingly. I do not suppose that this kind of indulgence has ever been conceded before or since. Jail apartheid, even when the inmates are accused of conspiracy and common purpose, is more pervasive than in the outside world. Perhaps this unique break-down in tradition was the fruit of our stubborn struggles and the authorities were anxious to avoid another *cause célèbre* hitting the national and world headlines. But whatever the reason, I was regularly escorted through the race barrier to spend evenings chatting with our comrades among whom were some of the legendary giants of the movement for liberation – Walter Sisulu, Nelson Mandela, JB Marks, Duma Nokwe and so on.

They slept on coir mats on the concrete floor covered by blankets which smelt of prison. The cell walls were dark in colour and the single bulb gave off a candle's light. A tin bucket in the corner provided the night toilet. The light was switched off at an early hour and I was then escorted back to our white men's prison palace, to our beds, mattresses, white sheets, bedside tables, a separate ablution block, our own control over the lights and generally all the mod cons usually advertised in the 'To Let' columns.

This experience once again raised the question in my mind: could a white group such as ours on whom relative privilege is showered (even when rounded up in the battle for racial equality) be trusted to share the same depth of anger and sense of commitment as those who feel the lash of race humiliation every moment of their lives? The emphasis given to such questions by out-and-out black racists should not (I have always thought) make us ignore the strands of reality which lie behind such sensitivities. I have refused to assume the guilt of white racism merely because of the accident of colour. Nevertheless, the coincidence of colour had always slotted us into privilege, and now in jail it was more blatant than ever. Yet the strong, warm voices we heard from that police van in the lane outside our wall spoke unmistakably of a common brotherhood.

For me personally one of the most exciting hours during my detention was on the afternoon of Thursday, 14 July. I wrote about it to Ruth:

'I was told I had a visitor. I walked into an office and there sat Shawn, Gillian and Robyn in their school uniforms, beaming from ear to ear … an excited, happy welcome. Robyn stood there giggling loudly for minutes … the hour passed by so quickly. They're the same as always … Robyn with that charmingly wicked look and eyes surreptitiously pointed in the direction of the warder whispering "Can't I steal you just for one day?", eyes goggling at the sight of big keys. Gillian – affectionate and quiet – complaining that I hadn't said goodbye to her when I was arrested. Searching questions on all sorts of topics. She's keen as a razor and sensitive, but controlled. And Shawn, the same old lovable self. An open face and a personality that exudes charm. They all clambered on to my lap and held me tight for an hour. Between hugs Robyn started where she left off, rearranging my hair and nose-rubbing. At the beginning I thought it would be difficult for us. But as it turned out – not one tear. They are so natural and seem to have an outline grasp of what it's all about. I can't wait for all of us to be one family again … There is little in this world which gives one such a feeling of optimism as a child's smile. Their comments and questions about the whys and wherefores of being detained make the whole thing look so ludicrous …'

A flow of beautiful letters from Ruth kept our family unit together. Her perceptions about the children and her capacity to paint them so skilfully made me know them better than ever before. Her letters were self-reflective and caressing, even though she claimed in one of them that 'loving is meant for the touch not the writing pad'.

'We spend so much time and energy over the formalities of living that in the daily rush values become obscured by chores and duties. These weeks have in many ways been a purification and a retreat, and the cluttering trivialities have dropped away to reveal the clean sharp lines of the form that is our life together in all its fullness.'

She reflected on her new temporary environment and the people she found herself with.

'By the sound of it your wonderful company have the best brought out of them by confinement; though it's largely the company, not the confinement, I'm sure, with the exceptions that are thrown into the vortex. One meets rather different types particularly in other situations. People who seem to think the world, or their world, owes them a living ... after all they spent the best years of their lives ... etc etc. We can't put them all in the same tub and float them, but they're often the kind of people who put number one first and blow most else. They've all got acute personal problems, but above all what I hold against them is their notion that those who don't elevate personal problems above all else have none. You know the line: leftists are so inhuman – no understanding – so hard – so impersonal. Those types I could cheerfully crack. Though one doesn't. And as people they've some fine qualities. But if one doesn't wear a heart on each sleeve it's sometimes presumed one hasn't one.'

A typical admiring insight into the children:

'They are natural and at ease and not obstreperous like so many others. Shawn picks up admirers like girls gathering daisies and most adults go for her like a shot. She has several "boyfriends" (most of them four times her age) who demand their daily cuddle from her. She's polite but not over-touchy. Gilly is tender but dependable and can get a mischievous glint in her eye. Robyn is a quacktail but a very attractive one. I thought her "Dear Dabby" letter priceless. They really shouldn't put five-year-olds in school, should they? It's like emptying the woods of sprites.'

In the middle of the hunger strike she wrote:

'I too find letter-writing a self-imposed restriction, there are all the subjects that are taboo under the emergency having to be left out. The age and spirit of great letter writing has passed and anyway the stilted conversation piece is poor recompose for the rough and tumble of free discussion and being together. But however reticent we are because of the nature of things – and prying eyes turn letters into public posters when they are meant to be for man and wife – the main thing remains:

we are hopeful, because you are, and we are strong because of you. All
of you ... I can hardly bear to think of what you are going through this
week. If I try to say some of it I would unnerve myself or write the trite
heroics that do sound slushy on paper ... It needs an experience like this
to sift us all out, I expect, and put us to the test but the agony is none the
less for recognising this ...

'Those good times and all the comforts we were able to surround
ourselves with fit into their right place now, I find. We acquired so many
possessions but leaving them flat suddenly one morning is really no ca-
lamity ... the kids talk about you as though you went off to work in the
morning and are due home any time after five.'

My release came at the close of the fifth month, but in the final stage
the place of detention became lonelier and lonelier. Every few days from
the beginning of July one or more of our comrades was released, until
towards the end they seemed to be holding out against five of us. I wrote
to Ruth how odd it seemed to see ex-detainees on the other side of the
fence as visitors: '... as usual they looked far sadder than we did ... I've
never seen a man with such a look of sadness as Harold when he left us
behind.'

However, our contact with the outside world increased immeasurably
with the illegal acquisition of a radio and its most important accessory
under these conditions, an ear-phone. We had never been permitted access to newspapers but we managed somehow to see them from time to
time, not least with the help of prisoners serving long-term sentences. A
jail gathers together people with above-average skills and ingenuity, and
the jail authorities never really win the battle to prevent evasion of regulations. When one of our comrades was being kept in an isolation cell an
old-timer who was now a trusty made a device from an empty toothpaste
tube to serve him regularly with hot coffee through the keyhole.

The radio unfortunately did not survive for long. A major cricket test
series was being played and, as partisans against the all-white South African team and as cricket enthusiasts, we assiduously followed the ball-
by-ball commentary. We happened to be sitting around our kitchen table
and it was my turn to convey the commentary I was receiving through
the ear-phone. The game had reached an exciting moment; an important
South African wicket had fallen and I, infected by the commentator's
excited voice, half stood up to repeat the venomous scream 'Howzat',
triumphantly showing an umpire's finger and shouting a number of con-
gratulatory phrases.

A moment later I was to discover the reason for the rather unusual
grimaces on the faces of my comrades and their slightly twisting hand

movements. They were trying to signal a warning that standing right behind me was a warder! The latter must have concluded that I had lost my mind until he noticed the wire from the ear-phone leading into a pocket, which hid the small radio. In return for not being charged under the prison regulations, the warder accepted the radio as a gift, and he honoured an undertaking to keep us informed of all major developments on the cricket field.

By the end of July the interrogations were complete. We had previously taken a decision that none of us would answer any questions other than supplying our names and addresses. It did not require a great deal of courage to carry out such a decision. Interrogation procedure was astonishing by today's standards. It complied strictly with a set of imperatives laid down by the English courts and generally known as 'the judges' rules'. My own interrogation lasted a mere few minutes. The police officer in charge addressed me as 'Advocate Slovo', politely offered me a chair, enquired after my health (it struck me afterwards that I had technically broken my pledge by answering 'Fine, thank you'), and then went on to warn me that I was not obliged to say anything but anything I did say would be taken down in writing and might be used as evidence. They philosophically accepted my statement that I would in the circumstances refuse to answer any questions, and that was that. What a far cry from Ruth's '117 days'; in a mere three years the police brute became the judge, and his rules if they had been codified would have read: 'You are obliged to answer every question even if it incriminates you or those close to you and if you choose not to, we will torture you mentally and physically until we have broken you or killed you or forced you to kill yourself.'

But this nightmare was still to come. Clarice, my handsome sister-in-law, drove me back to Johannesburg on a day that heralded the beginning of spring. My senses were completely intoxicated by what seemed to be unending free space in all directions.

The move towards violence

I t did not take long for things to get back to 'normal', at least for the Party. Our District Committees and units began functioning with their full complements once again and the executive section of the Central Committee with headquarters in Johannesburg resumed their collaboration with the leadership of the ANC. There was perhaps no other period in our history when the Party played such a seminal role in the unfolding of the struggle as in the years between 1960 and 1963. The ANC had just been outlawed. Its structures as a mass organisation made it more difficult for it to swing into underground activity at the grassroots level. As happened when the Party was banned in 1950, its national leadership included inherited elements whose staying power in risky, illegal conditions had still to be tested.

It was becoming more and more clear that we were in for a long haul. While the sabotage campaign continued sporadically, the thought of the leadership began to turn to the next phase of the strategy, which was now irreversibly committed to revolutionary violence as the only remaining option.

By the end of April 1963 the High Command of MK prepared a document (code-named Operation Mayibuye) containing proposals for the stage-by-stage preparation for the launching of 'people's war'. The document, which opened with the words 'The time for small thinking is over', won broad general approval from the leaderships of the ANC and the SACP. But the pace and even the eventual feasibility of implementation would depend on the success or otherwise of numerous preliminary steps, not the least of which depended upon the readiness and capacity of newly independent Africa to provide the necessary assistance.

In brief, Operation Mayibuye spelt out the following objectives:

Hundreds of activists would leave the country to be trained in the techniques and art of organising and leading a guerrilla struggle. At the end of their training they would, with the help of some of the newly independent African states, return with the minimum necessary armed equipment to a widespread set of strategic areas which had already been selected. In the meantime a network of full-time organisers was to be appointed to prepare these areas both politically and organisationally, more especially to ensure a relatively speedy integration of the local populace into the armed struggle. All these organisational preparations would be accompanied by intensive national campaigns of mass mobilisation including a national anti-pass campaign. The precise timing of guerrilla action would depend on the implementation of all these preparatory steps.

I have attempted elsewhere (*South Africa: No Middle Road*) to discuss Operation Mayibuye, the complete frustration of its main purpose and the enemy reprisals which left the whole movement abysmally weak in the years that followed. Hindsight, that most infallible (and sometimes irritating) critic, will surely demonstrate how utterly unreal our expectations were. But the national underground leadership which met at the Rivonia headquarters to discuss the plan felt, by and large, that its objectives were obtainable. Not for the first time in the history of radical struggle did the optimism of will displace the pessimism of intelligence leading, at best, to an heroic failure.

But heroic failures (as long as we don't consciously plan for them and we learn not to repeat them) have their own way of contributing to ultimate success. It could even be said that absolute victory in a social war is more often than not the climax of a long series of defeats in the course of which the revolutionary steel is tempered. It is in that sense that the 1905 defeat in Tsarist Russia contributed to the victory of 1917.

This same thought struck home when I was in Cuba in 1977 as part of an ANC delegation led by Oliver Tambo. In Santiago de Cuba we were shown the Moncada Barracks (now a children's palace) and the farmhouse some 30 kilometres away where, in 1956, a small group of revolutionaries led by Fidel Castro assembled to launch a frontal assault on Moncada with an assortment of carbines. Like Rome's Appian Way, the route from the farmhouse to the barracks is today marked with monument after monument to the martyrs who fell in this attempt. When we eventually met Castro he was questioned by Tambo about this episode and he confided that if he had his life all over again, he would not have launched this assault on the barracks. Yet, his arrest and imprisonment and his famous 'History will Absolve Me' court speech provided a significant stimulus to the process which led to Batista's destruction some three years later.

And by what act was that achieved? One hundred and twelve men left Mexico in that rickety Granma and all except 12 (including Castro and Che Guevara) were either captured or killed. Within 18 months these 12 marched into Havana at the head of a 10 000 strong victorious guerrilla army. Can there be any doubt that if Batista's bullets had found 12 other targets, the landing would have been another heroic failure stimulating other Castros and Guevaras to find a better way?

The ANC, to its credit, had refused to dissolve itself when it was banned. But it had begun the phase of illegality with a national leadership elected during the legal period which (like the Party before it) included a sprinkling of personalities who could not be expected (personally or politically) to face the rigours of clandestinity. Even among the rest there were a few who were by persuasion locked irreversibly into the long tradition of non-violence.

Indeed, that grand old man of the ANC, Chief Albert Luthuli, whose presidential leadership had made immeasurable contributions to the radical struggle of the 1950s, was not a party to the decision, nor was he ever to endorse it. It was a measure of his greatness that despite his deep Christian commitment to non-violence, he never forbade or condemned the new path, blaming it on the regime's intransigence rather than on those who created MK.

In general, if the issue had been placed before the ANC leadership as a whole some of them would undoubtedly have rejected the steps which were already being planned. These steps required the utmost secrecy which would have been undermined by a more generalised debate. In addition, the ANC's underground life was barely a year old and the process of creating effective underground structures was still far from complete. It seemed likely that an open acknowledgement by the ANC that MK was its military wing would encourage a more concentrated enemy assault on structures which still needed more time to mature in the new conditions.

During this period the top working collective of the ANC was situated in Johannesburg and consisted of Kotane, Marks, Mandela, Sisulu, Nokwe and a few others. It was this body, together with the Central Committee of the Party, which took the plunge into the new phase of revolutionary violence. For the reasons already mentioned, both leaderships agreed that MK should have, no formal link with the two organisations and that for the time being it should project itself as an independent body acting in support of the aims of the liberation movement.

But whatever the public position might have been, the two organisations were in firm control. A High Command was appointed consisting, in the first place, of Mandela representing the ANC's working group in Johannesburg and me representing our Central Committee. We were asked to make recommendations on the rest of the High Command, and these were considered and decided upon by the ANC and Party leaderships. The High Command was then charged with the task of creating regional commands and MK units in all the urban centres.

For its part, the Central Committee had already made approaches to the Chinese Communist Party for facilities to train a batch of top-level cadres in the art of people's war. By September 1961 a group including Raymond Mhlaba, Andrew Mlangeni, Wilton Mkwayi, Joe Gqabi and Patrick Mtembu left the country illegally and spent six months training in China. On their return they became members of the High Command, which also, at different stages, co-opted Govan Mbeki, Walter Sisulu and Joe Modise. Regional commands were established in Johannesburg, Durban, Cape Town and Port Elizabeth. In all these urban centres the Party had well-functioning District Committees and underground units. The regional commands and sabotage units, which began to act in December 1961, contained a fair proportion of Party cadres.

In the months between August 1960 and December 1961 decisions were taken by the leadership of both movements that left an indelible stamp on the future course of the struggle; they also set the scene for the next major journey of my life. The first of these decisions concerned Nelson Mandela.

By a happy coincidence, Nelson's ban against attending gatherings had expired in time for him to be present and provide leadership for the All-in-African Conference which met in March 1961 in Pietermaritzburg to consider a response to the impending declaration of a republic on 31 May 1961. He was elected leader of a National Action Council which was mandated to campaign for a national convention and launch mass action in protest against yet another major constitutional transformation in which blacks had no say.

On 13 May 1961, on behalf of the National Action Council, Nelson Mandela made a public call for a protest national general strike from 29 to 31 May.

It was at this time that the first really fundamental break with the past came. The decision no longer sounds startling, but it pioneered a new approach to clandestine work. In order to prevent the authorities from immobilising Mandela by serving him with a renewed series of bans, he left home and led the campaign from an underground headquarters. But of even greater significance was the subsequent decision that he should not present himself to a police station for arrest and trial in connection with charges arising out of his leadership of the general strike. Quite an intense debate raged around this question at top levels of the movement.

Those who argued that he should give himself up were certainly not motivated by a belief in the sanctity of the racist laws: they were, rather, still prisoners of a well-tested tradition of struggle in which such tactics had played a positive mobilising role, particularly in the last few decades. It was argued that people had been conditioned to expect a leader not to 'run away' but to spit defiance at the ruling classes by contemptuously accepting its punishment. The motive was not self-flagellation; it was a tactic which had helped to inject a spirit of sacrifice into the struggle by emphasising that the leadership was also ready to accept the suffering involved.

But the very impact of the non-violent campaigns of the 1950s was clearly leading to a radical change of mood. In most of the rural areas in which the people took to struggle (Pondoland, Sekhukhuneland, Zeerust etc) organised violence was more and more in evidence. Despite the emergency, the Pondoland Rebellion was still alive towards the end of 1960, and more than one Pondo delegation visited ANC leaders to discuss, among other things, the supply of arms. Another indicator of the reluctance to follow old-style pacifist forms of struggle was the poor response to the PAC's March 1960 exhortation that the people should assemble at police stations to hand in their pass books and invite arrest. In Sobukwe's own area a mere handful responded. But what gave the most food for thought was the disappointing response to the call by Nelson for a general strike on 31 May 1961. The people were becoming less responsive to the type of demonstration that demanded of them the discipline of legalism and non-violence in contrast to the growing violence and ferocity of the state.

The decision that Mandela should become a fugitive, and henceforth live the life of a professional revolutionary, was a major watershed in our history. It pointed the way to a qualitatively different style of clandestine work and set the scene for the complete break with pacifism or 'legalism' which was made soon afterwards.

Nelson was fully aware of the implications of the decision for himself and for those close to him. The flourishing legal practice of Mandela and Tambo (Tambo had left the country in March 1960 by decision of the ANC leadership) was shut down as the senior partners had a fair proportion of the staff dispersed to their posts in the movement, both inside and outside the country. For me, one of the by-products of this decision was that Nelson and I were thrown together more than ever before. My affection and admiration for him grew. There was nothing flabby or condescending about Nelson. Ideologically he had taken giant strides since we confronted one another in the corridors of the University during the early 1950s on the role of the Party in the struggle. His keen intelligence taught him to grasp the class basis of national oppression. But the hurt of a life whose every waking moment was dominated by white arrogance left scars.

Long before this period I remember meeting him by chance outside His Majesty's Buildings in Eloff Street. We both spontaneously shook hands, and this simple gesture of brotherhood attracted scores of white eyes, some with a look of surprise, but most filled with venom. This incident remains stark in my memory after something like thirty years. Imagine the accumulation in his memory of a multitude of such humiliations! Mandela and Kotane, although their class origins were completely different, shared a national sensitivity whose sting was sometimes felt even by some of their closest non-African collaborators. But, at the end of the day, neither of them was dominated by purely national politics, and it was precisely their proud bearing as African patriots which attracted wide sympathy for their more basic class positions.

The intensive discussions on the 1961 Anti-Republic strike sharply posed the necessity to break with the old policy of non-violence and militant pacifism; this policy was attracting less and less response from the people and increasingly disenchanted the youth. The discussions led to the formation of Umkhonto we Sizwe which launched its campaign of sabotage on 16 December 1961. In the proclamation accompanying the opening shots of the campaign, MK announced it was an independent organisation acting in support of the national liberation movement as represented by the ANC and its allies.

The short accounts that have been published about the formation of MK have been drawn from the court speeches by Nelson Mandela and Bram Fischer in their respective trials. Understandably, the racist courtroom is not the most appropriate forum for establishing this kind of history, and some elaboration is required.

By June 1961 the Central Committee of our Party and the Johannesburg Working Group of the ANC had reached a consensus on the need for a military wing and to prepare for its initial phase of armed action. There were many tactical reasons why this military wing was to launch itself without any form of consultation with the Congress movement as a whole. The Congress movement consisted of the ANC, Coloured People's Congress, South African Indian Congress, Sactu and the Congress of Democrats. Apart from the ANC, these organisations were legal. To have opened a dialogue with them on the armed struggle would have threatened their legality and (in the light of their broadly based composition) would also have jeopardised the secrecy of the undertaking. Since it was impossible for the Congress Alliance to sponsor the move towards revolutionary violence, there remained only the two organisations which had been driven underground – the ANC and the SACP. Why, then, was it also considered necessary to avoid a public organisational link between MK and the latter two organisations? The answer is connected with the fact that the ANC had only relatively recently been driven underground and faced transition problems from legality to illegality.

The public posture of MK as an independent body was formally maintained until the end of 1962 when in a London speech Robert Resha referred to it as the military wing of the ANC. From later discussions with him I am convinced he did this in the genuine belief that the movement had by now abandoned the 'independent' posture. The sabotage campaign was being attributed to the ANC in the press and other media, and there were no disclaimers. Robert was part of the external team negotiating training facilities and other forms of help from African states for the armed struggle on the basis that the ANC's military wing was already on the go inside the country. He was also influenced by a desire to counter the PAC's stepped-up propaganda campaign which attempted to paint a picture of the ANC as a moderate and passive organisation. In any event, from the time Robert made his speech the true character of

MK became more and more known without any further formal declarations.

Although the important role which the Party played in the creation and building of MK was not generally known, the close collaboration between the ANC's working group and the Party's Central Committee ensured that the affairs of MK were controlled in a true spirit of fraternal partnership between the two organisations. After 1963, with the virtually complete destruction of internal leadership of both organisations, MK was to come almost exclusively under the direction of the ANC's external mission, and Party involvement in its affairs was negligible. Of course, leading Party members did play a prominent role in the ANC's external mission. But they were not (as was the case in the earlier period) part of a Party leadership collective.

The reasons for this *lacuna* in Party involvement in MK are twofold. It took a little while before an organised external Central Committee emerged, and until this happened there was no authoritative Party collective. Secondly, the main external base for many years after the post-1963 period was Tanzania. Influential sections of the newly independent country not only accepted the myth that the PAC was the more militant and more revolutionary movement, but they were also infected by narrow black nationalist ideology which made them suspicious of the ANC's traditions of non-racism and its links with a communist organisation. At this stage the setting-up of an organised Party leadership presence seemed to some, including a few leading Communists, a provocative measure.

The first phase of armed action in 1961 was a sabotage campaign directed against government installations. Instructions were issued to avoid attacks which would lead to injury or loss of life. No one believed that the tactic of sabotage could, on its own, lead to the collapse of the racist state. It was the first phase of 'controlled violence' designed to serve a number of purposes. It would be a graphic pointer to the need for carefully planned action rather than spontaneous or terrorist acts of retaliation which were already in evidence. (An example was the Poqo-type violence which had nothing in common with people's war.) And it would demonstrate that the responsibility for the slide towards bloody civil war lay squarely with the regime.

The point was strongly featured in the proclamation accompanying the first sabotage acts which expressed the hope that 'even at this late hour' the actions would awaken everyone to a sense of realisation of the disastrous situation to which the regime's policy was leading, and would bring the government and its supporters to their senses before it was too late and before matters reached the desperate stage of civil war. In addition, armed propaganda was designed to emphasise the break with the period of non-violent campaigning and to create an atmosphere in which young militants would be inspired to join underground combat units.

Theory apart, this venture into a new area of struggle found us ill-equipped at many levels. Among the lot of us we did not have a single pistol. No one we knew had ever engaged in urban sabotage with home-made explosives. Some of us had been in the army but, for all practical purposes, our knowledge of the techniques required for this early phase of the struggle was extremely rudimentary. The most experienced military man among us was Jack Hodgson, who was appointed to the Johannesburg regional command of MK. Unlike me, Jack had really been through the war – a veteran of the Abyssinian campaign and a 'desert rat' during the early stages of the North African war, he was demobilised for medical reasons. He returned to civilian life to become one of the full-time leaders of the ex-service organisation, the Springbok Legion.

I have learned not to assume that every person who puts on a communist garb is necessarily a dedicated revolutionary. But Jack certainly wore that garb with distinction. He expected neither position nor personal recognition in return for sacrifice. Jack and Rica's flat became our Johannesburg bomb factory. Sacks of permanganate of potash were bought and we spent days with pestles and mortars grinding this substance to a fine power. After 16 December most of our houses were raided in search of clues.

By a stroke of enormous luck the Hodgson flat was not among the targets. Had the police gone there they would have found that permanganate of potash permeated walls, curtains, carpets and every crevice. We had learned that this substance, more commonly used in washing lettuce, mixed with an aluminium powder and catalysed by a drop of acid, could make an effective explosion. For timing devices we had to experiment with various thicknesses of paper and cardboard to establish the time it took for the acid to eat through. The acid was placed in a small bottle whose outlet was covered by a specific thickness of paper or cardboard, and, just before placing the device in the target area, one had to turn the bottle upside down.

It was with this rather primitive device that I set out to burn the Johannesburg Drill Hall which had housed the preparatory examination of the Treason Trial. I had reconnoitred it carefully on more than one occasion and had chosen this spot which would have ignited not only the enormous wooden floor but also the hundreds of wooden chairs which covered it. But when the moment came I found that the military authorities had decided to have their monthly spring-clean. I entered the hall through a side door and found myself in the presence of about 50 black cleaners who were removing the chairs, polishing the floor etc. I wandered through the complex in an attempt to locate another suitable spot. It was past five in the afternoon and the administrative offices seemed empty of staff.

I chose an office with huge wooden cupboards, turned the acid bottle upside down and was about to place the carrier bag behind one of the cupboards when a clipped military voice came from behind me: 'Can I do anything for you, sir?' Although I feared it might be too late, I had prepared for this moment. I told him my brother had received call-up papers but was about to take an important exam, and could I be informed who I should see about a possible exemption. The sergeant major, who obviously had no inkling of my real intentions, politely asked me to follow him. I did so with racing pulse knowing that the acid in that small bottle had begun to eat away at the flimsy cardboard. Had our kitchen laboratory calculated the 15 minutes correctly?

Fortunately for both of us the officer dealing with exemptions had already left and I was politely advised to come back another day. I gave him a sweaty hand and walked briskly away. As soon as I decently could, I opened the tennis ball cylinder box which housed all the ingredients and snatched out the bottle. The three or four minutes which preceded this were perhaps the longest in my whole life. We were to discover the following day that Molefe, the first MK cadre to die in action, was killed in the vicinity of his target by a premature explosion which must have been caused by a defect in the acid bottle cover. Some hours after the Drill Hall incident I felt somewhat redeemed when, as part of a team of Jack Hodgson and Rusty Bernstein, we dealt successfully with a manhole on the Johannesburg/Pretoria road which housed the telephone cables between the two cities.

I don't know why luck should be called a lady, but (accepting her sex) she once again held me by the hand in early 1962. A message came from the Western Cape MK Regional Command for a supply of TNT. Jack Tarshish, who was involved in the sabotage campaign in Cape Town, sent up a certain Mr Goldstein, one of his business associates, to collect the supplies. Using a prearranged telephonic code, Mr Goldstein was contacted at the Victoria Hotel in Plein Street and an arrangement was made to deliver the parcel to the reception desk at an appointed hour. Since we had no previous knowledge of Mr Goldstein's reliability we took the normal precaution of avoiding personal contact by effecting the delivery many hours earlier than the appointed time.

That same night I attended an MK High Command meeting which discussed, among other things, a communication we had received from Govan Mbeki who had gone on a political mission to Cape Town. Govan's letter needed a very urgent response. Forgetting about the 'classroom' precautions which we had previously taken in regard to Mr Goldstein, we decided to use him as a courier for our reply. I was asked to see him and, very early the next morning, I set out for his hotel. On the way I had a tyre burst and no spare wheel. I made my way back to the house on foot to borrow Ruth's car but by the time I reached the hotel Mr Goldstein had already left for the airport.

Mr Goldstein was an agent for the security police. At the Cape Town airport Jack Tarshish walked right into the trap. He was tried and sentenced to 12 years imprisonment – the longest sentence that had, to date, been imposed on any movement activist. Explaining the relative severity of the sentence, the judge stated that Tarshish was endangering the lives of the aircraft's passengers by carrying TNT. TNT is a stable industrial product which can only be exploded by a detonator. In any case, as we discovered much later, this particular batch of TNT could not even have been exploded with a detonator; it was part of a larger doctored consignment which had been sold to us by a person who also happened to be a police agent. None of this would have saved me from joining Tarshish in the dock but for that fortuitous tyre blow-out. As for Mr Goldstein, soon after Jack's trial was over he ran off to Israel.

The first to be sent to jail for an act of sabotage was Ben Turok, secretary of the South African Congress of Democrats. On 16 December 1961 an incendiary device wrapped in a brown paper bag had been left in the drawer of a desk in the Native Divorce Court, then housed on the same block as the Rissik Street Post Office. The device was found by the police virtually intact; it had started burning but snuffed itself out by the lack of oxygen in the drawer. The scorched remains of the brown paper bag had on it a number of palm and finger prints whose identify could not immediately be traced.

Five months later Turok was among those arrested in a police swoop designed to interfere with mass demonstrations which were being planned for 31 May 1962 in protest against the celebrations of the first anniversary of the declaration of the Republic. The arrest gave the police a special bonus; they had now discovered that the prints found on the wrapping paper of the incendiary device coincided exactly with those taken from Turok when he was detained.

In the trial which followed before Mr Justice Simon Kuper, I acted as junior to Senior Counsel George Coleman, who later became an appeal court judge. Coleman did not share my special knowledge of the 16 December events. He was always convinced that, on the evidence, there should have been an acquittal. We could not dispute the evidence that the prints found on the wrapping paper (the only evidence offered by the state) were indeed Turok's. But certain factors emerged in the trial, which, at the very least, should not have led to the dismissal of Turok's version, under oath, as being false beyond any reasonable doubt.

Turok testified that the Congress of Democrats office in which he worked was frequented by numerous political activists, some of whom favoured the move towards violence. It was reasonably possible that a discarded paper packet (of the type normally provided when one purchases small quantities of stationery, paper bags etc.), could have been picked up in the office by the actual culprit. If Turok had previously handled the paper packet, the prints implanted would remain there virtually permanently (like a watermark) because paper absorbs the body salts which describe the fingerprint pattern. A substance known as ninhydrin is used to make this pattern visible even if the salts have been absorbed centuries ago. What added some credibility to Turok's hypothesis was the expert defence evidence that the distance between the palm prints and fingertip prints was such that they could not have been implanted while holding the tennis ball cylinder which housed the incendiary device; the juxtaposition of the two prints was more consistent with the possibility that they were placed there at an earlier time.

There was an element of poetic irony about the outcome of the trial. Turok was indeed guilty. At the same time the main ingredients of his defence were based on true facts. He wore gloves from the moment the device was delivered to him until he had deposited it at the target. At first, it seemed to me that the police had taken an educated guess as to who the culprit was and 'planted' the fingerprint evidence.

But what really happened was this. While Jack Hodgson was busy distributing the incendiary devices on 16 December one of them prematurely caught fire in his motor car. He managed to dispose of the offending device but the flames had already charred the outer wrappings of the others. When Turok received his own parcel, he naturally felt uneasy about the attention that its outer charred wrapping would attract on his journey to the target area. To avoid this he rewrapped the device in the old paper packet which he found in the boot of his car and which unfortunately bore his prints from a much earlier handling. Without these fortuitous interventions Turok's arraignment (and the consequent three-year jail sentence) would never have occurred. Seemingly, poetic justice sometimes visits the good as well as the evil.

My involvement in the Turok case was to have other consequences. A short while after Turok's appeal had been dismissed by the Appellate Division of the Supreme Court, Mr Justice Simon Kuper was shot dead by an assassin who fired at him through the window of his lounge. This event gave the 'dirty tricks' department of the Security Branch an early trial run in the series of campaigns of slander and misinformation about me. The rumour was spread that the killing was in revenge for Turok's conviction and that I had helped to organise it. Judge Kuper's daughter, a colleague of mine at the Bar and, like her father, a most warm and gentle person, stopped greeting me and would not join a common room table if I was seated there. Some years later when I was already in exile, the 'journalist' Gerard Ludi was used to spread the same innuendo about me in the press – an act all the more cowardly since bans imposed upon me prevented the press from publishing any response from me. Ludi had been an activist in the underground and was blackmailed into becoming a police nark after he had been arrested under the Immorality Act while fornicating with a black prostitute in the back of his car.

Unfortunately, one of the beneficiaries of the Turok trial was Bartholomew Hlapane. I was briefed to defend him on a charge of being in possession of Communist Party underground literature. He was stopped at a road block outside Soweto and a few hundred copies of the Sotho version of the party programme were discovered in a suitcase in his boot. His defence was that the suitcase belonged to a friend who had asked him to help transport it to Soweto. It sounded an unlikely story, particularly since he was unable to produce the 'friend', and a conviction seemed probable.

While arguing on Hlapane's behalf I was punctuating a point by fiddling with a few copies of the exhibit pamphlets in front of me. Suddenly I noticed something, the significance of which would have completely escaped me but for the Turok trial. Many of the pages of the exhibit pamphlets in my hand had a pink haze on their surfaces, a sign that the chemical ninhydrin had been applied to establish fingerprint identification. Since no fingerprint evidence was given I safely assumed that Hlapane's fingerprints were not found. I indignantly protested the impropriety of the prosecution's failure to lead evidence on the fingerprint tests which would have provided some corroboration of Hlapane's version. I invoked the well-established maxim that the prosecutor has a duty to place *all* the facts before the court, including those which favour the accused.

On an embarrassed admission by the prosecutor (after consulting with the officer-in-charge of the case) that the tests had been carried out but had indeed proved negative, the magistrate acquitted Hlapane without any further argument. Hlapane was later detained in the post-Rivonia swoops and became one of the most notorious police collaborators in the trials which took place in the 1960s and 1970s. He was one of the 'star' witnesses in the US Senate's Denton Committee in 1981 or thereabouts which investigated communist subversion in the South African liberation struggle. In 1983 he was executed for his treachery by a unit of Umkhonto we Sizwe. Had I not been made aware in the Turok trial of the ninhydrin method of uncovering fingerprints, it is a speculative possibility that Hlapane would have gone to jail in the first place and may not have made himself available as one of the best-known Mr Xs in numerous political trials.

The wish expressed in the MK manifesto that even at this late hour the government and its supporters would be brought to their senses before 'matters reach the desperate stage of civil war' fell on deaf ears. The regime responded with a series of laws which made sabotage a capital crime and gave the security services a free hand to detain without trial and engage in torture in the police cells – all this with no access to legal assistance and without scrutiny by the courts.

Release Mandela!

Nelson Mandela was arrested on 5 August 1962, at a specially prepared roadblock after he had addressed a number of clandestine meetings in Durban. It was a truly depressing moment. An enormous slice of our future plans depended upon his presence among us. In addition, the circumstances of his arrest had about them the smell of some Judas in our ranks whose identity could not be pinpointed.

Within a few days of the arrest a decision was taken that everything possible should be done to organise his escape. A commission which included Joe Modise, Harold Wolpe and me was given a full mandate to plan and carry out this task.

We spent session after session at the underground headquarters at Rivonia floating schemes, which, in varying degrees, bordered on the unreal and the fantastic. Could not the artist among us, Arthur Goldreich, make a plastic mask which would enable Mandela to change places with another prisoner who was being taken to court on some minor offence? Could we not take advantage of the blanketed emissaries from the Transkei Royal House who came in groups to the Fort to greet their royal cousin? The idea was that Mandela would surreptitiously cover himself in one of the visitor's blankets and walk out a free man as part of the group.

But we had to find a man who not only had the right kind of physical characteristics (here again the use of the plastic mask was argued for) but who was also brave enough to remain behind as a hostage. A big enough bribe at a high enough level might do the trick? But could we expect even corrupt white officialdom to become accomplices in the liberation of South Africa's most celebrated black revolutionary? The answer to this question was to emerge a little later. In the meanwhile we continued to exchange dreams.

In the end we opted for the following scheme: assuming the Fort to be impregnable, we turned our attention to the Johannesburg Magistrate's Court in which Nelson was due to appear. It sounded simple enough. Each day between 12.30 and 2.30 court proceedings are adjourned and the accused are taken down the steps leading from the dock into a basement where they are locked up in individual cells until the court resumes. Nelson must escape during one of these luncheon adjournments. But how? Stage by stage we grappled with the obstacles until, in the end, we knew we would make it!

It is now 12.45 pm and Nelson is seated on the concrete bunk in his basement cell. Joe Modise's ex-Sophiatown network extends right into the police force, and one of its members is in charge of the basement cells. He is prepared to leave Nelson's cell door unlocked, but that is not enough; during the lunch adjournment warder and prisoner cannot get out of the basement until the white custodian of the courtroom key unlocks the door leading from the basement to the dock.

The African interpreter in the very court which interests us happens to be a friendly man, embittered by his experiences of he way in which the white man's justice works. His name is Mzwai and Harold knows him well enough to risk an approach. We ask him about the vital key. He says 'No problem.' It appears that the clerk of the court leaves the key every day in the same drawer during the 11 am tea adjournment. 'I can pass it to you as long as it is back in place within a few minutes.' For the next week or two the desk in my chambers is covered with an endless variety of different types of plasticine and other modelling materials. We find just what we are looking for – a rather dense sculptor's modelling clay which hardens extremely fast when exposed to air. Back at the court

Mzwai is as good as his word. At five past eleven the key is in my hand. In the lavatory I make two impressions, and, within a few minutes, the clay becomes rock hard and the mould is ready. By the time clerk shouts 'Silence in the court' the key is back in its usual place.

Issy Rosenberg owns an engineering works in Ophirton. He is pleased with the mould and the key is safely cast by him personally on a Sunday. A few days later Mzwai arrives at my office beaming; he has tested the key and, as he puts it, 'it's open sesame'. On our drawing board Nelson is now out of his basement cell and, with the key, enters the deserted courtroom. But there is yet another problem! The external doors of the complex which houses all the courtrooms are apparently kept locked during the adjournment. Joe Modise locks himself into a lavatory and spends more than one lunch hour carrying out reconnaissance. He finds a door, abutting on the lane used by supply trucks, which is open and unguarded. He tests the position by making a few safe exits. The rest is easy: a getaway car and, in our minds' eye, Nelson is back at Rivonia within 30 minutes.

But what about Nelson's face which would be recognised by any one of the hundreds of people who fill the streets and pavements outside the court building (including many policemen and court employees)? They would surely raise an alarm long before he reached the getaway car. We begin to work on a disguise.

Over dinner at the Delmonica restaurant in Commissioner Street, Cecil Williams, a Party member and full-time theatre director, introduces me to a professional wigmaker with radical social attitudes. He agrees to make, free of charge, an Indian-looking wig, moustache and beard for a subject whose identity is never discussed. 'A stage job is easy,' he says. 'The footlights and make-up hide glaring defects in the material and the fit.' He has a stock of passable straight black hair but he needs very precise measurements. He is obviously a perfectionist and, through Cecil Williams, I receive a list of intimidating length – the distances between the top lip and the bottom of the nose, and the bottom lip and the tip of the chin, the length of the mouth when in repose, the distance from a central point of the bottom of the chin curling round the shape of the face to the ear, the circumference of the head just above the ears and so on and so forth.

We face the formidable task of measuring a man under police custody in the Johannesburg Fort. The solution we arrive at clearly would not have the approval of the ethics committee of the Johannesburg Bar Council. I am given the task, as Mandela's legal representative, to carry out this mission in the course of my almost daily consultations with him in the jail's interview room.

The interview room is about seven metres square and is completely bare except for a large table and two chairs. At the open door a prison warder holds vigil to prevent the passing of unauthorised items to the prisoner. Nelson sits with his back to the door and I sit opposite him facing the warder. I ask the warder to close the door because I am not prepared to interview the accused within earshot. When he gives me an expected refusal I tell him that, in the circumstances, I shall conduct the interview in writing. He shrugs and the operation begins.

I convey my intentions to Nelson in writing and I pass him a length of cotton. He carefully measures the first position, breaks off the cotton and passes it back to me. I stick the piece with sellotape into an exercise book and record next to it what part of the head or face it has measured. We have to do this slowly and without ostentation, and I spend countless interviews trying to complete the process. In the case of some parts, such as the circumference of the head, the odd nature of the manoeuvre involved may just alert the warder that something is happening outside the normal routine of a lawyer-client relationship. Nelson therefore takes some cotton and carries out some of the measurements in the privacy of his cell. After some weeks the measurements are now complete and over another Wiener Schnitzel at the Delmonica I deliver the cotton book to our friend.

The finished product together with some specially prepared adhesive for the skin is returned to me by Cecil Williams. That night the escape committee is meeting to hear a progress report, and Joe Modise and I decide to have a bit of fun. I report that Joe has been held up and will be a little late. While we are sitting there a completely strange Indian with a well-groomed beard and moustache throws open the door and stares at us. A panic scatter movement by all because it looks like the beginning of a police raid, but Joe relieves the tension immediately with his loud, distinctive laugh and the removal of the wig. If it works so well for someone who has not been measured, Nelson's safe passage to the get-away car seems assured.

The only remaining problem is to find a way of delivering the disguise items and the key to Nelson for safe-keeping until D-Day. The plan for this is finalised after Joe Modise sees Winnie. The way in which an accused presents himself in court is of some importance and a well-groomed suit with a matching quiet tie is usually a good start. An ANC tailor in Soweto expertly inserts the items in the shoulder padding of Nelson's best court suit and he receives it without incident. Nothing more to do except nervously wait out the two weeks which are left for Nelson's court appearance.

But something else is in the wind, the precise meaning of which is yet unclear. It is a Sunday morning and I receive a telephone call from Attorney Bearman who has an office in Chancellor House, the same building in which the firm of Mandela and Tambo use to conduct their legal practice. He has a message from one of his clients who is awaiting trial on a charge of fraud that the officer in command of the Fort would like to see me urgently at his official residence adjacent to the jail. This is an extraordinary request. Has something gone wrong? Am I being trapped? I rush over to Bram Fischer to discuss what my response should be. We both speculate that had there been a leak it would by now have become a police matter. There is no way of guessing what it is about and we decide I should go.

I ring the Colonel from a public phone, and at the arranged time he is waiting for me on the large *stoep* of his colonial-style residence. I carry a briefcase containing a cassette machine with the record button already depressed. He gestures towards his front door, but I tell him I prefer the garden. He agrees.

'I will be brief,' he begins. 'I take it you people are interested in freeing Mandela?'

I wonder whether he notices the shock waves which pass through me as I mutter the time-gaining stop-gap. 'What do you mean?'

He comes straight to the point. He explains that because of his outspoken support for the opposition United Party he has no hope of further advancement in the prison service. In any case he has had enough of it and would like to opt for early retirement. His mind has turned to small farming: he needs open space after spending the better part of his working life locked up with his prisoners. 'For £7 000 you can have Mandela,' he says.

If this is a trap to implicate me in a corruption charge I must at least have the advantage of the right kind of tape-recorded answer. I tell him that, as an officer of the Supreme Court, I can hardly make myself a party to such a scheme and that in any case, I have every confidence that my client will be acquitted at the end of his trial. He is shrewd enough to suspect the real motive behind my immediate response and asks me, anyway, to give it some thought and to have a cup of tea with him on my next visit to the Fort. The first opportunity I have of replaying the recording is in my motor car, and to my extreme disappointment hardly a word is audible!

That night we discuss and discuss. There is no way we can be certain that the offer is genuine. We are very tempted to follow it up even though the other scheme on which we have been working for months seems poised for success. The political impact of an escape and Nelson's return to the underground are very weighty factors. As to whether the Colonel can be trusted, there is no outside evidence and, since I have been the sole contact, much depends on my own assessments. My impressions during the interview incline me to believe that the Colonel is in honest search of a dirty penny. We decide to go ahead with the negotiations.

Seven thousand pounds is a goodly proportion of our total resources and we can't risk losing it through any double-dealing colonel. We also continue to lean primarily on the main scheme. I arrange another meeting with the Colonel, this time in a pub in Hillbrow. I tell him that my client's friends are ready to go ahead subject to two conditions. They are not prepared to hand over any portion of the money until Nelson is safely in their hands. And, since there is a chance (which we know does not exist) that Nelson might be acquitted, the go-ahead for the plan will be given only when such an outcome appeares unlikely. In case we pull off the original plan, we are forced to play for time and money.

He is not so happy about the conditions and raises the question of a down payment as a gesture of good faith. I tell him this may be possible at the stage when I give him the green light. This kind of arrangement, I say, depends solely on mutual trust; without it both of us will be in deep trouble. We agree to leave it at that.

The crucial day is approaching and excitement about the trial mounts. Leaflets are pouring out calling for solidarity demonstrations with Mandela, posters and stickers start appearing on walls and buildings, 'Release Mandela' slogans are chalked or painted over a wide area. In the escape committee we all inexplicably feel uneasy about the rising momentum of the campaign; we speculate whether police preparations against possible demonstrations will lead to measures in and around the court building which will frustrate our project. But there is no way even of hinting to the local political levels that they should tone down on what has become the most important issue of the day.

Two days before Nelson is due to appear in court I journey to the Fort for another lawyer-client consultation with him. I write out the usual requisition for the prisoner and wait in an interview room. A few minutes later the warder returns: 'Sorry, sir, the prisoner is no longer here. They took him to Pretoria where he will be tried.'

I ask to see the Colonel and he receives me. He wonders, as I do, whether there has been a leak. I assure him that if there has, it could only have been from me.

He says: 'Well, they pipped us at the post,' and I cannot help responding: 'In more ways than one, Colonel.'

Part 2

Reflections

Introduction

I n July 1991, Joe was diagnosed as having multiple myeloma, bone marrow cancer. He was quite lucky in getting an early diagnosis. In June he was sitting late in his ANC office in Sauer Street, Johannesburg, giving an interview to a French journalist. One of the topics they discussed was the security of the ANC building. Lo and behold, when they tried to leave the building they found they had been locked in on their floor. Joe attempted to climb out through the louvres over the door before someone came to their rescue. In the following weeks he complained of a sore chest and wondered if he had done himself an injury. X-rays indicated there were no cracked ribs but the pains continued. Joe also experienced an unusual level of fatigue and his doctor decided that a series of check-up tests should be undertaken; the diagnosis of bone marrow cancer was proffered.

The first months were rough going. It is a disease which, when it takes a grip, often gallops towards a speedy end. The average prognosis is two years, but with significant variability – one French politician worked with this condition for 13 years. Other people, however, only first discover that they have the cancer when their kidneys pack up, which is usually quite close to the end. But after half a dozen shaky months, Joe seemed to turn around and begin to respond to the tandem treatment of chemotherapy and homeopathy. He got back into the full swing of work and enjoyed another fruitful three years before the beginning of the real crunch in August 1994.

In 1991, Joe got one spate of personal letters, and then another in the last six months. Of course there were letters from lifelong friends, but others were well-wishing letters from strangers. Some were from Christians who begged him to see the light, that there was still a chance to save his soul and redeem himself from an otherwise useless life. Others simply and generously said they were praying from him even if he was not himself a Christian.

There were also dozens and dozens of caring phone calls, whether from Graca Machel in Maputo, 'I want you and Joe to know that I and the people of Mozambique are thinking of you at this time', or the many male political friends and colleagues who were more typically inhibited in their putting pen to paper.

I have chosen very few letters to be included here, in what I have called *Prologue to Dying*. For the most part, they tell something of the personal, to complement the portrait of his life that the autobiographical chapters present. I have also included the short address that Madiba, President Nelson Mandela, gave at Bloemfontein, at the 49th ANC National Congress, informing Joe of the decision of the National Executive to confer on him the *Isithwalandwe Seaparankoe* Award. Lionel Abrahams's poem, 'At Revolution's End', which opens this section, poignantly identifies Joe's need to find harmony to approach his imminent death. The piece by Philip van Niekerk is based on the last interviews Joe gave and includes some of Joe's last retrospective comments. The swan-song of the section is the SACP collage of some of Joe's best pithy statements in recent years.

The funeral was a massive affair, and the atmosphere is well captured in the piece written by Mark Gevisser. There were many speakers: Mandela presented a comprehensive biographical sketch complemented by John Gomomo, Jeremy Cronin and Barney Pityana. But the speech which astonished the crowd was that of Chief Rabbi Cyril Harris; it is included here. The family speech is also printed here. It is customary for a male family member to speak at the graveside, but for the remaining family of strong women – wife, daughters, step-daughters, grand-daughter, sister and nieces – that custom seemed questionable, and we asked that our request to break tradition should be accepted.

When the deceased is such a public person, public property so to speak, it is difficult to find some private space for family and friends to share their intimacy of bereavement. My daughters, Tessa and Kyla, suggested a small private gathering of Joe's closest friends and family members; Kyla's idea of 'small' was a group of about 30 people! In the end we were helped to organise an event at the Johannesburg City Hall, which had figured so largely in Joe's early political history and again at the end of his life when we were concert subscribers. This was the secular place Joe would have liked to have had for his funeral but which was rejected because of size and security concerns.

Each member of the family was asked who they would like to have with us for the evening; immediate family, Joe's close friends as well as comrades and colleagues with whom we knew Joe shared an affectionate relationship. The idea was to be both inclusive and exclusive. We failed in some instances (we know of at least one terrible oversight) but, under enormous strain, we tried! The evening was wonderful. As Alexei Makarov has written, 'The farewell party made a very strong impression on me, something I never experienced before. It was not funereal but rather a party of friends, people who knew him well, who could sit together and talk. The atmosphere was so friendly, almost family-like and relaxed, as if Joe was amongst us and had just left the room and would be back in a minute.' Cyril, Barney, Harold and Alexei made major speeches; Pallo told two of Joe's best jokes, his (Pallo's) own favourite and mine. Many people got up spontaneously to speak but the contributions were interspersed with two of Joe's favourite pieces of classical music, the sombre but magnificent Beethoven's *Eroica*, a moving rendering of Mahler's Symphony No 5, *Adagietto*, and on the lighter side some folk-songs which we had so often sung together on car journeys, *I gave my love a cherry*, *This land belongs to you and me*, and *This train is bound for glory*.

We also received more than one thousand letters after Joe's death, several poems, and hundreds of people signed condolence books, not only at home but in South African embassies and trade missions all over the world. Many of the letters were from friends, but others were from strangers from all races and walks of life and across the political spectrum. Some of Joe's erstwhile foes paid their respects, Pik Botha, Abe Williams and Mangosuthu Buthelezi. Many letters were from communist parties and symbolised the internationalist aspect of Joe's life. I have chosen just a few international tributes. For the rest, it is difficult to make a choice. My guide has been to include the merest few, wherein the writer reflected on some aspect of Joe's life, how it touched them and others, or some anecdote which adds to building up an overall personal portrait.

To conclude the book it was suggested that I contribute the letter written to friends as an epilogue. I had written this over the days immediately following Joe's death. His dying was so intensely private; so many friends respected Joe's wish not to have visitors whilst very much wanting to express their caring and having a sense of what was happening. I felt for their exclusion, but afterwards found that I did not feel talkative; putting something to paper seemed to be my answer. I did not expect to share this letter beyond a more immediate circle of friends, but months later, I have found that there is some healing of the rawness of feeling which makes the wider sharing acceptable.

Helena Dolny
August 1995

Prologue to Dying

At Revolution's End

The mild-eyed white-haired wedding guest
carries behind spectacles and pallor
huge secrets of fragility and power.
Astute, patient strategist of an apocalypse,
he is at last a Cabinet Minister
in the achieved glorious government, at last is tasked to build,
but has to formulate a policy
to meet approaching death.

I know about him more perhaps than most
(more than he guesses) yet not enough
of his dangerous history – what sacrifices
might his perfect purpose justify? –
to share the certainty of those who love,
or those who fear and hate him.
Besides who-knows-how-many deep debates
and plots, his serial of missions under cover,
specified bullets and labelled bombs,
he has survived the great dialectical disappointment:
retaining his visionary certainty,
the Jewish atheist (dreamer or schemer)
has claimed an armed judgemental Jesus Christ
as warrior in his People's war.

What – in our skin or genes, schemes
for survival, teachers' creeds,
the streets we've lived in, scars
of the years, secrets of the couch –
elects the rhetoric that direct
and rouse our different heart?
This politician's passion of faith
shifts and hammers history's mass,
and sends down states, while mine
dictates the fall of syllables.
We could be neighbours, brothers,

but the poems we each can hear
are hieroglyphic to the other.

He has been sitting at his table
remote at the core of a silence
which even his magnificent daughters
seem reluctant to breach.
A white shadow covers him,
a cold flame slowly consumes
his material life.

He rises and walks in my direction.
I'm holding my table with a boastful anecdote,
and when his eye catches mine and he asks,
with a curious urgency, 'Are you
saying something to me?' I wave him
aside. He swerves away, and I slowly
grow to know that now
when his is weakest and strongest
something might have been spoken.

Lionel Abrahams

The ANC's highest honour

Nelson Mandela presented Joe Slovo with the ANC's
Isithwalandwe Seaparankoe award at the organisation's
49th National Congress in Bloemfontein on
16 December 1994.

Comrade Joe Slovo,

Your militant and unswerving commitment to the ANC embodies many
values which we wish to honour today.

There are some people who, by pursuing their own convictions and
without being self-conscious about it, touch the lives of millions of others. Such has been your life.

I am not sure, comrade Joe, it you ever thought of yourself as a white
South African. Nevertheless, the fact remains that your decades of activism have served as an outstanding example for hundreds and thousands
of activists coming into our ranks, and indeed for millions of other South
Africans. In a country in which there is a racially oppressed majority,
non-racism is not an outlook that can be simply taken for granted. You
have contributed immensely, through your personal example, to nurturing
that outlook which is so evident in our ranks and, increasingly, in our
country today. Let those politicians who have based themselves on narrow ethnic constituencies, supposedly to safeguard minority interests, now
ponder on your example.

Comrade Joe, you also symbolise and personify the alliance of the
ANC and the SACP. It is an alliance whose durability continues to bewilder our opponents. They fail to understand its deep historical roots
and its ongoing practical relevance. In your recent capacity as Minister of
Housing, I believe that you are underlining what that alliance is all about.
It is about a common commitment to overcoming, as the absolute priority, the terrible legacy of national oppression. It is an alliance based on
serving the social needs of our people.

Your contributions to our struggle are many. But it is, I think, especially as a strategic thinker that you are held most dear by so many in our
ranks. You have played a role, often a central role, in most of the out-

176

standing strategic documents of our struggle. In the decades of exile I know that yours was a crucial role in the regrouping and consolidation of Umkhonto we Sizwe.

You have always been able to respond practically and dynamically to changing circumstances. You have had the courage of your convictions, spelling out the implications of new situations which sometimes we, as a movement, have found hard to admit. I think, most recently, of your contributions to analysing the complex negotiations process.

We are extremely fortunate to have within our ranks such an outstanding revolutionary, who has combined a rigorous mind with attention to practical organisational work. It is with a sense of real pride and emotion that I announce today the decision of the National Executive to confer upon you, comrade Joe Slovo, the *Isithwalandwe Seaparankoe* Award.

President Nelson Mandela

Letters

A letter from Ymile Kennedy, one of the many Joe
received from South African Christians

Upington, 18 November 1994
His honourary Mr Slovo,

It has been nearly one and a half years that I have been praying for you.
Yes, I know it sounds really stupid to think that a devoted Christian lady
is praying for a staunch Communist Minister ... spending more time on
prayer for him than anybody else, except my own family. These things
do work strange! Through this letter I'm not trying to impress you with
my devotion to Jesus Christ, but really to tell you that I care for you. The
moment Johan Heyns [a clergyman assassinated by a right-winger in
1994] set foot in our home here in Upington last year we decided that we
will spend special time to pray for Mr Slovo! Now that my dear friend,
Johan, is not there any more, I thought it necessary to let you know how
this man cared for you – he always kept me up to date with your health. I
also know that in Pretoria, where Johan had a special Bible study group,
they also prayed very specially for you Mr Slovo.

I want to tell you that we love you, because Jesus that lives in us, also
loves you and also died for you on the cross. He planted that love in my
heart for you – every time I see you on TV and in the papers I just know
that Jesus loves you – and he cares for you. He knows about your suffering and He would like to stand by you, but it is you and you alone that
has to choose to follow Him or not. Mr Slovo, trust me – He is real!...

Mr Slovo, Johan is with this God of ours at the moment, but I'm still
here to let you know Jesus loves you and is still interested in you – I
want to assure you, that even if you don't understand it, I'll keep on
praying for you till you or I have left this world! Please let me know if
ever you come to a point where you would like me to pray specifically
for something special.

May my God bless you, and our family on the enclosed Xmas card
are praying for you to come to meet the one and only living God we
serve and love. He is so real!

Love in Christ Jesus,
Ymile Kennedy (Mrs)

PS. We stay in Upington – my husband is an export grape farmer, and I used to be a ballet and art teacher, but at the moment spend most of my time assisting my husband on the farm. We have three lovely daughters – enough of us for the time!

Extracts from Bridget's letters

Bridget O'Laughlin became a friend and colleague of mine in Mozambique when I was a junior staff member at the Centre of African Studies. But of greater relevance is that she was, at the time of Ruth First's death, very close to her and very much part of Joe and Ruth's social life. Bridget, along with Pallo Jordan and Aquino de Braganza, was also injured in the bomb blast which claimed Ruth's life. While recovering in hospital she learned she was pregnant; her baby girl was named after Ruth. In the subsequent years she remained close to both of us. Her choice of how to deal with the problem of our being thousands of miles apart, while Joe approached death, was through writing conversational letters.

22 September 1994
Dear Joe,

I wanted you to know how much I appreciated your coming to Brussels, and above all sitting through that dinner to be with us all. Only that will of yours could have kept such fatigue under control. You were very generous.

I also realised that conversations will be difficult for you, and even more so attempts at telephone conversation, so I've decided to write you a letter from time to time as a sort of alternative visit. Don't worry, I don't expect you to answer ...

This is a light teaching term for me, so I hope to get quite a lot done on my book on agrarian policy in Mozambique. It's dedicated to Ruth, so when I finish it, expect it to be good, and I will finish it. I am now working on an introduction, having finished the sections on the shaping of colonial agrarian society. Too much thus far revolves around the political basis of Frelimo policy and the nature of socialism in Africa ...

In part I'm still trying to work out a satisfactory response to what you said in a conversation we had on the beach in Cape Town (which I'm sure you have forgotten, but which is still bothering me). Anyway I've actually gone as far as to read seriously some of the post-modernist stuff on the African state – there is some good writing, and 'thick description' as the anthropological guru behind some of this would say ...

30 October 1994
Dear Joe,

Marc brought back photos from your garden and you looked a lot better than in Brussels, your face returning back to poking fun at the world and destiny. I was relieved.

Our conversation on the beach was about Frelimo's suppression of civil society. I cannot (and do not want to try) to reproduce our positions, but I thought you had an excessively spontaneous vision of civil society. We have a clear (if not very effective in the US) vision of how a communist party should work to shape civil society in a pre-revolutionary context, but what does it do when it holds power? This is perhaps an anachronistic question, but anyway ... I don't agree that all mass organisations should be subordinated to the party, but in a revolutionary process all histories are not equal. The catholic church had a strong rural base in Mozambique, particularly in Zambezia and Tete; it also had an extremely powerful and conservative hierarchy contesting for power at a national level.

1 November 1994
Dear Helena,

Thanks for the photographs. It was a relief to talk to Marc and also to see the later photographs. What scared me in Brussels was not so much the exhaustion in Joe's body, but the fear in his face – which I have never seen before. Getting yourselves into a better point of equilibrium is a mammoth achievement. I'm not being romantic about future prospects of the weight of the process though ...

21 December 1994
Dear Helena and Joe,

I could try and use all of this technology we now have access to and design a computer greeting card … Actually I did all my work more quickly pre-Windows and the fancy programmes with the 100 000 options … But after saying that, I should add that we have now been joined up, or at least the computer in the documentation centre has, to the internal ISS system and they have been receiving the *Weekly Mail* by E-mail. So, I have been able to follow events in South Africa again. First I skim and then I run searches on Slovo, housing, land and agriculture to see if I missed anything. But oh how I still miss the feel of paper in my hand, the way words jump off the page with a real newspaper, reading the banalities, which I'm not willing to do on a computer screen …

I went to a conference on land reform in Southern Africa which had two Cape Town land lawyers in attendance. I learned quite a bit, but it made me wonder again about the importance of judicial systems in your transition process. If the ANC had not had so many competent lawyers, would you have tolerated the complexity of legal language in asking fundamental questions? Is there really protection for people's interests in all this litigation?

I heard that you broke your arm, Joe. I suppose that means that your bones are brittle and that you must take care. I hope it is not too great a hindrance to your work, and that the pain is controllable. I'll phone sometimes soon just to hear your voices. I miss you.

27 December 1994
Dear Joe,

It's a wonderful wailing day of gales, like in Cape Town, where the water can get dumped on you from below as well as from above. The Dutch are disappointed because there was a spell of freezing weather over Christmas, and they had hoped to skate on the canals – this rain ruins that dream …

I woke thinking about that time we went to Santa Caroline, the only true and beautiful tropical island that I've been on (or likely to visit). I can recapture the feeling of the sun and sand and sea and colours at the edge of dreams, but when awake what comes through are the rather awful, but funny moments. There was the man who came up to us when we took a break at Quissico (you were smoking a cigar) and said 'hello *baas*' to you. There was Ruth abandoning herself to total bad humour and her headache when the sea becalmed. I can still see her scowl as she tried to shelter

181

under the edge of the boat. And there was real hardness in your voice when you looked more closely at the tyres after we discovered the puncture and said,'You were trying to kill me' (not us). I think that was the only time I ever saw the look of a guilty child on Ruth's face, but she still summoned up the courage to say, 'They wouldn't look like that if you didn't drive so fast.'

Well, enough of this meandering. I think you know it's just a way of telling you that I care about you and miss you, including some of your jokes. Helena's told me you are now drawing in quickly toward your centre. You've given us all so much energy from that centre. You always will.

3 January 1995
Dear Joe and Helena,

The pages that follow are a copy of a letter that Nuno wrote to *Noticias*. It is a little long, but has some wonderful lines in it. Don't worry, Joe, I don't expect you to get together the remnants of your Portuguese; the lines are good even in translation. I just thought that it illustrated one of the gifts that you've bequeathed to the communists of Southern Africa – that recognition that conviction and wit are not incompatible ...

This year we hung, near the top of the tree, the crystal you gave me years ago, Helena, from Zimbabwe I think. I usually keep it packed away in a box with other jewellery. I'm glad I thought of this use. It reflects everything beautifully – sun, artificial Christmas lights, tinsel – and it made me think of all of you.

The problem for us all is how to find a way from this great distance to give you the support of our love without sharpening the pain. Even if we were the masters of words, it wouldn't be enough. I would like you both to be able to feel physically the support that comes from moving linked in rhythm and affection. The secret of your guitar.

The following is a selection of letters received in the days
prior to Joe's death wherein each person finds their own
way to let go.

24 December 1994: From Gill and Isky, London-based friends
Dear Joe,

I cried on the phone, along with Helena, hearing that this may be the
beginning of the end. Isky and I both had a strong urge to say goodbye,
and so this is our farewell message. To say thanks for the friendship and
fun, jokes and red socks along with the serious business. My mind is
awash with memories ... two special ones: your teaching me that there
are no indiscreet questions, but only indiscreet answers; and the deep joy
you brought to my special friend Helena.

We hope you know how much you are admired for the part you played
in the transformation of South Africa. Others will continue what you started
even if they cannot take your place.

My thoughts are with you all – Helena, Shawn, Gillian, Robyn, Tessa
and Kyla.
    Gill

I have composed this letter many times in my head, yet when it comes to
writing something down, I seem to stare at the keyboard with a blank
mind. You may well add that my mind is blank most of the time! Your
humour was always good and refreshing. In some dark times you somehow managed to find a different way of seeing things and the ability to
find a reason to smile was wonderful.

Even though your life is an example of someone who has taken the
world very seriously, nevertheless you have managed to combine that with
a very humorous approach, a mixture which I and many others found both
charming and somehow made you approachable.
    Isky

We'll always be there for Helena – Go in peace, friend.
    Gill and Isky

27 December 1994: From Claire, a comrade-friend from Lusaka
My very dear Helena,

Gonda just phoned me ... I am thinking of you. I am thinking of him. For both of you, so hard a time that no word can smoothen reality. I try to imagine how he must feel after having taken this decision, and how one can understand and feel with him. Decide: enough is enough, I rounded up my life. A doer who accepts to wait ... and retain his dignity and his intrinsic courage. Sometimes, I wish he would know the deep meaning he has in my life, the symbol of humanity he has always been and will always be for me. It should be comforting to him to recognise the decisive imprint he leaves on so many people who had the honour to come close to him. So much of the unspoken ...

Why do I write you, not him, all this? I don't believe that he would care, now, about what people who have been at the margin of his life, do think and feel about him. You are the one suffering and remaining, and you understand and share. You have to prepare yourself to lose so much more ... another dimension. It is so difficult to prepare oneself, to be prepared ... One believes one is so far, one has gone far enough in preparing oneself ... how much courage has one yet to have? Remembrance will help, when you will have time for yourself. But now, you only know what you can still give to him, with your personality and your courage ...

your friend, Claire.

27 December 1994: From Audrey Coleman
Dearest Joe,

I am sitting on my bed looking out at the grey but tranquil sea, the lagoon at low tide, and the mountains shadowed by a sky mottled by grey and white clouds, with occasional patches of blue. You know how tranquil the scene is. All the quiet, people blissfully enjoying their siestas. It has rained the past four days but at noon it stopped and the sun is struggling through.

After speaking to Helena I pondered as to whether I should get on a plane to come for a day to see you, but decided that the less pressure and visitors at this time the better it will be for you and to rather write this note.

I have only known you for a few years, but having had the privilege of having you in my house on your return from exile I had the opportunity to get to know you well. You are very important to me. Thinking back on our relationship I realise I found it very easy to criticise and argue with you but not easy to verbalise my intense admiration, despite your bad habits of smoking, breaking things, eg my ashtray and chipping the bath etc!!!

I admire your integrity, maturity and courage. You gave your life willingly to the struggle but your contribution in these last years has been the most valuable. Your mooting the sunset clause and handling of the housing portfolio are only two major outstanding ones. The transition occurred peacefully maybe because of the sunset clause despite all the criticism including mine. You stuck to your guns.

I was so pleased you were appropriately honoured at [the ANC] Conference. Your going will create a tremendous vacuum, difficult to fill. The likes of myself will come and go without leaving a ripple but you my dear Joe will live on in our hearts and will be recorded in history ...

Goodbye my dear.

All the Coleman family hold you in the highest esteem and join me in this letter of farewell.

With our love,
Audrey, Max and the family

30 December 1994: From Nadine Gordimer
Dear Joe,

When I came back from a two and a half months' stint at Harvard I was delighted to hear that you had been given the great Award. No-one could merit it more than you; I am sure it gives you such pleasure, as the idea that it has come to you gives us – all the people who admire your wonderful transformation from leader in the liberation battlefields to Minister of Housing; and fulfilling the latter post superbly, into the bargain. As I told people in the USA who asked about your present activities, you're the man who knows how, and when the time demands it, to beat AK-47s into bricks and mortar!

The award is the only one worth receiving in our country, of course, perhaps with the exception of the one we kids used to learn about in school, the Wolraad Woltemade (was it called) which I seem to remember as originating in the politically clear feat of a man plunging into the waves on horseback to rescue someone. The other apartheid equivalents of the Iron Cross should, indeed, be melted down: we might think of instituting some new ones.

Reinhold and I send our warmest congratulations. You're the comrade, in all senses of the word, of all South Africans, whether they recognise this or not. Our man for all seasons.
Love, Nadine

*5 January 1995: From Gonda Perez, a close friend
from the days in Lusaka*
Dear Joe,

This is a short note to say thank you ... Thank you for the joy you
brought into our lives – this brings back memories of Lusaka parties
(your 60th was the best one), memories of red socks peeping out of a
serious suit and crystal wine glasses flying as you try to make a point ...
Thank you too for all I learnt from you ... you didn't mind stupid questions and patiently explained things. Thank you for development, friendship
... the list gets longer.

There have been times I've been angry at you, fortunately by the time
we met I've gotten over it (sunset clauses come to mind). You were
probably right ... we might not have been where we are today without it.

Lots of love
Gonda

*2 January 1995: From David Goldblatt, who although not a friend,
shares his insight of Joe during the negotiations process*
Dear Joe,

May I take the liberty of telling you that I admire you greatly for what
you have done in the past years in the negotiations and then in government, for all of us, your fellow South Africans?

... I got an inkling of the magnitude of your effort when I spent from
3 pm until about 1.30 am at the World Trade Centre one day, while
waiting to photograph Cyril and Roelf. Whenever the parties were not in
session you were sitting at a table in the ANC office reading documents
and making notes. I watched you. The strain showed – you had been at it
since 9 am I was told – but you kept on, seemingly inexhaustible, never
losing what I can only describe as a sort of – forgive the term – benign
quietude.

What can one say to an old communist? I can only think of that old
movement song, 'Harry Pollett was a Bolshie, one of Lenin's lads ...'
and say with certainty, you will not be 'brought up for trial before the
Holy Ghost, for spreading disaffection among the Heavenly Host ...' Your
place among the angels who have transcended all parties is assured!

David

Prologue to Dying

From Marge Urban, who shared the exile trek with us from Maputo to Lusaka to Johannesburg

Joe, you taught me not to lead away from my aces ... (Anyway I gave
    up bridge!)

In the midst of your own bereavement you remembered missing com-
    rades ...

You brought me strawberries on a lonely birthday in Lusaka ...

You played and danced with my son Ernesto when he was little ...

You were the face of change he, and we, knew and could talk to.

Your time should have been longer.

Good-bye

Marge

4 January 1995: From Barney Pityana in Cape Town

Dear Comrades JS and Helena,

I write as one of many South Africans who wish you well as JS battles with ill-health at this time. I wish to assure you both of our prayers for courageous endurance as well as peace of mind and body.

Comrade JS is much loved and respected. We are sad that his tenure in government couldn't be longer. We are assured that his long association with our common struggle, his role in the negotiation which brought our present dispensation into place and the strong and caring direction he has given, in government, to the needs of our people, especially the poor and needy, are all worthy of the greatest honour. Than you for giving quality, integrity and intellect to our struggle and to political life in our country. For all that we are truly grateful. We would that you had more years to enjoy the fruit of our struggle. As you now struggle with equal fortitude we thank you for the example you show us and pray that you may be at peace.

Helena, these are difficult times for you, in particular. Allow us to thank you and to wish you power to withstand, resources to cope and serenity to endure. Please be assured of our love and support. Distant we may be physically but we bear you both in our thoughts.

With all best wishes, Barney

5 January 1995: From Harold Wolpe, Joe's oldest and
most intimate friend
Dear Joe Slo

I spent a good deal of time with you last Thursday morning struggling to find the words to express my thoughts about our long friendship and comradeship. But not only do I not have the skills to encompass the complexities of nearly 50 years in a spoken sentence (without sounding trite) and all the more so, because you and I never theorised our friendship but merely took pleasure from being, doing, and speaking together.

But the* moment to say something has arrived and yet it is no less difficult away from you and in writing. Nevertheless I want to say how much I have valued and enjoyed our friendship in all its varied aspects – despite (or maybe because of) your false allegations concerning my football hooliganism and your attempt to burn down my London house, among other things! It is difficult to imagine a world without you.

AnnMarie and I and also Peta, Tessa and Nick admire not only your great accomplishments but also the remarkable way in which these have left unaffected your personal relations with friends. We all send our fondest love and wish you *hamba kahle.*

I sign the letter in the way you always greeted me on the telephone –

Wolpe!

White hero of black revolution faces up to his final struggle

Philip van Niekerk's piece written for *The Observer* is
based on one of the last interviews that Joe gave to
journalists as Minister of Housing. Joe offered some
retrospection on his life, and the political choices he made.

J oe Slovo's private struggle with cancer has suddenly taken on a
very public dimension in South Africa. A dramatic weight loss
and gaunt appearance, brought on by an unfavourable response
to new medication, unleashed speculation about whether the old communist, the most senior white person in the African National Congress, had
fought his last political and personal battle.

In an interview in his Pretoria office last week, it was hard to tell
which was the more fragile, Slovo's health or his humour. 'I'm in a stable condition,' he snapped. 'I'm doing my work, as you see. You chaps
go on and on about it. Like all of us, when we can't do our jobs, we'll
say so.' His sharp response was softened by a flash of the old Slovo wit.
'Life is a terminal illness,' he added, 'We'll all go.'

Despite his illness, Slovo is enjoying life as a Cabinet Minister, sa-
vouring 'the most challenging, happiest period' of his 68 years. He puffs
contentedly on a cigarillo, but will not allow himself to be photographed
smoking it.

Talk about Slovo's health has overshadowed his achievements as Housing Minister. Into his domain falls one of the most visible inheritances of
apartheid: nine million homeless people packed mostly into squalid
squatter camps ringing the cities.

'Housing is the yardstick by which Nelson Mandela's government
will be judged in its primary task of delivering a better life to black
South Africans. The target is one million houses in five years. But before
the building can start, an impasse has to be broken. Law and order has
collapsed in many townships, and a boycott of mortgage repayments,
rents and service repayments has grown. The result is that banks have
red-lined black areas. The banks fear to tread because of the complete

breakdown of civil law enforcement,' said Slovo. 'They have got something like 18 000 properties for which they've received judgment for eviction, and are unable to implement. We have cases where the sheriff comes to carry out the court's decree and gets necklaced (murdered by having a petrol-doused tyre placed around his neck and set alight). You can't deliver houses in that environment.'

To end the stand-off, Slovo has put together the most pragmatic of compacts: coaxing the banks back into the township market by deploying state funds to underwrite mortgages, while cajoling black residents into resuming monthly payments with the carrot of community improvement and the stick of eviction threats. 'We have spent this period charting the path ahead, ensuring that all the relevant stake-holders are with us. From early next year the fruits of this will start to show themselves.'

If employing private investment and individual ownership is an odd policy for an avowed communist, Slovo's plans to house the millions who cannot afford mortgages are even more unorthodox: the state will provide sites with the basics of electricity, water and sewage and a foundation. 'But the responsibility for putting a roof over heads will depend on mobilising the sweat equity of the people themselves', a sentiment Margaret Thatcher would have no quarrel with.

'You cannot build an economy or a society purely on the basis of entitlement,' said Slovo, who for many years admired the Eastern bloc societies where the state was meant to provide from the cradle to the grave. 'People have to make a contribution. They have to have a sense of ownership which they don't get from being given blocks of rented accommodation which they don't own, don't have a stake in and haven't helped to design.'

Slovo is contrite about his life-long support for the Soviet Union and its satellites. 'I was wrong and I am ashamed of some of the traps I was led into,' he said. He explained: 'If you've ever been a member of an official delegation you learn less about a country than sitting in the British Museum. You don't meet the people, you don't actually see the conditions. People said there were gulags, millions of people incarcerated there. We were assured there was no such thing. We didn't have the opportunities to actually check.' He admitted his own doubts began in the mid-1960s but he chose to remain silent because he had seen the alternative at close hand. His wife, the fiercely unorthodox and independent author and academic Ruth First, was, he said, sidelined by the movement.

'The choice you face is whether you can continue to contribute to the struggle or not. At that stage, independence was just not tolerated. It was part of the sickness we tried to get away from eventually. For me the question was: do I now take a lecturer's job in London? In retrospect I would have made a big mistake if I'd allowed my doubts, which were growing and growing, to lead to a withdrawal.' It is in that context that Slovo's contribution makes sense. He is a pragmatist, prepared to compromise principles to achieve the larger goal of national liberation.

He savours the twists of fortune that have taken him from membership of a 'relatively powerless grouping' in the 1940s, through exile and armed struggle to the beginnings of reconstruction. At every point Joe Slovo was a key player.

'What more could one person expect out of one life? I could happily lay down and die now,' he said. But beneath the self-confidence, Slovo betrayed a vulnerability, as the subject he least likes to talk about resurfaced on its own. 'I have cancer. What can I tell you? I also have feelings.'

The SACP's tribute

As a final piece in this section, I have chosen the SACP's collage of pithy comments made by Joe in recent years on some of the themes that preoccupied him throughout this eventful and heroic period.

On the leading role of the ANC
'We've had examples of radical youth, and quite a few radical workers too have come to join us and said: "We're not joining the ANC, we're waiting for the party to come out," and we've told them on that basis there's no place for them in the party because they'll have to be re-educated politically. And it's not because we want to have a presence in the ANC, it's because we believe that the task of the party has been and must continue to be, to strengthen the most important national force.'

The armed struggle
'In 1961 history left us with no option but to engage in armed action as a necessary part of the political struggle. It was a moment in which (to use Lenin's words) untimely inaction would have been worse than untimely action. We could not refuse to fight. We had to learn how to do so. And, in many respects, we had to learn on the ground, in the hard school of revolutionary practice.'

On religion
'It is my contention that there is a major convergence between the ethical content of Marxism and all that is best in the world's religions. But it must also be conceded that in the name of both Marxism and religion great damage has been done to the human condition. Both ideologies have produced martyrs in the cause of liberation and tyrants in the cause of oppression.

'Let us (socialists and believers) stop concentrating exclusively on the debate about whether there is or not a paradise in heaven. Let us work together to build a paradise on earth. As for myself, if I eventually find a paradise in heaven, I will regard it as a bonus.'

On the apartheid regime's disinformation campaign against him
'For the past decade and a half they have been saying that I am a KGB colonel. I must be the most unsuccessful spy in the world – in 15 years I haven't had a promotion!'

The working class and the national democratic struggle
'If we pose the question by asking only whether our struggle is a national struggle or a class struggle, we will inevitably get a wrong answer. The right question is: what is the relationship between these two categories? A failure to understand the class content of the national struggle and the national content of the class struggle in existing conditions can hold back the advance of both the democratic and socialist transformations which we seek.'

Has socialism failed?
'For our part, we firmly believe in the future of socialism; nor do we dismiss its whole past as an unmitigated failure ... But it is more vital than ever to subject the past of existing socialism to an unsparing critique in order to draw the necessary lessons. To do so openly is an assertion of justified confidence in the future of socialism and its inherent moral superiority. And we should not allow ourselves to be inhibited merely because an exposure of failures will inevitably provide ammunition to the traditional enemies of socialism: our silence will, in any case, present them with even more powerful ammunition.' (1989)

Has capitalism succeeded?
'The wretched of this earth make up over 90 percent of humanity. They live either in capitalist or capitalist-orientated societies. For them if socialism is not the answer, there is no answer at all.' (December 1991)

On his return to SA from 27 years' exile
'As I was saying before I was so rudely interrupted ...'

The negotiations
'The starting point for developing a framework within which to approach some large questions in the negotiating process is to answer the question: why are we negotiating? We are negotiating because towards the end of the 1980s we concluded that, as a result of its escalating crisis, the apartheid power bloc was no longer able to continue ruling in the old way and was genuinely seeking some break with the past. At the same time, we were clearly not dealing with a defeated enemy, and an early revolution-

ary seizure of power by the liberation movement could not be realistically posed.' (September 1992)

'For the past three years we politicians have all had our say. It is time now for the people to have their day. For the past three years we politicians have spoken to each other, at each other and past each other. We have been at bilaterals and multilaterals. But beyond the walls of the World Trade Centre there is growing impatience with our speechifying.' (March 1993)

On certain English liberals
'Bashing the Afrikaner is a popular pastime among certain English liberals and it gets my goat ... It stems from a combination of English jingoism and an attempt to evade collective white guilt for our racist inheritance by oiling it all onto the Afrikaners. It also creates a smokescreen over the real roots of racism by giving pride of place to the ethnic factor rather than to economic exploitation. Mealy-mouthed shedding of responsibility and blaming it all on the Boers is, at best, ahistorical and, at worst, a form of racism. If any one group is to blame for the modern foundation of apartheid it is the non-Afrikaner upper strata which dominated the seat of power for more than 75 years before 1948. I am not arguing for one randlord, one bullet, but we must get our history straight.'

The SACP's secret weapon
'Commentators continue to be puzzled by the staying power of the SACP in a world in which socialist parties are in decline. It is time to divulge one of the lesser known secrets of our public relations success. No, we have no contract with Saatchi & Saatchi who are already working for the NP. We rely on the firm of De Klerk and Botha, whose public relations work for our party is unsolicited, unintended and free.

Every time this old firm launches a salvo against us, our popularity rating among blacks takes a further leap.'

On multi-party democracy
'The single party state, except at rare moments in history, is a recipe for tyranny. What we've learnt from the Soviet experience and from the African experience is that the concept of the party as a vanguard which has the right to rule by virtue of calling itself something and which is entrenched in the constitution as a permanent godfather of this society, is a disaster.'

The challenges of a new SA

'It is our task to give millions of South Africans an essential piece of dignity in their lives – the dignity that comes from having a solid roof over your head, running water and other services in an established community.'

Looking back

'As far as I am concerned, what I did, I did without any regrets. I decided long ago in my life that there is only one target, and that target is to remove the racist regime and obtain power for the people.' (December 1994)

The Funeral

Slovo: They came to claim their hero

He was endearingly messy and relaxed in life – and so was his farewell. Mark Gevisser reports on the symbolism that emerged at Joe Slovo's funeral. (*The Mail & Guardian*, 20 January 1995)

As I drove the 12 kilometres from Orlando to Avalon on Sunday, crawling through the human avenue of thousands of people, a young man rushed up to me, carrying a stone. The impulse was to flinch – I am white, this is Soweto – but I was confounded: 'I'm not going to make it there in time,' he cried. 'Please put this stone on his grave for me.'

There were other stones at Joe Slovo's graveside; those lobbed by the crowd, that succeeded in chasing people off the scaffolding where the pleas and commands of Cyril Ramaphosa failed. It was a shocking moment, mob justice of a sort, applauded even by those on the podium: the rule of the stone prevailing over the words of the leaders. A symbol, perhaps, of the ANC's losing control over its constituency?

Earlier, in the Orlando Stadium, 40 000 people sat, immobile through long ponderous speeches. Reverend Barney Pityana offered an academic exegesis on faith and liberation; Cosatu's John Gomomo waded through treacle-thick exhortations to the working class; the South African Communist Party's Charles Nqakula fashioned overwrought populist imagery that failed nonetheless to ignite the crowd. The crowd showed only three moments of palpable engagement: when President Nelson Mandela entered the stadium, when he finished his speech and when Mzwakhe Mbuli sang his praise poems.

Slovo's interment was this country's major public event since Mandela's inauguration eight months ago. It was, on paper, the first state funeral of the new South Africa. In fact, it was neither a state funeral nor a struggle funeral. It had neither the pomp and ritual of the former nor the fervent engagement of the latter. It was something in between; a transition funeral holding a mass of contradictions and ambivalences reflecting, perfectly, the transitional nature of the tripartite alliance of the ANC, the SACP and Cosatu.

There were obvious ironies: the words of *The Internationale* printed on government paper; the presence of Joe-Hunter Number One, Pik Botha, sitting decorously next to Mandela just behind the hammer and sickle fashioned of roses beneath the podium. These ironies were not lost on the speakers. Mandela himself called it 'nothing less than the tragedy of South Africa' that Slovo's 'humanity, pragmatism and industriousness' were realised by whites 'only now, after 40 years of banning and that these qualities are extolled by some, as if they were new'.

Just as the alliance itself is struggling with the dual roles of mass movement and governing political party, so too did the funeral. It was there, for example, in the space between Ramaphosa and Thabo Mbeki at the graveside; the former on the crowd-mike, trying to control the people; the latter seated and dignified with his wife up on the podium, only intervening at the very last minute to quieten the crowd for Helena Dolny's speech.

And one saw it, most acutely, in the absence (or presence) of the military. Mbeki and other ANC heavyweights arrived at the graveside in Nyalas laid on to transport them from their cars through the mud. Later, township people climbed atop them to get a better view, a casual display of new ownership. But then, when the soldiers tried to clear them off, things turned nasty. Once more they were 'comrades' against *boere*: insults – and mudclods – were traded.

The decision to cart Slovo's coffin through Soweto on a South African National Defence Force gun-carriage had intense symbolic significance. In the popular imagination of those tens of thousands lining the streets, Slovo was first and foremost a military commander who, with a great mind and a handful of committed cadres, defeated the armed might of his own people. The gun-carriage that carried him was thus his final trophy; the material of oppression commandeered for his final ride.

But where were the Impalas flying overhead trailing the colours of the SACP? Why were there only two soldiers giving the final salute rather than the 24 Howitzers? Where was the swagger of military might so essential to the public display of patriotism that takes place at a state event?

The answer lies, once more, in the ambivalence of the ANC to its new-found executive power. On one hand, military might now belongs to the people it used to oppress; it is controlled by the ANC itself. On the other, it carries with it the memory, from funerals past, of teargas and bullets, of the disruption rather than the facilitation of mourning.

Battalions of soldiers and barriers around the graveside would have prevented the possibility of a tragic crowd crush but the ANC, as the new government, would have inevitably found itself on the wrong side of such barriers, separated from the people it purports to represent.

And so there was also intense and very self-conscious political significance to the fact that Umkhonto we Sizwe, rather than the South African National Defence Force or the police, buried Joe Slovo.

Umkhonto, remember, no longer exists. It thus came across as an assertion of ANC's liberation-movement self over its government-self.

And an unsuccessful assertion at that, for the MK cadres deployed at the graveside were unable to prevent the near-chaos. Indeed, the firing of their AK-47s , as the coffin was lowered into the earth, was barely heard above the hubbub of the crowd.

Perhaps that's appropriate. Because in the banner headlines proclaiming 'Unruly crowds at graveside', one essential and unforgettable truth is lost: the whole of Soweto came out to bury one white man, as they had never buried anyone before.

The true funeral took place neither in the stuffy confines of Orlando Stadium, where there was too much order and discipline, nor in the muddy chaos of Avalon Cemetery, where there was not enough. Rather, it took place along the way between the two; where the people of Soweto could mourn and celebrate unmediated; where they could sing 'Hamba Kahle Umkhonto' with the gusto lacking at the graveside or in the stadium; and stand outside their homes with buckets of water, just as they did during earlier funerals when it was needed to ward off teargas.

When Chris Hani was buried, the tension brought out the anger of urban life. The people were seething, ominous, jealous of their space.

The crowds along the route of Slovo's procession presented that other basic urban mood, the laughing, ribald air of a carnival – in which people shouted 'Vivo!' instead of 'Viva!' and traded earthy humour with the cars that passed.

There was celebration in the air, an irreverence and delight that seemed to match, perfectly and perhaps unwittingly, the 'wine, women and song' that those who knew him better were commemorating.

At the end of the funeral, Dolny spoke about her husband. Finally, the family of this public man was staking its claim to his memory. Dolny's speech was moving, generous, brilliant: she claimed him back without requiring the masses to relinquish him. He was, she said, 'endearingly messy and relaxed'. Perhaps the same could be said about his funeral. –

Slovo was, according to his wishes, buried by a mass of people, with all its contradictory impulses, rather than by a taut state ideology. Perhaps the alliance should be praised, rather than criticised, for not managing the memory of Joe Slovo more effectively.

How reassuring that South Africans are trapped neither in struggle nor in blind allegiance to their leaders.

A Jewish Tribute

Cyril Harris, Chief Rabbi of the Union of Orthodox
Synagogues of South Africa, at the state funeral on
15 January 1995.

W e gather together today to mourn the passing of Joe Slovo and to give thanks for his great life. We give thanks for the quality of his character. He possessed a wondrous mixture of contradictory traits – he was an intellectual who had his feet very much on the ground; a theorist who always put the needs of the people first; a man who faced the turbulence of volatile times with gentleness and good humour; a white man who with every fibre of his being fought to improve the lot of his black brothers and sisters.

We give thanks for his humanity. There are two major motivations towards helping fellow human beings. One is religious. The Fatherhood of Almighty God betokens the brotherhood and sisterhood of humankind. We are all God's children, responsible for the well-being of everyone on earth, commanded to reach out the hand of help to the other.

Social justice and benevolent action are as old as the Bible. The prophet Amos, for example, stoutly defended the oppressed, thundered with indignation against the idle rich for their ill-treatment of the poor: 'Let justice well up as the waters, and righteousness as a mighty stream' (Amos 5:24).

The second motivation is humanitarian – it springs from a deep sense of identification with the oppressed, the ability to hear their cry, an acute awareness of the realities of poverty, a personal anguish at the suffering of fellow human beings. This was Joe Slovo's way. His humanity was boundless and inspirational; he became the true champion of the oppressed. Let not those religious people who acquiesced, passively or wrongly, with the inequalities of yesteryear, let not those religious people dare to condemn Joe Slovo, a humanist socialist, who fought all his life for basic decency, to reinstate the dignity to which all human beings are entitled.

He was proud to acknowledge the Jewish roots of his compassion. Brought up as a child in a Lithuanian ghetto, he experienced at first hand the degradation and misery of being unfairly treated for no proper reason.

So in the South Africa he grew to love, he determined that no one should be singled out for unfair treatment for no proper reason. It was not enough to avoid harming others – positively and purposefully one had to strive to ameliorate widespread poverty and hardship, to build a society based on harmony and equality, in which every single individual would be respected. This was the driving force of his life's work: to achieve in an egalitarian, non-racial society the betterment of the living conditions of the entire population.

Another great freedom fighter, the Rev. Martin Luther King, once said, 'We are all inextricably bound together in a single garment of destiny.' Joe Slovo brought the fulfilment of that dream, that we are all part of one big caring human family, so much closer.

We should appreciate that it is not genius, nor glory, nor even love which truly reflect the human soul – it is kindness. Countless millions of people, touched by the humanity and kindness of Joe Slovo, will forever cherish him in their hearts.

We give thanks for his bravery. Unflinching throughout the struggle, he never gave up in the darkest hours but soldiered on to tackle seemingly insurmountable difficulties. Thank goodness he witnessed in great joy the deserved success of the founding of the new democratic South Africa, with all the promise it carries for our future.

And he was so brave in his terminal illness. Not for a moment did he give up his arduous task at the Ministry of Housing; he summoned reserves of energy when he had no strength left. He showed us all the triumph of the human spirit over sickness, fatigue and adversity.

There is an old Rabbinic teaching, a beautiful one, that just before a person dies, an angel comes to him from Heaven and asks the vital question: 'Tell me, is the world a better place because of your life which is about to end? Is the world a better place because of the efforts you exerted? Is the world a better place because you were around?'

For Joe Slovo, we give the answer Yes, a resounding Yes. The world *is* a better place, thanks to you, Joe, and your remarkable life.

Joe, we say farewell to you. We will always remember you with pride and affection. *Shalom*, dear brother, *Shalom*. Rest in eternal peace.

At the Graveside

I t is not usual to have a woman speaking at the graveside of the burial of a family member. But as Joe's immediate family are all women, it is also hardly appropriate to have a man speak on our behalf. And so we have chosen to break with custom and hope you will accept our reasons for doing so. I want to begin by speaking of various dimensions of Joe's life:

The shaping of the man
As a family, we have listened to many people in this past week singing Joe's praises, what a great man he was.

Clearly Joe has contributed to the history of this country, but there also needs to be recognition of how much this country and his wider international exposure contributed to the making of Joe.

He was shaped by history, by people and by his family.

He was born at a most opportune time. He listened to immigrants debate the Russian Revolution, he experienced the anti-fascist war, and the whole notion of apartheid was an anathema to him from his earliest working experience. The obituary you have in front of you not only describes what part he has played but also illustrates the opportunities open to him and that he learnt from.

People have mentioned his astute ability in negotiations as a tactician while not compromising on principles. I think this is one lesson he took most sharply from Mozambique's Nkomati Accord which he saw as not only detrimental to the ANC but to the Mozambican nation as a whole.

At a personal level, his politics were shaped not only by Marx, Lenin and the Vietnamese military strategists, but also by South Africa's greats – Yusuf Dadoo, Oliver Tambo, Madiba and Walter Sisulu. His tendencies towards being a hack were kept in check by Ruth, his first wife, his intellectual challenge and reinforced especially by Harold Wolpe and Pallo Jordan. His personal circle offered him a wide range of international political debate.

As a family of women, we would also like to think that Joe became one of the more sensitive of our leadership on gender issues. This should have been the result of his continuously being given a hard time at home where there was unrelenting tension that being a socialist did not just mean representing a certain line in debates but demanded a certain code of practice at the personal level.

People have spoken of the sacrifices that Joe made. There is no doubt that there were rough periods. But a sense of sacrifice did not dominate Joe's life. He acknowledged that he got so much from the struggle. He enjoyed an enormous sense of achievement, of fulfilment, and savoured his good fortune at having had such a life especially since his return from exile. Whilst he contributed to history, history also shaped him and offered him amazing opportunities which he never took for granted.

Joe at a personal family level

A few words about Joe and family. At a family level, Joe also had a sense of good fortune. We, his family, loved him and he felt this deeply. He also showed his love, sometimes gently, sometimes joyfully, sometime passionately. He occasionally referred to other comrades' lives that were fraught with personal difficulty. He counted his lucky stars that his was otherwise, even though he found the demands we made on him occasionally created tensions.

As a family, while we may be able to list what my husband, what my father, step-father failed to do because he was too busy, we can also identify important invaluable gifts that he gave us.

He taught us a sense of perspective and priority as he struggled for what he could change and accepted what could not be changed.

He taught us the importance of incorruptibility as part of the essence of self-respect. While appreciating opportunities to enjoy the good life, he refused to use his position to get himself, or us, anything that wasn't his due.

There is one extra special gift which he passed on to all of us – and that is a self-confidence, a sense and strength of identity. His strength and persona did not overwhelm us in our lives but rather enriched the persons that we have become.

Joe as part of a wider family

I would also like to speak of Joe as part of a wider family. He enjoyed long-standing loyal friendships with a wide range of people within and beyond his political circle.

I have tried to think why he was so endearing to so many people – a quality often referred to – and I have chosen just three points.

Firstly, he never got too big for his boots, but would respectfully engage in discussion with whoever he met on a journey, on a visit, in the camps, in ANC houses or with whoever he might find at home.

Secondly, he was endearingly messy and relaxed. People related easily to the things he enjoyed in life at an everyday level – the peanuts, whisky, cigars, red socks, wine, women and song.

Thirdly, while people have mentioned his humour over and over again, what was so very special was his ability to tell stories against himself and laugh at himself.

Finally, we would like to talk of ourselves as part of a wider family. This week, we have listened to people thanking us for putting up with the deprivation we must have experienced because of Joe's role in politics. But what we realised is that Joe's involvement meant that we are also part of a very large and generous family, both at the political and personal level. People have been wonderful for us, not only this week, but for a long time. We have felt tremendously supported and we are left with the deepest, warmest feeling in our hearts.

We, as family, stand here together, to say to all of you, people of South Africa,

Thank you.

International Tributes

From Mozambique

In January 1995, Mozambican Television produced a
documentary: *Joe Slovo, Freedom Fighter*. They
introduced the programme as follows:

A t dawn on January 6th, a man died who throughout his life was an example of courage, coherence and dedication. With his death one of the last giants of a certain generation disappeared, a generation which sacrificed itself to its very end for the cause of the liberation of the African continent. Eduardo Mondlane, Patrice Lumumba, Amilcar Cabral, Agostino Neto and Samora Machel have already passed away. Now the time of Joe Slovo has arrived: the world has lost a freedom fighter.'

The programme continued with interviews of a dozen people who were a close part of Joe's life in the seven years he lived in Mozambique. Extracts of those interviews follow:

Raul Honwana, Professor of Literature, whose family was
an integral part of Mozambique's own struggle against
colonialism.

'The loss of Joe Slovo, as a political person, as a militant, is of great significance. My reading of this tragedy is that it affects not only Africa but the whole world and that stories of the people's revolutions and leaders are being lost.

'It is inconceivable that Joe Slovo could have lived in another place, in another age, if not this one, this epoch, none other than here – Southern Africa.

'He had an enormous moral and political stature which cannot be claimed only by South Africa. It belongs to us more widely. He belonged to this period, to a certain period of struggle and politics, of which we are also a part. As a political person, a man who so deeply participated in our contemporary history, his contribution was so large that his loss has to be perceived as not only our loss, but as a loss to all of humanity.'

Polly Gaster, a founding member of the Committee for Freedom for Mozambique, Angola and Guinea Bissau in the late 1960s and currently Director of the Public Information Bureau, Maputo.

'The man I knew well was an unpretentious person, a family man, a political man, a man for the masses, a militant. He worked hard but was a jovial man who liked to relax and who loved to joke. He was a man who was an able teacher, never one of those arrogant people who thought he knew more than others; he always respected the other person and engaged in dialogue. He was capable of changing his mind, which is not very common.

'Going to the funeral was an extraordinary experience. I think this decision of his, being a white man, to wish to be buried in a cemetery for blacks (I'd never realised that South Africa had different cemeteries for black and white people, but of course, once you think about it, it's a logical consequence of apartheid), was an act which was totally consistent with the way he lived his life.

'Joe was the person who never carried himself as a white militant, but first and foremost as a militant. But the fact that he behaved as a militant and was white, captured the hearts of the people.'

Ze Forjaz, director of the Faculty of Architecture, Maputo.

'Joe was the most agreeable person you could possibly have as company. First, he was one of the best joke-tellers I have ever known. His specialities were both socialist and Jewish jokes. He knew them all and took enormous pleasure from their telling. Secondly, he had a pleasant disposition, always in a good mood from day to day. I saw a lot of him and Ruth – they were close and often here at home.

'Before he left Mozambique he had been writing a book and read some of it to me. It was about moments of his life. It wasn't an autobiography as such – rather it was selected episodes of his life, mostly ones he considered interesting, ironic, jocular and humorous. He took a great pleasure in recalling these and writing them up. I don't know if Helena, his widow, knows what happened to them. I must take it up with her because really they were wonderful pieces of prose, of not only an historic but also a humorous value.

'I will ask to be excused for harping so insistently on Joe's trait of humour, but it is perhaps because this aspect of his personality was not well known. In South Africa he had been made out to be fearsome, an ogre, when in reality he was a cuddly bear, a teddy bear – a person with a great spontaneous friendliness. Many of the people Joe encountered at my house became his good friends.

'For example, he played the guitar, and played badly – he never had time to practise properly – but he liked to play, and met up with George Povey, the American doctor, quite a few times here at home. Both played badly, but they enjoyed singing and knew an enormous number of folk-songs, which they played and sang with gusto. Joe sang well, and had a good ear.

'I remember in 1993, staying at his home in Johannesburg. He got up early every morning at 5 am to go swimming, even though he was already suffering from the cancer that eventually killed him. He was home by 7 am, and we had breakfast, and then he went off to his office, still in the ANC headquarters at this time. He went about his life with great energy, but a calm energy, a well-directed, well-placed energy, focused on whatever task he was undertaking.

'Yet he knew he was going to die shortly. He was incapable of mis-leading himself and couldn't take on any metaphysical belief. He accepted this knowledge with courage and simplicity. Courage – it seems odd to have to have courage to do something that we all have to do – but he knew that to die was natural, and accepted his own forthcoming death.'

From Cuba

Extracts from 'A Brief Remembrance of Joe Slovo', by
Angel Dalmau, the Cuban Ambassador to South Africa.

G iven my responsibility at the Southern African desk of the Party
Headquarters in Havana I regularly met ANC and SACP leaders either in Cuba or in Luanda, Lusaka, Harare, Maputo and
other places.

I first met Joe in Luanda in 1978. Until then I had heard of him as the
white legend within the ANC; from then onwards I came to know Slovo
the man, the revolutionary, the communist and now the legend again. I
am deeply proud to have been his friend.

Joe visited Cuba many times representing the ANC. He always did it
in search of practical support for the liberation of his people. And he got
it. Joe liked Cuba for many reasons. There he found people who shared
his main political thinking and a strong political motivation for African
freedom fighting. Cubans also thoroughly enjoyed his jokes.

When the negotiations at Kempton Park were about to be derailed,
Joe Slovo came up with his sunset clause. At the time I was Ambassador
to Namibia and trying from there to more or less follow the negotiating
process. I observed – in confusion – strong reactions against the sunset
clause and even accusations against Joe for becoming 'politically soft and
giving up'. But my confusion lasted only for a couple of days. First I got
a copy of the document and, without claiming at all to be an expert on
South African politics, I understood its intentions; secondly, I had faith in
Joe's integrity as a man who would not spoil the real meaning of his
entire life for peanuts, as he didn't.

Joe was a deep thinker who could express big ideas in few words.
Among these many ideas I have made mine one that shall accompany me
forever:

'The wretched of this earth make up over 90 percent of humanity.
They live either in capitalist or capitalist-orientated societies. For them if
socialism is not the answer, there is no answer at all.'

Very well said, dear Joe.

From Italy

Extracts translated from 'In Memory of Joe Slovo' by
Italian activist Dina Forti, published in *Politica
Internazionale*, no. 4, 1994. Forti is an 80-year-old,
life-long communist, who knew Joe well for almost three
decades.

I will try to say something of Joe Slovo as a person. This is not intended to be a political evaluation, even if Joe was a political person and his life was therefore also part of the world of politics.

I met Joe for the first time in 1965 in London at a seminar on apartheid. I was very struck by his contribution, by its lucidity, its force of argument and its brilliant dialectic. During the course of that week, I met Joe on various occasions, not just during the meeting but also outside, at lunch, at his home. I soon understood the important characteristics of his personality. He was at the same time a leader, a man capable of expressing his thoughts with great efficacy, capable of extreme commitment; later, this commitment was to mean the responsibility for the life and death of many people. But Joe was a calm person at the same time, with a great sense of humour.

From then on we met frequently, both in Rome, which he loved, and abroad. I met him as representative of the ANC and as a leading member of the SACP. Especially after 1968, we frequently had hard and even bitter discussions. Our friendship became closer and our meeting often daily when Joe and Ruth were living in Mozambique, where I too lived and worked from 1979 to 1983.

I will always remember 17 August 1982, towards evening, when, as soon as I heard the terrible news of the criminal attack against Ruth First, I went to their house. Joe was distraught, but calm. For some weeks he had given up smoking, and in that moment he had a tremendous desire to light a cigarette. 'I can't,' he said, 'Ruth asked me to give it up for good, therefore I can't, but please pour me a whisky.'

During the evening, with friends around him – the Mozambicans, the South African comrades in Maputo – Joe often had to break off the discussion to telephone the daughters. When he managed to reach them

(Gillian and Robin in London, and Shawn in the United States), he spoke with such gentleness, finding the most tender words to tell them what had happened and to ask them to take the first possible flight to Maputo. But when he spoke to Ruth's mother, already over 80 years old, he could not keep back the tears.

He knew his life was in danger every day; he was number one enemy of the apartheid regime, but he carried himself calmly, as if his physical person was not involved.

The last meetings I had with Joe were very special, because they were in South Africa, the land he loved so much. In 1992, one evening, before going out to dinner, he wanted me to visit his new home in Johannesburg of which he was really proud. That evening he told me he was seriously ill. He said it almost smiling: 'I've got cancer and I have to go to hospital for chemotherapy. It's very tiring, but I still manage to get a lot of work done, and that's the important thing.' He was happy to be so involved, this time back inside his own country. We never thought, during our conversations in the previous years, that this moment would have arrived so soon.

After the ANC's success in the elections, after the formation of the government in which he was given one of the most important and difficult ministries, that of Housing, Joe's illness became worse. Despite this, he wanted to keep the commitment he had made with Helena, to have a holiday in Italy.

When they came to Italy in September 1994 Joe was very ill: he could hardly speak, and he could not swallow his food – Joe, who loved Italian cooking so much. But after a week's rest (perhaps the first for ages) he seemed better and we were able to talk at length, of South Africa, of Italy, even of me.

On 23 December, I phoned Joe in Johannesburg. Helena told me he had fallen and fractured a bone and that this had aggravated his condition, but he wanted to speak to me. His voice was weak, and he said how hot it was (it was full summer), nevertheless he wanted news of the political situation in Italy. He replied to my questions regarding the Congress of the ANC which had just finished, he asked after me, and thanked me for my telephone call.

That was Joe, strong and calm right to the end.

From China

'Joe Slovo: A brilliant teacher'
by Shu Zhan, of the Chinese Association of International
Understanding, (revised and edited version of an article
first published in *CHINAFRICA*, May 1995).

A t the time of his death, Joe Slovo was the national chairperson of the South African Communist Party (SACP) and Housing Minister of the new Government of National Unity. The spontaneous outpouring of grief was so great, it took hours of continuous dialing for me to reach his personal fax machine in order to leave a message of condolence for his family.

I was stunned and could barely believe he was gone. How could it be true that this great man has left us when South Africa needs men of his stature? In the film *A World Apart*, Joe gently kisses his sleeping daughter goodbye and disappears into the darkness before dawn. At the celebration for the victory of the ANC in the national elections, he sang and danced with gay abandon.

Opening my journal, I was reminded of accompanying him on a visit to the Palace Museum in Beijing, and sitting with him in his home in Johannesburg while he talked of the prospects facing the new South Africa. Emotions at his passing overwhelmed me, and tears of sorrow smeared the pages of my journal.

Although I began reading Joe's works some ten years ago, it was on a visit to South Africa in the summer of 1992 that we first met. We had several chances to meet in the years after that, but our schedules restricted our contact. Still, from our first meetings, we felt as if we had known each other for many years; I through his writings, and he through years of contact through our respective political organisations.

During our first meeting I came face to face with the rapid intellect I had only heard of before. He had wit and wisdom, but he was cautious in his speech. His sharp analysis of great changes in the world and his original views toward the complicated situation in South Africa deeply impressed me. He slowly voiced his thoughts, often hitting the mark with a single comment.

'It is not that socialism is no longer full of vigour, but that the dog-matists have made mistakes. We have many faults, too. The wonder of China's reform and opening over the past ten years or so has proven this exactly. We must be practical and realistic toward the current changes and reform in South Africa. We must explore a road of our own.'

But at our first meeting, I didn't fully grasp the profound significance of his words. In the winter of 1992, I read his article *Negotiations: What Room is there for Compromise?* in which he resolutely put forward the suggestion to adjust proposals for immediate majority-rule and supported power-sharing based on an insightful analysis of the international situ-ation and a minute comparison of diverse camps in South Africa. And later, he participated in the arduous negotiations and patiently persuaded his colleagues to devote their efforts to the formation of a government of national unity.

Joe made friends according to personality, not status. When we got together again during his visit to China on holidays, he asked many ques-tions of me and chatted about both international affairs and domestic matters. He even guessed my age correctly, which surprised me, as I have often been told that I look young for my age. He explained with a smile, 'It is not difficult to guess, knowing you were sent to the countryside to live and work in the later 1960s.' I wondered at his deep understanding of China's history and current situation.

I was impressed by his careful research as I acted as an interpreter for him in an interview with Chinese economist, Professor Dong Furen. They debated the nature of public ownership and the nature of socialism. Com-rade Joe described an air-conditioning factory he had visited in Wenzhou. Five successful men had now issued bonds and created shareholders and defined the factory as 'publicly owned'. Joe's concern was over the defi-nition of public ownership, that to define shareholding as public ownership is to describe 40 percent of the western capitalist economies. He said to Dong Furen, '... we need theoretical clarity on the nature of public own-ership ... surely as theoreticians and Marxists one needs to identify the nature of the different forms of ownership and be vigilant, because eco-nomic forms of production contribute to ideology. We need to understand what is the nature of socialist public ownership. I accept there is no Chi-nese wall between capitalism and socialism, but after taking power in South Africa, we will still need these capitalist forms because they have not exhausted their contribution to economic development to lay the basis for socialist transformation.'

Their dialogue began to explore the very nature of socialism. Professor Dong pointed out that there are different schools of socialist transformation –

Marxist, Marxist-Leninist, Social Democrat – and that people need to rethink and reunderstand socialism through practice. They noted that there were questions raised by Marx which may have been correct at the time but which now seem outdated, and other concepts which surely must have always been wrong – for example, Marx's suggestion that the market can disappear because the economy operates on the basis of a unified plan. They concluded that any theory must undergo a process of development, that this represents the advance of human understanding. 'We cannot expect Marxism-Leninism to predict and tell us all truths. This is itself against Marxist theory in that this approach is no longer dialectic.'

Through the April and May of 1994, I was invited to lecture in South Africa. This was during the heated election campaigns. Each day, the South African people could see Joe on TV as he canvassed the townships, speaking to the electorate and sitting across the negotiating table from his political rivals as they compared programmes for the advancement of the nation. All this was done smoothly despite his progressing illness.

On the evening of the ANC election victory, I called to congratulate him. Two days later, Comrade Dolny picked up my colleague and me and brought us to their home. It was their little daughter's birthday. As we waited in the backyard for him to join the party, Helena told us that he had not rested a single day in the past months. He was that day attending an important meeting with President Nelson Mandela to decide the organisation of the new cabinet. By the time Joe returned, night had fallen; the 20 minutes of our chat were interrupted seven times by phone calls.

As we parted, he grasped our hands and said he would come to China again. His tired eyes revealed his reluctance to let us part. He asked his two bodyguards to take us back to our apartments. We worried about his safety, but he insisted that the danger was outside his home, and he would not let us return unescorted. He had hardly finished bidding us farewell when the phone rang. He hurried back, turning twice to say goodbye. None of us thought it would be a final farewell.

In the only two photos I have of us together, he smiles kindly at me. Last December, I sent a Christmas card to him, wishing he would recover well enough to visit Beijing again in the summer.

I can't overstate my pride at having been able to study the great works of Joe Slovo and in being able to say that I was one of his many students and friends. The opportunities I enjoyed to work with this great revolutionary will be treasured in my mind for the rest of my days. Joe has left the world with a grand legacy of words and deeds. His personal example and his teachings, his faith and firmness, his sincerity and cordiality will linger, always bringing benefit to all who learn from his life.

From Russia

'Joe in my life'
by Alexei Makarov.

M y whole career was associated with South Africa and the liberation struggle of its people, especially from the early 1970s. The association began earlier, in 1963, when I graduated from the language school and was sent as an interpreter to Odessa, where the first MK group was being trained. It included Joe Modise and Ronnie Kasrils. Later, when I came to work with the Soviet Afro-Asian Solidarity Committee in 1970 and then with the International Department of the CPSU, I came in contact with the major liberation movement leaders.

I met JB Marks, I attended Moses Kotane when he was in hospital, and I have a very warm memory of the late ANC president Oliver Tambo. But the two persons closest to me among the South Africans were Yusuf Dadoo and Joe Slovo. Yusuf was much older than I, and my attitude to him was that of a youngster to an elder. He was an outstanding human being in the strict sense of the word, and you knew he would never betray you. I am really happy that our relations went beyond my official obligations. But with Joe the relationship was deeper and closer.

I worked at the CPSU from 1972 to 1977, and I would meet Joe – not often, just a few times a year when he came to the Soviet Union. I had an impression of an energetic and dynamic man. He inevitably attracted the attention of the audience, though I cannot remember that he tried to impose himself on others. From the first meeting, I had a sense of a man of erudition, a man who knows what he is doing and what he is saying. He had the aura of inner strength and confidence, and one could see among the comrades, black and white, there was respect for him. He was full of humour, charged with it, and liked to crack jokes and tell anecdotes.

My other memory is of him smoking cigars. Later he gave up smoking, but at that time whenever he came to Moscow he used to seek me out to accompany him to the cigar shop. There was plenty of good Cuban stuff, and you could buy those cigars rather cheaply. I had the impression that Joe would spend all his pocket money – the allowance in roubles comrades got when visiting the USSR – on Coronas and other brands.

For me, throughout his life, Joe retained independence of mind and action although he was always part of a team and had a strict sense of party discipline. No, he did not have his own agenda, but he listened to his internal voice and his internal principles. As I see it now, whatever he did was subordinated to one, and only one, goal – destruction of the apartheid system and liberation of the South African people.

His attitude towards the Soviet Union was one of great respect for its political support and material assistance to the liberation movement. This attitude, I know, was honest and sincere. Questioning certain practices in the USSR and other socialist countries (which he never brought out into the open), at the same time he deeply believed in socialism as a system that could best cater for the interests and needs of the people.

A vivid example of this is one of his later papers, *Has Socialism Failed?*, written at the time of the *perestroika* process in the USSR, accompanied by anti-communist attacks. He could not accept the arbitrary decision to disband the CPSU and did not welcome reforms that led to the destruction of socialist achievements in the USSR and setting the country on a course of primitive capitalist transformations. In one of our discussions in 1992, he did not conceal his negative attitude to the reforms started in Russia earlier that year, comparing them unfavourably with the reform policies of the Chinese authorities of gradual market changes under the control of the Communist Party.

I developed a sense of him as a man who was strong politically, theoretically and as an organiser. Was he a KGB agent? Certainly this was rubbish cooked up by the South African propaganda machine to stain the name of this man whom they could fear as no one else. When speaking at the farewell party for Joe I joked that having heard the rumours about him published in a South African newspaper, we had a meeting in the International Department to think it over. Our final conclusion was that the rumour was false for the simple reason that being only a colonel in the KGB Joe could not claim to have a dacha on Lake Baikal – for that he would have to be at least a general!

Our close personal relationship evolved after Joe's trip to the place of his birth, the village of Obelei in Lithuania where he spent his first years before his family departed to South Africa. He never concealed his wish to visit that place, though he was never pushy. There was always a positive attitude towards being able to meet his wish, but there was a problem. That part of Lithuania was a restricted area for foreigners, and arranging a visit for Joe presented some difficulties, even for the CPSU International Department. Somebody had to take the initiative and push it through the appropriate channels.

The permission was eventually granted and the visit was scheduled for September 1981, immediately after a meeting of the Central Committee of the SACP in Moscow. As always, Joe was very busy, and his schedule was tight, so he only had two days available for the trip to his birthplace. I think he welcomed the idea that it was to be me who would accompany him. By that time we had developed friendly relations. Besides, I was no longer a party official for him and that made him feel at ease. As he admitted later, that trip was something very personal for him and had nothing to do with his official standing.

During the two days we spent together I saw him as just a normal human being, not a political leader or a theoretician. A kind of magnetism had developed that drew us closer together. The content and depth of our discussions changed. We talked at length about the Soviet Union, its problems, the problems of socialism.

At that time, like many in my country, I thought much about these issues. It was the general critical mood of the people around me. You could feel it in many ways, though it did not materialise in open debate, which in fact was not possible. There were too many discrepancies between the official theory and real life that brought more questions than answers. I couldn't discuss these things with many people, just with a few friends, and Joe became one of them. He had a solid background, saw the world, never hesitated to defend his own point of view, and at the same time was an interested and active partner in conversation. I also knew that I could be secure talking to him on many matters.

Joe was a wonderful interlocutor. He never imposed his own opinion and carefully avoided criticising any particular country or political leader. But his contribution was immense because he went deep in his analysis and stimulated innovative thinking.

We talked much about South Africa and he was quite open with me on many issues. I do not mean unconditionally open – we never touched on particular persons and he never revealed any Party decisions which were secret at the time. I learned to look at South Africa through his eyes. This really helped me understand the dimensions of the power struggle, the strength of the internal resistance and that of the ANC and SACP in organising and guiding this struggle.

For a few years we lived in Mozambique during the same period. In Maputo I came to know his wife, Ruth First, as I was a regular guest at his house. He frequently popped into my flat for lunch. He liked socialising and from time to time took me to parties. I came to know many comrades. I met with Joe's daughters and later with his future wife, Helena Dolny. I felt I was admitted to his whole family. Joe became part of my life and I felt very attached to him. We enjoyed our shared understanding of each other – these emotions went deep.

Our meetings continued in South Africa after I came in March 1991 to open the USSR diplomatic mission in Pretoria. We met regularly whether officially, privately or on special occasions, like his 65th birthday party. We last met at Johannesburg airport on 6 November 1994 while checking in for the same flight to Cape Town. Since I had last seen him in his ministerial office in Pretoria a few months before, his appearance had changed dramatically.

We agreed to talk on the plane. After the meal was served, I came to look for him. He was asleep. I called his name and he woke up. 'We must meet,' he said. 'Look how thin I grow, but I still feel strong. I just have to. It is hard for me to find time for you till the end of the Parliamentary session (18 November), but after that give me a call. I shall be glad to see you.'

That meeting never happened. I last saw him in mid-December at the ANC National Congress in Bloemfontein. He left very quickly after receiving the *Isithwalandwe Seaparankoe* Award from Madiba.

I think the South African liberation movement has given rise to a galaxy of wonderful personalities. The South African people, and indeed the whole world, owe to them the elimination of one of the most vicious political systems and securing a miraculous peaceful transition to a new democratic dispensation. Joe Slovo should be singled out as one of them. He was outstanding in his grasp of big ideas and big developments, by his vision of the future and at the same time understanding the intricate problems of the ongoing process. I feel honoured and proud to have been close to, and to have have shared a friendship with, this extraordinary man.

South Africans Remember

In Memory of JS

Cyril Ramaphosa
City Hall Private Memorial, 14 January 1995.

M uch has been said and written about JS since he died. Listening to some of those who have been paying moving tributes to JS, one has heard them say, 'What I'm about to say has already been said by others.'

I believe there is much more to be said about JS. Much more than the heavy political tributes we have heard and read. This private ceremony gives us the opportunity to say what has not found its way into speeches at memorial services or the print media. It gives us the chance to celebrate JS, and be with him for the last time and tell him and his family what he meant to us.

James Motlatsi, the President of the National Union of Mineworkers, and I first met JS in a hotel room in the mid-1980s. He struck us as a complete contrast of what South Africans were fed by the NP government propaganda. He was a warm, jolly and robust bespectacled man with a good listening ear. The party had just published a pamphlet commemorating the 1946 miners' strike. He wanted to know whether we would be agreeable to the distribution of some 2 000 copies of the pamphlet amongst the mineworkers. He was taken aback when we said we wanted 10 000 copies. The party dispatched the pamphlet through the underground network and we had it distributed amongst our members. What impressed us most was the speed with which JS organised the dispatch of the pamphlets. We knew then that we were dealing with an efficient and effective revolutionary who could keep his word.

Serving with JS on the National Executive Committee of the ANC was a privilege. Our work on the NEC gave me, and I guess many others, a rare opportunity to have a deeper insight into the intellect and the clarity of thought of one of the outstanding revolutionaries of our time. Whenever JS spoke in NEC meetings everyone sat up and listened because his contributions were always of a strategic nature and far-sighted and focused on the broader objective.

It was during negotiations that I came to know JS a lot better and got close to him. He was without any doubt one of our outstanding negotiators. Every hour spent with JS in the negotiating chamber was an hour in history. During negotiations sessions JS would write notes to me on pieces of paper – not on negotiations strategy or tactics – but on issues many would call trivialities. I once recall when the Inkatha Freedom Party, Lucas Mangope's party and COSAG were being difficult, he passed a note to me saying he was considering joining a monastery to get away from these unreasonable people. He quickly sent another note saying it might actually be a better idea to go to a nunnery. A minute later another note came where he said since he might find Mrs Gouws (of COSAG) and Mangope's daughter-in-law there he had decided not to join the nunnery after all.

Throughout the negotiations JS never compromised himself, his principles or the positions of the movement. He may be the father of the sunset clause which gave birth to the Government of National Unity, but let it be known that he never compromised an iota of his convictions.

We all know that JS was demonised by the National Party who called him all sorts of things including a KGB colonel. He resented this label because in their propaganda he remained a colonel for decades and was never promoted. He often said, 'Surely they must know that I have much more than just a pretty face. They do a great disservice to my intelligence.' Notwithstanding all this, JS had a respect for his adversaries and was able to see what was good in people like Roelf Meyer and Fanie van der Merwe. Even when his adversaries were down he was not given to rubbing their noses in the mud.

Working with JS also enabled me to have a rare insight into JS the romantic. I am one of those who can testify to the fact that JS loved you very deeply, Helena, and always wanted to please you and make you happy. He was at times torn between setting aside time to spend with you and the grueling task of negotiations. I recall him agonising whether he should go with you to China or stay with us negotiating at Kempton Park. He sought my opinion, and I told him that if he went he would be leaving at the most critical time. He decided to go but I knew his heart was with us. I thought I would find it difficult to forgive you, Helena. But as it turned out, not much was achieved during his absence and I am rather glad he went, because like all of us he was tired and needed a rest. He came back rejuvenated and we were able to draw a lot from his renewed strength. So I do forgive.

JS's job as Minister of Housing was, he told me, the most meaningful job he had ever done throughout his life. Nothing he had done previously could ever be compared with his last mission. We can now all confirm that this last mission is accomplished. He has left us a formidable legacy.

You have passed the torch to us. Rest assured that we will not allow the flame to be extinguished. We will hold it high. You will always remain a symbol of commitment and dedication in the struggle to achieve a better life for our people.

'Joe was my friend and I was his'

Barney Simon,
City Hall Private Memorial, 14 January 1995.

W hat made us friends had little to do with politics or theatre. We spent little time discussing either. In fact, because of exile, life and work, we spent very little time together. All I know is that our best times were rare and quiet and alone, when we shared the comfort of our trust in each other. I found Joe through Ruth and I found her in the Rivonia days, her time of greatest fragility and transformation, when, with Joe in exile, she was isolated by bannings and restrictions and ravaged by her 117 days of solitary confinement.

When she joined Joe in exile, I visited them whenever I passed through London. My earliest memory of those times seems more fantastic than real. A glorious Sunday morning in London – that's fantasy already. Joe and Ruth bare-shouldered in bed surrounded by newspapers, coffee and toast which they invited me to join. Not even a *dared* dream less than a year before.

In contrast, a few years later, I witnessed their bitter arguments over Czechoslovakia and Joe's stubborn defence of the Russian invasion. I remember equally vividly during those days the times that he and I spent wandering on Hampstead Heath and his yearning questions about our country and the people and the places that he had loved and left behind. It was here that our bonding began. To this day, when I think of Hampstead Heath, more essential than the Houses of Parliament, I don't think of England, I think of Joe.

On 1982, weeks after Ruth's assassination, I remember Joe's enveloping embrace at the Riverside Studios when we dedicated the opening night of *Woza Albert* to her and added her name to our list of heroes. And I also remember the next day and the coffee bar we abandoned to walk and weep together on the Heath.

Our next meeting was in Mozambique, after the Nkomati Accord. Joe was subdued. He had lost light. I had never before seen him so despondent, so truly hurt. He had been instructed to leave Mozambique with the rest of the ANC, and he was moved from the safety of his home in the

Government Compound to the unguarded danger of an ordinary suburban house. He was fetching me for a lunch that he had prepared around a precious piece of pork.

When we climbed into his parked car I found an envelope, type-addressed to him, lying on my seat. A clear bulls-eye for any of the many who wanted to make him a target. We had the only argument that I can recall. At least I argued. Joe just shrugged and smiled and mumbled something I didn't even care to hear. It was a very hot and humid day, and the pork, as precious as it was, lay heavily within us, particularly me, the visitor to Mozambique. I was offered a rest in the only air-conditioned space, his bedroom upstairs. I lay down on his bed, and as I turned to doze I faced into his open wardrobe and the AK-47 that leaned in waiting among the shadows of his clothes.

There is a Hasidic saying that God created man because He loves to listen to stories. If that's the case, then, despite himself, Joe had to be one of the Lord's biggest favourites. He could spin a yarn and tell a joke with the cream of us down here below. In fact I made Joe a proposition. We would film him telling 365 jokes and replace the daily religious programme on TV with a daily Joke with Joe. I thought it would do wonders for our country. But he wouldn't take me up on it. I suspect that he didn't know 365 jokes.

It's not that I'm pushing God. I have my doubts about Him myself, but I suspect that Joe's life, as varied and difficult as it was, was always punctuated by miracles. The clearest one was Joe himself and his extra-ordinary faith in life that is always in the now. His genius for pragmatic transformation, his capacity for astonishment. I remember in 1990, when he first came home, trying to get him to come into my garage studio to see my greatest treasure, my Jackson Hlongwane throne. He was immovable on my backyard stairs, staring at the sky. It was dove-grey and imprinted with two perfect rainbows. 'Gee, Barney,' he said, 'Look at that! Can you believe it! Just look at that!' I was ashamed of even trying to move him on.

The other was Helena. She had to be some kind of divine assignation. He was granted a woman who was his best friend, his challenge, his lover and his wife. She brought blessings to his days, and through the courage and joy that she engendered in him, brought blessings to our country. Miracles can be cruel too.

The last that I will mention, and it one that I am still struggling to respect, was the assignation of Joe's death. I have learnt through my witnessing of him in these last three years that death is not simply the enemy of life but can also be its friend. I have learnt that if we can find the courage, and love is the greatest source of that, the knowledge that our years are limited can illuminate our every day and help us enrich what surrounds us. Maimonides wrote in *The Guide for the Perplexed*, 'When the blessed man is near death, his knowledge increases mightily, and his love for the object of his knowledge becomes more intense, and it is in this delight that his soul separates from his body.'

Hamba kahle, Joe.

My life-long friend

Harold Wolpe,
City Hall Private Memorial, 14 January 1995.

W|e, relatives, close comrades and friends of Joe, express our collective deep grief and sense of loss. Personally, after 48 years of steadfast friendship, it is virtually impossible to accept the fact of Joe's death; to accept that there will be no more phone calls with his declamatory greeting, 'Wolpe!', and my equally declamatory response, 'Slovo!', an exchange which somehow signified our strong bond and mutual affection.

However, we are here also to celebrate the person he was and his extraordinary accomplishments. It has been frequently asserted that Joe sacrificed himself to the liberation struggle, but as Joe's wife, Helena Dolny, has aptly pointed out, he hugely enjoyed his political work. Indeed, he said many years ago in London, in the dark period immediately following Rivonia, when his full-time role in the movement was first defined, that he had been offered the perfect job.

Of course there were personal costs. We know of the stresses experienced by Joe's daughters, Shawn, Gillian and Robyn because of the political involvement of the parents, the trauma of Ruth's assassination and their fears generated by the threats on Joe's life.

The most dramatic demonstration of the value Joe placed on his job was the way in which throughout the whole period of his illness he enmeshed himself in political work, first, in negotiations, then in the election campaign and finally, during the worst phase of illness, in the housing ministry. When cancer was first diagnosed, his express wish was to live to see the ANC's election victory.

Yet, while there was no doubt about Joe's will and desire to go on with his political work, his capacity to continue to do so became increasingly uncertain because of the gravity of his illness. That he was able to function as effectively as he did was due not only to his own courage and determination but, in large measure, to the loving care of him by Helena to whom I want to pay tribute.

Joe's contribution to the definition of the basic elements of the negotiated settlement – power-sharing and the sunset clauses – and his brilliant orchestration, with the support of his director-general of Housing, Billy Cobbett (whose devoted personal assistance to Joe and Helena in the last days of Joe's life must be recorded), have been universally acclaimed in both the South African and the international media and across the political spectrum. But it is important to recognise that the way in which this has been expressed often has the effect of devaluing both Joe's work and, indeed, the policy of the national liberation movement prior to February 1990.

The implication is that what changed was Joe, not the situation, and that from being an ogre (terrorist and dogmatist) he became, through a process of individual reform, a pragmatic hero pursuing only what is immediately possible without thought for more long-term goals. The idea that Joe had cleansed himself of his revolutionary past and this made it possible for him to argue for compromise is entirely without foundation. His argument for power-sharing and the sunset clauses was as much rooted in his view of revolutionary theory as earlier the armed struggle had been.

It is of fundamental importance that the positive assessment of Joe should not be restricted to the period of reconstruction, but should be understood also in relation to the pivotal role he played in bringing about the conditions which made the present possible.

That role was not unrelated to his entire approach to theory and analysis. Despite the orthodoxies about the socialist bloc and about the theory of the South African revolution which pervaded the liberation movement and, indeed, despite his own adherence to these, Joe never allowed himself to be trapped in an iron cage of orthodoxy. The richness and innovativeness of his theoretical and strategic contributions derived, to an important degree, from his preparedness to engage in written and oral debate.

I cannot resist the telling of a little bit of personal history.

I remember meeting Joe for the first time at Wits University early in 1946, but he had a different recollection. According to Joe, when we were about 11 years old I, as the doyen of local soccer, kicked him off the Yeoville sports ground when he attempted to join a scratch football game on a Sunday morning! Years later, shortly before our joint 60th birthday party in London, he sent me a cable from Lusaka which read: 'Congratulations on the 60th birthday of the world's first football hooligan!'

Joe began his studies towards a law degree in 1946 when I was already a second year social science student. And so we met at registration and discovered that we shared intellectual, political and sporting interests. We went to rugby and cricket tests and discussed deep philosophical and political issues in the intervals; we spent endless hours on weekends and during vacations playing snooker for Coca-Colas; we argued over books and films and topics in our university courses. But above all, our time and energies, outside of study, we spent on politics.

Joe was already a seasoned political militant, having joined the Communist Party before entering the army, and he was soon drawn into leadership roles. But he and I did practical work together. Among the highlights was our week-long distribution, in the dead of the night, in the mining compounds, of leaflets to African mineworkers during the 1946 strike and the organisation of food raids in Johannesburg on shops holding back food in short supply in 1947.

On 1 June 1963, my wife AnnMarie and I had a clandestine farewell dinner with Joe and his wife Ruth First – he was to leave the country the next day for a few weeks on a mission for MK. In the event he spent some 27 years in exile which carried for Joe, as for other leaders of the national liberation movement, long periods of personal isolation from family and close friends. In part this was alleviated by his visits to London where he often stayed with us. We used to focus on Marxist theory as Joe grappled with strategic issues and I pursued academic research. We often became angry and aggressive with one another as each attempted to claim superiority in the argument. Indeed, in certain areas – political economy, swimming, snooker, squash (he once broke my front tooth in a viciously fought game) – our relationship was distinctly competitive.

There are many anecdotes to relate of an entirely personal character. Among these was the occasion when, while staying on his own at our house in London, he nearly succeeded in burning it down. The pop-up toaster, apparently faulty, failed to pop up the toast while Joe was in the bath. After a while he noticed that the steam of the hot water was actually smoke from a fire. He rushed down, extinguished the fire, but could not open windows to allow smoke to escape because of anti-burglar devices. He immediately telephoned me at Essex where I worked, angrily demanding why I did not own a pop-up toaster!

One of the reasons why Joe's political judgments inspired great trust was the profound confidence he had in his own theoretical, analytical and political abilities. What was remarkable, however, was that he was a man entirely without pretensions who retained always the common touch in his relations and, indeed, perhaps paradoxically, a wonderful modesty.

Lack of pretension, modesty and wit were powerfully attractive traits. The wit which was so integral to his personality was never more aptly expressed in the last anecdote he recounted to me a few days before his death. I congratulated him on the *Isithwalandwe Seaparankoe* Award, and he told me that when he was informed at the NEC meeting that he was to be honoured, he responded with the following story.

'Some 50 years ago, an accused was tried before Judge Greenberg and a jury. After the evidence and argument, the 12-person jury retired for a couple of hours and on his return the spokesman was asked, "What is your verdict?" The Judge was furious at the answer, "Not Guilty" and asked on what grounds. The spokesman replied, "Insanity" at which point the Judge asked, "What, all 12 of you?" '

Thus, with wit and honour, Joe ended a brilliant political career. A more fitting conclusion to his life could hardly be imagined.

Internationalist and Communist

Pallo Jordan,
Memorial meeting at St George's Cathedral, Cape Town.

S ince the day when Comrade Joe Slovo passed from this existence we have heard a lot about Joe Slovo the Minister of Housing. We have also seen innumerable, and not undeserved, tributes
to the role Comrade Joe Slovo played in the negotiations process.

What has unfortunately been lost is the Joe Slovo known to millions
of our people. What seems to have been misplaced is the Joe Slovo so
dearly loved and admired; the Joe Slovo known to his comrades in the
national liberation movement.

Today I want to recall Joe Slovo the revolutionary, because that is the
true meaning of his adult life.

As a militant democrat and as a communist, Joe Slovo threw himself
body and soul into the national liberation movement, joining the then
Communist Party of South Africa at the age of 16. He committed himself
fully to the struggles of the people in his chosen home, South Africa,
becoming an ardent patriot in the true sense of that word, meaning a love
for one's country and all its people, not merely blind support of the government in power.

After the banning of the Communist Party and the illegalisation of
advocacy of Marxism in 1950, Joe Slovo was among the group which
reconstituted the Communist Party as the underground SACP in 1953.
Because of his undoubted talent he rose quickly into its leading bodies
and retained that status until the end of his life. Despite the terrible disap-
pointments associated with the name of socialism, Joe never wavered in
his commitment to socialism as both an honourable cause and a realisable
goal.

In a world in which people, especially those involved in liberation
politics, were compelled to choose sides, many found it very difficult to
voice their misgivings about the flaws of existing socialism publicly. On
both sides of that great divide, at the height of the Cold War, there was
little room to accommodate critical supporters.

232

Comrade Joe preferred to maintain a public silence about his doubts, questions and very far-reaching criticisms of all the socialist countries. He confided these to his friends and colleagues but not publicly. Though I have been one of his sternest critics, I can, however, appreciate his motives.

Though he held very firm views on a whole range of issues, Joe was never dogmatic, let alone rigid. He had a great capacity for concrete analysis, employing his Marxist learning to dissect and comprehend a living reality. He repeatedly emphasised that there was no strategy that could hold good for all time, and that tactics necessarily had to be adapted and readapted to suit changing political and social circumstances.

Joe Slovo distinguished himself both as a strategist and as a practical man of action. He was instrumental in the slow rebuilding of the movement's underground after the reverses that followed the Rivonia arrests. The document, *ANC Programme, Strategy and Tactics*, adopted at Morogoro in 1969, bears the indelible print of his ideas. As one of the commanders of the Special Operations Unit of Umkhonto we Sizwe, he was responsible for planning some of the more spectacular attacks launched inside South Africa between 1978 and 1982. During the 1980s, he was among the small group of comrades active in drafting the so-called *Green Book*, which served as the central strategic document for our movement before the Kabwe conference of 1985.

During the 1970s, both inside and outside the SACP, Joe's writings were critical interventions at key moments in the struggle. In 1977 he published an outstanding essay, entitled *No Middle Road*, which was the virtual bible of activists in the mass democratic movement and the underground during the late 1970s and the 1980s.

. With the coming of *glasnost*, it was once again Slovo's incisive intellect that initiated the SACP's reappraisal. His pamphlet *Has Socialism Failed?* remains unique among South African Marxist writings for the wide-ranging debate it provoked. Though there were sharp exchanges, acrimonious and heated arguments about that pamphlet, Joe never allowed these to degenerate into personal animosities and always showed himself willing to engage with his critics, both at home and abroad.

Because of his immense talent, Joe Slovo was chosen by the NEC of the ANC to assist our late comrade president OR Tambo in supervising and directing 'Operation Vulindela', whose purpose was to begin the transfer of the external leadership of the movement inside the country.

To those whose memories have faded, it seems incomprehensible that the lovable man, who became our first Minister of Housing, was not too long ago the primary target of virtually every dirty tricks specialist and assassination squad leader in the employ of the apartheid government. The enemy made him the target of every conceivable form of character assassination, including the absurd smear that he was a colonel in the KGB!

Joe earned the ire of the apartheid government, their propagandists and their supporters for precisely the same reasons as he was loved and admired by the oppressed and exploited. Second to Oliver Tambo, he was probably the best-loved leader of the ANC, both inside and outside South Africa. In the camps of Umkhonto we Sizwe he was a living legend whose name was invoked in marching songs and the chants that accompanied the *toyi-toyi*.

Many a foreign friend has marveled at the generosity of spirit of the oppressed majority, who have not yielded to the temptation of becoming anti-white. That generosity of spirit owes much to the sterling example of people like Joe Slovo, and many other white comrades, most of them communists, who gave every fibre of their being to the struggle for freedom.

As a government minister Joe brought to bear the virtues of hard work, discipline and levelheadedness that had served him so well in the national liberation movement. He did not shirk from taking tough decisions but he was always very sensitive to the real needs of the most deprived. One journalist recently remarked that in the past seven months Slovo did more for housing than had been done in four decades. That is a measure of Joe Slovo and his achievements, but it is also a damning indictment of all those who preceded him.

I have no doubt that the life and work of this remarkable man will continue to inspire revolutionaries. When, one day, a definitive history of the communist movement in South Africa is written, there will be a number of outstanding men and women whose names will be recorded as having played a decisive role. Joe's name will feature very prominently on that list.

He will feature on that list because he embraced and lived by Marx's eleventh thesis on Feuerbach: 'Philosophers have interpreted the world in different ways; the point however is to change it.'

I consider it an honour to have known and worked with him and to have been counted among his friends.

Friend and Colleague

From Billy Cobbett, director-general, Ministry of Housing.

Dear Helena,

In the week since Joe died, I have been wondering how best to add my thoughts to the floods of correspondence that you have been receiving. I would like to share some of my personal observations and memories that I was fortunate enough to share by virtue of a very close working relationship with Joe over the last eight months.

While I know there was a sense of frustration that Joe felt at not being able to complete a job he had begun so well and enjoyed so completely, I also know that Joe died a happy and satisfied man.

In about August, by which time he had more than come to terms with the nature of his job, Joe and I were sitting in the Business Class lounge at Jan Smuts airport waiting to fly to Cape Town. He then told me that he had seen his doctors, and that the diagnosis was sufficiently clear that he knew he was going to die. How long he had he did not know, but he spoke of having less than a year.

He then discussed how he felt fortunate that, after all of his life and having had cancer for a statistically lengthy period, he was still able to serve long enough to become a minister in the Government of National Unity and, in particular, to have become the Minister of Housing.

When I asked him whether he might retire as his health deteriorated, he said that if he gave up his job, he would be dead within a month. At that time, he still had the challenges of the banks, the Summit Accord and White Paper to keep his mind focused.

Maybe the most powerful image I have of Joe occurred when we were in the Eastern Cape (this was the trip during which he suffered the embarrassment of having the plane called off the runway to come and fetch us). Joe and I were with the MEC in a helicopter, visiting different areas in the Eastern Cape. We had visited Duncan Village, and had then seemingly brought the entire community of Butterworth to a complete standstill by landing in the middle of the town. We received a message via the President's office that there was a major land invasion occurring

235

in Umtata, and that JS should try and intervene. We cancelled Port Elizabeth and flew to Umtata.

The story ends with the image I have referred to: Joe, climbing up on the back of a tractor, addressing about 300 land invaders in a field outside Umtata. Rather than retreat to populism, he spelt out in very clear and unambiguous terms the consequences of their action, and the fact that they could expect no support from the Government. What particularly angered him was that the land was not being invaded by urban or rural poor, but by people who arrived in their 4x4s and, as he pointed out to one vociferous objector, 'My friend, you are better dressed than I am.' The land invasion was stopped.

Public commentators have voiced the smug opinion that 'Joe changed' upon realising the realities of his office. On the contrary, in his time at the ministry, it was Joe who most strongly insisted on designing policies that would have the best chance of assisting the poor. I remember he once called me into his office and said words to the effect that all the clever technical policy being designed was wonderful, but we were not sufficiently addressing the needs of the poor.

On any occasion when he addressed large audiences, he always told people to keep pushing, keep up the pressure on him and the government and to keep him on his toes.

What Joe brought to his Ministry was a level of political intellect and 'feel' that cannot be taught, and which cannot be replaced. His decisive interventions were to instinctively guide housing through a politically challenging time. He would hate me to observe that I cannot think of a time when he made a wrong call.

His greatest triumph, I believe, was not the White Paper or the deal with the banks – it was the National Housing Summit and National Housing Accord. Both of these he conceptualised and planned himself – indeed, if he had followed my advice on the summit, it would have been a weak and ordinary event. He demonstrated what was possible, and pulled off the most significant event of reconciliation and consensus in the history of housing in the country.

Throughout this he always kept his humility and his humour. His favourite ice-breaker on meeting new people in the industry was, when referred to as 'minister', to look behind him to see who they were referring to. What other minister introduced himself to his entire staff, within four hours of assuming office, and put them at ease by telling his favourite Che Guevara joke? And it worked.

The more I write, the more I remember, the less sad I feel. The loss is indescribable – and I can do no more than to give thanks that I had the honour and pleasure of those eight intense months with Joe Slovo, my minister and my friend. I miss him terribly, and always will.

Now to the purpose of this letter. The real person I want to thank is Helena Dolny. I had Joe because Joe had you. Without you, Joe would not have lasted as long as he did.

I know. Joe told me. Thank you.

Clandestine Hero

A personal tribute by Lenasia activist Ismail Momoniat,
The Indicator, 26-31 January 1995.

I first met Joe Slovo (JS as we called him) during the TIC/NIC-led Indian delegation that met with the then-banned ANC in Lusaka in 1988. We were all aware of the vilification campaign mounted by the South African government against him. Meeting him in the flesh turned out to be a memorable experience.

We were impressed because we met a leader who was not only willing to listen, but was clearly concerned about the fears of the Indian community. He understood the suffering of the Indian community under the Group Areas Act and apartheid and was very familiar with the contribution of Indian South Africans in the struggle. He complimented the delegation on the success of the anti-tricameral election campaigns.

Our delegation was even more impressed that a communist like Joe Slovo fully appreciated the religious and cultural concerns of the Indian community. Indeed, Joe Slovo and Thabo Mbeki went out of their way to open up religious and cultural contact for the Indian community with countries like India and in the Middle East, even though there was an international boycott of South Africa.

I also got to know Joe Slovo at another level through my involvement in the underground structures of the liberation movement. Many activists like myself saw the need to link our activities in the UDF and TIC with the ANC. We valued the political analysis coming from the ANC alliance. But such formal links were illegal and dangerous. Joe Slovo understood the dangers and proved to be a disciplined leader who was able to guide us, and yet to conceal such activities from the security police.

It was under his leadership that the delegates from within the country were able to attend an underground congress of the SACP in Cuba in 1989. This was also concealed from the security police. This was no mean feat when you consider the dark days of the State of Emergency.

Recollections

Ronald Segal,
Memorial meeting, London, January 1995.

J oe broke all the rules that seemed to govern the characters of other people I have known. An apparently undeviating apologist for Soviet policy until almost the last of the Soviet system, he told me the sharpest and funniest anti-Soviet jokes I ever heard. He was considered and controlled in his judgment, but he played the wildest game of bridge, intermittently driving his partners to distraction, though never, somehow, to ill-tempered recrimination. He was a realist and at times might have passed as a cynic, but was essentially an optimist. Few people I have known experienced such anguish in their lives. It might so easily have made him sour and mean. My wife and children all came to call him 'Joy'.

We spent so many times together, and I do not believe that it is because of some sentimental censorship that I remember them as such happy ones. Among them, none remains as vivid in my mind as the last, and not because of that. It was a fortnight or so before he died, and I had arranged with Helena that they would visit me and my family in the house I had rented for a few weeks at Fresnaye in Cape Town. Shortly before they were due to arrive, Helena phoned to say that they might not be able to come, since he did not seem up to it. But they did, because he insisted, and he climbed, so painfully, the steps to the sitting room and walked on to the balcony for the view across Sea Point to the sea.

He drank half of the Scotch I poured for him, and talked, and then, for a little while, with a mat he took from the table in front of him, played peek-a-boo with my one-year-old granddaughter. Recalling it, I want to cry, but find myself smiling instead.

Condolences

Joe Slovo was a fighter, an unforgettable man, full of humour, valour in thought and display. He was a heart to heart, flesh and blood communist. I learned a lot from him. Rest in peace. Go well, Ngwenya.
Comrade Lt General Moloi, SANDF (MK Cde 'A' Lambert)

Comrade Joe was a true human being for our country. A challenge to be humane. With him, the racial issue was defied and one cherished to be human. Rest in peace, Comrade Joe. You did what you could.
Wally Serote

Dear Helena
There will be so many flowers in tribute to Joe, that mine would be lost. So please, if you like, buy yourself a plant or shrub, and plant it in your garden which Joe enjoyed so much — as a thank you to him from me. Much, much love, as ever,
Your loving Mum

Dear Helena
I never actually met Joe, but of course he was such a public figure that I grew to admire and respect him. Apart from his obvious political impact on the lives of ordinary people, Joe did a whole lot of good to entire strangers by demonstrating how not to give up, to despair. I certainly know of one instance in which his example has been used as encouragement to an elderly woman with cancer. What intrigues me was how Joe, by sheer good work, convinced people who did not know him and who differed with him fundamentally in ideology, that he was a good person doing good work worthy of support. I cannot see this happening anywhere in the world other than in our country over the past few years. He leaves a good feeling.
Love, *Jonathan*
(a colleague from Wits University)

Dear Mrs Slovo
We only met once but I wish to tell you that I am very sorry that you lost your husband. Your husband and mine (Prof J Heyns) had a few quality talks with one another and my husband had a very great regard for Mr Slovo. As a Christian my husband often prayed for Mr Slovo. I'll be thinking of you.
Kind regards, *Renee Heyns*
(widow of the Rev Johan Heyns who was assassinated in 1994)

Dear Helena,
Dave has one key memory of Joe – the way he used to ring the bell of Mercers Rd and just be there before him – the only person who just 'appeared'. He epitomised Africa for Dave: people just being there without fuss. We also remember our warmth with you Helena, and Joe, in late 1991. At last after all those years of struggle, Joe could walk, and we with him, in a free South Africa.
Love and solidarity, *Pam Smith and Dave Wield*
(friends from London and Dar es Salaam)

Dear Helena,
I am pleased to have had the chance to meet and enjoy Joe during our brief encounter. I watched the episode the other night (while wearing my red socks too!). Those who watched it with me, without any knowledge of him other than that of old fears, were delighted. And ashamed of the success of the propaganda of the past. That propaganda is now in shreds. Thanks to Joe's humour and gentleness. To you and his children, my love and best wishes.
Pieter-Dirk Uys
(Satirist)

Dear Helena,
I wish to convey my sincerest condolences to you. Bereavement, and the period of adjustment which follows afterwards, are always traumatic. How much more so for those who were part of the private life of a public figure, for they have to share their grief and memories with thousands of strangers. Yet it is inevitable that someone like Joe, who directly and indirectly affected so many people's lives, would be mourned by most South Africans.

Recently I came across an interview given to *Homeless Talk* in late 1994. In it Joe discusses housing options with several homeless people. One of them tells Joe that several hundred people are sleeping at Park

Station, in old car-port shelters, to which Joe responds: 'Have you organised these communities, these homeless living on the street? I'm not saying the whole of Jo'burg, but these two or three hundred you're talking about – what ideas have you got for solving the problem?'

He then goes on to discuss their solutions, points out the strengths and weaknesses of each option, and in general encourages them. This approach to problem-solving was typical of the man. The leading by empowering, the interacting with all sorts of people without either down-playing his obvious abilities or being patronising, the holding of key roles in the ANC, SACP and government of South Africa whilst remaining unimpressed with the trappings of power – all of these made him special.

In the same interview to *Homeless Talk* he said, 'We cannot start off with the approach that any human being is beyond reach.' Perhaps it was his faith in the redeemability of human beings which produced a fighter so gentle, an intellectual so pragmatic, a compassionate man so firm and unwavering, a politician so human.

The interview ends with an invitation from the homeless to Joe: 'Come and see our place,' to which he replies, 'Well, invite me, and we'll see what we can fit in. The workload is very heavy at the moment, but write to us and we'll see what we can do.'

They then thank him for his time, and he responds: 'Don't thank me. That's my job and I'm being paid too much for it!'

The temptation to heap praise upon Joe is great, for a person combining so many extraordinary attributes, in such a quiet and unostentatious manner, is indeed rare. Yet sometimes praise for a leader can be a way for people to disempower themselves, to thrust the burden of struggle away from themselves and onto the shoulders of people 'up there'. I feel certain that Joe would not have wanted his virtues extolled if that was done in order to avoid our own moral responsibilities.

We cannot minimise the loss and pretend that all is as before. We are very much worse off without Joe Slovo. Yet all he ever promised us was the best of ourselves. The greatest tribute we could pay him is to live, as Joe did, with warmth and kindness, with great integrity, with courage, with a simple unaffected humility. I hope we will be able to live up to his legacy.

Hylton Applebaum (Liberty Life Foundation)

'Comrades who have made me'

On 20 May 1995, Thenjiwe Mtintso, SACP central committee member and parliamentarian, was the main speaker at the 'Unveiling of a Plaque' ceremony at the Joe Slovo Comprehensive School in Khayelitsha. Thenjiwe shared many personal recollections to illustrate some of the points she had learnt through working with JS: that you have opportunities, you make choices and then there's the issue of the level of commitment. Weeks later we sat down to recall the speech and elaborate on some of her recollections.

T he first time I met JS was in Maputo. I had only recently joined the ANC, having left South Africa and the Black Consciousness (BC) movement. He was the first ANC white that I came into contact with and I had an attitude towards whites. Our BC perception was that the ANC had whites who were controlling it. There was a PAC slogan, *'ANC Ngwethu, ingqondo Slovo'* (*Amandla! Ngawethu! Ingqondo! Yeka Slovo!* Power! To the People! The Brain! ... is Slovo's!). In addition, we in the BC were convinced that communists were white and were manipulating the ANC. I'd joined the ANC and SACP, but there were still these lingering suspicions and doubts.

I have never met Slovo, and I don't know what he looks like. A white man comes into the meeting, wearing these ugly hunter boots and these funny, shapeless trousers. He sits with Jacob Zuma and eats the brown bread and jam with us. I sit there, looking at him, eating this brown bread and jam and I am thinking, 'These whites, there's no reason for them to be involved. Why do they pretend, why should they pretend to be poor? This definitely is part of the whites' patronising and paternalistic attitude.'

I don't know it's Slovo. My prejudices have been reinforced in South Africa when we, as BC activists, would receive visits from some international groups. And when they visited us in the townships by day, they would be dressed scruffily in jeans and untidy shirts. But then, later, when we met some of the same ones at the house of Donald Woods and found them dressed differently, smartly, there was a sense of being patronised.

That evening, this very meeting, will be the first time I am meeting anyone from the leadership of the ANC, other than Chris (Hani) who has been my contact in Lesotho. The talking begins. I note that on Slovo's part there is an eagerness and keenness to listen, not just about what is happening in the units and our contact with Lesotho, but more widely about what is happening inside the country. The way he listens, does not interrupt, does not impose, begins to make me feel different. I am being listened to, and I feel a sense of confidence and self-importance that someone like Slovo wants to hear what it is that I have to say.

I have to begin to modify my attitude, but then Slovo always had the reputation of being an exceptional white.

But as the discussion went on, he entered into dialogue. We were discussing Black Consciousness, my understanding of the BC movement at home and its positions. He offers to the discussion a framework of class consciousness and class analysis, just in the way he is talking and contributing. I find I am learning from him, not through some formal classroom experience but through dialogue. That first experience of JS as the teacher, teaching through informal discussions, interaction and engagement was to become my life experience of JS as he touched my life at various stages.

I met him again when I was in the camps. We often had egg powder as a main food and also 'Mugabe', some tinned stuff sent from Zimbabwe – horrible stuff that smelt, that seemed to be tinned tripe and innards. Joe was one of the few people I saw eating this stuff – with relish. I know he liked good food, but he could also enjoy egg powder and Mugabe. There was no fuss, no complaint.

I realised then the extent of the choices he had made. I realised he could have had a good life but had chosen otherwise. By then I had read more about him and his background. I began to understand where Slovo was coming from – a very poor background, he hadn't done matric, but then after the war, given an opportunity, he became the best law student.

And then I understood the connections between opportunity, choice and commitment. Because, having got his opportunity and become a lawyer, he could have amassed wealth. But he had a hatred of exploitation which lead to a choice, and a commitment. And this is what I tried to say to the pupils in Khayelitsha: given an opportunity, most of us can achieve what we want. But of importance is what you do with that opportunity, ie the type of choices you make and the commitment to transformation of society – not just yourself. JS's life teaches us about opportunity, choices and commitment to transforming society to the benefit of the poor. As JS said in one of his last interviews: 'I did not waste my time.' Indeed, he did not waste his life.

He was revered in the camps. He was known as *ijuda*, the jew. When there were political discussions about new happenings, people would ask one another, 'and what does *ijuda* think?, what was his line?', and this was the line they would adopt. It was not because of a blind following of a leadership line, but this approach was based on an enormous trust. There were three comrade leaders who were most trusted: number one, OR Tambo; number two, JS; and number three Chris Hani, and in that order. The soldiers in the camps of the 1970s and 1980s will give you that order. It came from their experience of him in the camps. When he came, he listened, he made sense, he had a commitment which you yourself experienced.

I had come from a BC background with my suspicion of whites and expected as a black to be patronised and undermined, and more so because I was a woman. But I found comrade JS didn't treat me as a woman, but first and foremost as a person.

He was very important to those ANC comrades coming from a BC background. Remember our line was that we just wanted to leave the country to go and get guns and bring them back quickly. But through JS we came to a different understanding of the armed struggle. His emphasis was on the political. When I was working with the underground structures from Lesotho he would say it didn't matter how many guns we were getting into the country – what mattered is how many people were with us, and that the issue was not how many cadres had been sent into the country, but how many units had been created, political-military units, but his emphasis was always on the political.

He said what was important was not the gun, but the person behind the gun. He asked less about what operations had been carried out than about the success of political propaganda, and in this way he enhanced my understanding about having the support of the masses.

But what I enjoyed most about JS was not my experience of him in the meetings. It was the social interaction that takes place in the smoke breaks that was most important. And I remember in Mozambique, the success of the Sasol bombing and the excitement among comrades and JS saying, 'There's reason to drink!'

It was during meetings that I came to realise that JS was an impatient person, especially with long-winded people. I noticed that he used to start tapping his pen on the pad in front of him. And he had this way of sitting in meetings which reflected his state of engagement. He would start off facing the front, but then if the meeting was boring or the person long-winded, I noticed he would shift his body and end up sitting sideways with his shoulder to the meeting. And then I swear that there would come a time when he would just close off.

He would make me laugh. I especially remember one commissariat meeting in Mozambique. The comrade, well-known for being long-winded, who was speaking, adopted 'nitty-gritty' as his key phrase. He kept using it over and again. Joe was writing on his pad. I noticed that he registered every time the comrade said 'nitty-gritty'. Then he wrote something more at the bottom of the pad. I couldn't contain my curiosity and peeped over and saw he had written, 'CDE X HAS DISCOVERED THE MARVEL OF WORDS!' Now I couldn't contain my laughter!

The other special thing about him was that he would engage in a fight. Some white comrades would withdraw from verbal battle, conscious of their whiteness, but JS never used his whiteness to shirk responsibility.

Bravery isn't the right word, and yet he was brave. 'Courage, bravery and daring' are the type of words that immediately come to mind. I don't mean in the physical sense – although he didn't care too much about his physical security, didn't want bodyguards – but he had a daring, a bravery and courage in challenging and putting items on the agenda. At the 1989 Party Congress in Cuba, we met Fidel Castro and listened open-mouthed when he told Fidel that our next congress would be inside the country. He was attacked for this by comrades who feared it was an empty statement. JS said it was a commitment that he personally was prepared to risk making.

At that conference he also put 'negotiations' on the agenda. How could Cde Slovo dare to raise the issue of negotiation? Coming from the camps, as I was doing, negotiation was equated with 'compromise' and 'selling-out'. And he went as far as to raise the issue of 'compromise' by even using the word! That's what I mean by bravery, he was brave enough to raise these issues.

There was a fight at the SACP Central Committee after the publication of the document, *Negotiations: What Room for Compromise?* I do not know what would have happened if it wasn't that we have a CC with a certain style of working. There was enormous reaction. There was a sense of betrayal. And so Joe put himself up to be challenged – let's go through the roots, how this document came about, what was the process of logic of arriving at certain positions and how he came to decide to write the document. There was the opportunity given to fight, to reason it out.

It has been very important to me personally to witness this style, as I had a lack of confidence to put things forward, but as I observed JS proposing controversial points and being prepared to take on the challenge, it enhanced my own confidence.

At some stage last year I wanted to acknowledge this directly – so often we never say the positive things directly to a person. At the ANC congress I said to him, 'We may not be the best, but you should be proud. And you should know that all the time we felt you were there for us, and want to thank you for your life.' JS's touchy response was, 'What you're saying is I'm dying.' My response was, 'No, I'm saying thank you, I love you.'

My sense of loss of JS began when he became a minister. He started to be taken over, everyone saying what a wonderful minister he was. I wanted to say, 'Hey, this is our Slovo.' Part of my anger with his death and the statements made was the emphasis on this last part of his life as a minister, and not that person we knew in the past. I know it is good in some way because it is getting rid of the demonising that used to happen, but on the other hand I felt our Slovo was being stolen: Slovo, the communist, the Slovo of *No Middle Road*, the Slovo whose articles you hastened to look for in the *African Communist*, the Slovo who came from Shell House to Party meetings.

And I felt we were also losing the other side of JS, the one of comradeship and cadreship, of his settling down into a flat-out session of telling stories and jokes.

I do have an enormous sense of personal loss. Comrade JS was my last anchor. Chris (Hani) had gone, then OR (Tambo). All three were in a sense my political mentors, my security in the sense of feeling comfortable and safe to share my feelings, joys and fears with them. Now when I have doubts, I have the sense of a void.

I am, however, also grateful in that I was one of the lucky ones, to have been touched directly by his life.

One of the thoughts that struck me when I sat in this house after JS's death reflecting on his loss, was that I have lost comrades who made me and comrades that at any time I could turn to. I don't want to see them as father figures or brother figures, but at any time, with any of these three, whether it was about my personal life or my political life, I could say anything.

We say that no-one is indispensable. But we only had one Slovo. We won't have another.

Epilogue

Joe Slovo died on the morning of 6 January 1995.
Helena Dolny sent the following letter to family friends
just over a week later.

14 January 1995

Dear friends,

We read in the media that we were too distraught and grief-stricken to talk to the press. On the contrary, we shared a sense of quietude, of relief that Joe had let go of life after suffering, and a sense of achievement that as a group of carers there was a job well done. There could be no self-recrimination – Joe had died at home where he wanted to be. Quite simply, conversing with the media would have been an intrusion on our calm. For us, our parting with Joe was welcomed; there comes a point when loving a person means being able to let go and to help them let go more easily.

Joe had wanted privacy and was reluctant to have visitors. As friends, many of you have wanted to know about Joe's last days, without wanting to push us to speak more than we want to. It is part of your process of parting.

When you live with someone who has a terminal illness, when you see them suffering with stoicism, you spend time thinking about when you call it a day. In August, last year, Joe and I had watched a video recording of British playwright Dennis Potter's last TV interview. Potter was weeks away from death, in great pain, and continuing to write. 'The worst would be for me to die four pages from completing my last play,' he said. He sipped morphine and commented wryly that he needed enough to dull the pain, but not too much – so as to have a clear mind to be able to write. It has seemed to me, while living with Joe, that as long as there is an ability to continue to work creatively, as long as there is enjoyment of relationships and beauty, there is an extraordinary capacity to tolerate pain and that general feeling of being unwell. Our homeopath, speaking to Gillian, also said, 'Your father has unfinished business; people with unfinished business don't die quickly.'

Joe's final health crisis began in August. Since then we certainly learnt what Potter refers to as 'living in the present tense'. We took a break in Belgium and Italy, and the enormous generosity of friends and the exquisite beauty of Tuscany helped him to rally. He had unfinished business! He wanted to do, and did, the Bloemfontein Housing Summit and the

White Paper. On 2 December Joe came to the Eastern Cape looking forward to a well-earned rest. He delighted in the place and was overjoyed to feel and smell the sea again. However, the fall and fractured shoulder on the third day of the holiday was to prove the last straw. But you will remember that two days after the fall he presented the White Paper to a Cabinet meeting in Pretoria and joked about his injury. It was only after this that the trauma of injury set in.

At some stage I wondered if the fact of being on holiday, of Joe not being engaged in work, was contributing to his worsening condition. Billy Cobbett, his director-general, offered to return from holiday on Boxing Day. Billy arrived. He tuned in to Joe's needs with a manner and harmony which Joe accepted with ease. He was to prove an invaluable companion over the next ten days.

Joe's daughters arrived. And while Joe wanted them, his pride made him uncomfortable. It took some days for him to slowly accept his daughters as carers – but it happened.

The days passed with good moments interspersed. Harold and AnnMarie came for a day from Cape Town. Madiba arrived with a 'business-as-usual' attitude, telling Joe that he expected to see him at the Cabinet caucus on 5 January. Cyril managed to overcome his shock at seeing Joe's deterioration and chatted and joked wonderfully. On New Year's Eve Fazel and Helen, Gonda and Jaya joined us for champagne and fireworks. On New Year's Day Hillary visited and he smiled at the arrival of his granddaughter, Cassie. Hans, the reflexologist, boosted our morale by his generously coming from Cape Town; massage had worked well for Joe. Claire also arrived daily to take calls and care for us. On the 5th, Joe lay sleeping peacefully in the lounge while Hans and Kyla padded around him, taking down the Christmas decorations – a day early as we thought the next night might well be Joe's last.

Wednesday night, the 4th, had been a terrible night for Joe. He was so restless. Fazel stayed with him for the first part of the night and I took over at 2 am. 'He slept a little over an hour from 11 till just after midnight,' Fazel reported. The rest of the night Joe continued to be restless, taking a shower, moving often between the lounge, the veranda, the TV room, the bedroom. Just after dawn, we sat by the aquarium which Joe had relaxed by often in the last few days. He was hunched, shivering slightly whilst feeling hot. I noticed he was not wearing his spectacles, not focusing but withdrawing inside himself, barely communicative.

'Joe, you're not enjoying anything any more, are you?'

'No.'

'It's torture for you to be in so much discomfort and torturous for us to watch you in this way.'

Silence.

'Joe, all that willpower that you put into staying alive, can't you now put your remaining energy and willpower into dying more quickly?'

'I will.'

After this Joe slept.

On waking, Joe began his restless moving about again. Hans gave him a massage and he fell into a more peaceful sleep. The day progressed with Shawn, Gillian and Robyn taking turns to make Joe more comfortable. Joe had now accepted that they too could care for him. His weakening continued throughout the day; Gillian said she sat with him and willed him to die quickly. We had all reached this point.

At six in the evening there was an unexpected telephone call: Madiba will be here in ten minutes. I asked Joe if he wanted to put on a shirt. 'Yes.' I brushed his hair. He chose to sit by the window of our bedroom. I placed another chair close by so that they would hear each other easily.

Madiba greeted Joe in his warm and again, business-almost-as-usual manner. They sat with Joe's hand squeezing Madiba's in acknowledgement as Madiba carried the conversation forward. 'Well, Joe, today at the ANC Cabinet caucus we discussed ... I am sure these decisions would have your support.' Madiba then turned to me and recounted student days when they proposed that Joe should represent the law students, and the quick wit with which Joe had parried Harry Schwartz's opposition. We went on to discuss train journeys, one in 1948 for Madiba, one in 1982 for me when Joe had asked for some reconnaissance work to be done for Special Operations, and finally the Blue Train journey which Joe had so much enjoyed two weeks earlier – the soothing rhythm, the beauty of a Karoo landscape under an almost full moon during a night of fitful sleep.

Joe listened to the conversation, at intervals getting up and moving restlessly, from one chair to sitting on another chair, requesting help to take off his shirt and then shifting again. Towards the end of the visit, now sitting on the edge of the bed, Joe beckoned me to help him move again to a chair. When standing, he put his arms around me tenderly. Madiba commented, 'Helena, Joe is saying thank you.'

Joe moved to yet another chair next to Madiba who now began to bring the visit to a close. On finishing speaking, he bent over Joe and their heads rested together for a lengthy and poignant moment. 'Goodbye, Joe,' said Madiba and slowly began to move away. I thought Joe was going to complete the visit without uttering a word, but he decisively took Madiba's hand and said, 'Cheers'.

Epilogue

Two days later, sitting by Madiba at a meeting of the funeral committee, Madiba turned to me and said, 'Helena, when I visited Joe and he stood and embraced you, I think he was saying goodbye'. Tears filled my eyes and I nodded agreement. Yes, now I knew that was his final goodbye to me.

As Madiba left our bedroom he found Fazel, our doctor, waiting to examine Joe. Fazel broke the news that Joe's pulse was now weak and thready. 'I don't think he'll last the night.' This was good news.

Shawn, Gillian and Robyn were called to return. It was clear that Joe's restlessness was coming to a close, and he went to bed, which is where he had actually spent the least amount of time in the previous days. Hans asked for an oil burner and luckily we had a small ceramic one. He blended neroli (ultra-relaxing) with basil (to help release the grief of parting) and bergamot — a combination to create a peaceful atmosphere, making it easier to let go. The scent delicately pervaded the room as the hours went by. Fazel arrived and also gave Joe something to help him relax; a difficult night for Fazel who had become a friend to Joe over the years of his illness. Joe curled to the side and began to sleep more calmly, more deeply. Over the next four hours we sat with him, together, one by one, two by two in a varying harmony of giving each other supportive company while at other times respecting privacy. We played music gently in the background, Handel's *Messiah*, Respighi's *Fontane di Roma* and Mahler's 5th Symphony.

Just before 3 am Billy and I sat together, sensing the lengthening space between each beat of Joe's pulse, listening to the ever-slowing rhythm of his breathing. Then there was silence, all breathing had stopped. Billy called Fazel. Together they turned Joe on his back, arranged his head on the pillows. At last Joe's face had the serenity that we had not seen, even while resting, for some weeks. Shawn, Gillian and Robyn joined us. We played Mahler's 5th at a more celebratory level of volume. We each took a glass in our hands and, reiterating Joe's last word to Madiba, toasted Joe's departure.

'Cheers.'

With love and thanks
Helena